GRAND STAND FOR
NEW JOCKEY CLUB.
D.X. Murphy + Bro, Archts
Louisville, Ky

Scale, ¼ inch. 1894
⑥

A. Side Elevation.

Churchill Downs was designated a
National Historic Landmark by the
United States Department of the
Interior in 1986. It had been placed
on the National Register of Historic
Places in 1978.

CHURCHILL
DOWNS

CHURCHILL DOWNS

....

A Documentary History of America's Most Legendary Race Track

SAMUEL W. THOMAS

KENTUCKY DERBY MUSEUM
LOUISVILLE, KENTUCKY
1995

Published by the Kentucky Derby Museum in cooperation with Churchill Downs in recognition of the one hundredth anniversary of its legendary Twin Spires and the tenth anniversary of the museum. A private, not-for-profit institution, the Kentucky Derby Museum preserves and promotes the history and traditions associated with Thoroughbred racing and the Kentucky Derby, and is located adjacent to Churchill Downs.

Copyright © 1995
Kentucky Derby Museum
704 Central Avenue
P.O. Box 3513
Louisville, Kentucky 40201

ISBN 0-9617103-2-2

Book design and production: Julie Breeding/Plaschke Design Group, Inc., Louisville
Printed by Merrick Printing Company, Inc., Louisville
First printing: February 1995

Front endpaper: South elevation of grandstand proposed in 1894 by the architectural firm of D.X. Murphy & Bro.
Page 1: An unidentified gentleman poses on track shortly after grandstand had been completed in 1895.
Pages 2-3: The earliest known photograph of the familiar first turn of the Kentucky Derby captures the three horses in the 1905 race, won by Samuel S. Brown's Agile (in the lead).

CONTENTS

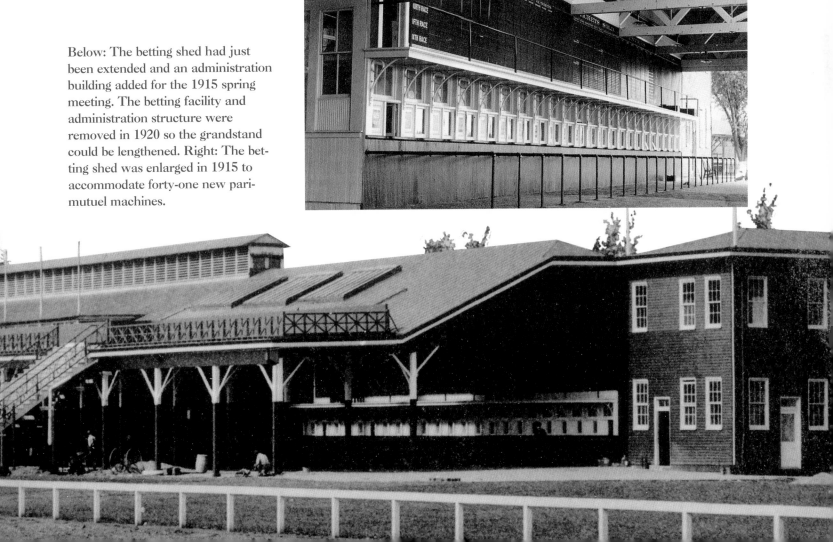

Below: The betting shed had just been extended and an administration building added for the 1915 spring meeting. The betting facility and administration structure were removed in 1920 so the grandstand could be lengthened. Right: The betting shed was enlarged in 1915 to accommodate forty-one new pari-mutuel machines.

INTRODUCTION

Those who visit Churchill Downs for the first time, gaze at the monstrous crazy-quilt structure, shake their heads in a puzzled way, and go away from there to classify it as something fantastic in architecture, and wondering how it ever happened.

—FROM *DOWN THE STRETCH: THE STORY OF MATT J. WINN*

"When the long-drawn tremolo of 'My Old Kentucky Home' lingers at next May's Derby, there will be nobody, we fancy, who will be insensible to a tone of keening. Matt Winn will be gone." And so commenced the editorial tribute of *The Courier-Journal* to "The Man Who Brought Legend To Louisville." He had died on 6 October 1949 at the age of 88. Matt Winn had witnessed the first Kentucky Derby as well as the seventy-fifth.

Beginning in 1902, when in mid-life he became part of a reorganization of Churchill Downs' management, "in charge of the amusement and catering features," Matt Winn was a driving force behind the track's ultimate success. But there was in addition to Col. Winn a significant cast of players who built Churchill Downs and kept enlarging its seating capacity and beautifying its grounds until in the evolution of spectator sports the Kentucky Derby had taken its place as a premier event. After 120 consecutive runnings, the Kentucky Derby continues to generate the spectacle and pageantry we have to come to anticipate on the first Saturday in May.

However, this book is not another account of the Kentucky Derby. It would be senseless to try to duplicate the handsome works by Joe Hirsch and Jim Bolus, *Kentucky Derby* (1988); Peter Chew, *The Kentucky Derby: The First 100 Years* (1974); Jim Bolus, *Run For The Roses: 100 Years At The Kentucky Derby* (1974); Bill Levy,

The Derby (1967); and Lamont Buchanan, *The Kentucky Derby Story* (1953); as well as Churchill Downs' own Derby milestone markers for the 75th and 100th runnings, and the track's extensive annual media guides. These accounts describe the Derby itself — the horses, the people, the contest. This book chronicles the development of the 120-year-old institution that provides the backdrop for the most popular racing event every year. Few architectural symbols are as well known or as easily identified as the twin spires of Churchill Downs. They are synonymous with the Kentucky Derby, and they are a national treasure. There is no more poignant moment in all of sports than the tradition of the parade to the post, set to the familiar strains of Stephen Foster's "My Old Kentucky Home." Memories and emotion gather under the hundred-year-old, steel-framed grandstand and simply explode in unison in the chorus, "Weep no more my lady."

This book is an outgrowth of research done for a project at the Kentucky Derby Museum to commemorate the hundredth anniversary of the building of the grandstand with its familiar lofty spires. Churchill Downs President Thomas H. Meeker was instrumental in getting the project underway. Randy W. Ray, the museum's former director, and Jenan Dorman, its deputy executive director, had requested the research, and it quickly became apparent to David E. Carrico, senior vice president at Churchill Downs, that little of the physical plant's development had been documented. Karl F. Schmitt, Jr., Churchill Downs' vice president for corporate communications, thought the research could be expanded into a book. Dan L. Parkerson, senior vice president and general manager, made the plant accessible through his working knowl-

edge of its every nook and cranny, gathered over more than three decades. Butch Lehr provided much information and insight about the track and its backside from his perspective as superintendent. With Jenan's guidance and oversight of the project this has been an opportunity to piece the story together. The book's publication was spearheaded by two members of the Kentucky Derby Museum's board of directors: Graham B. Cooke and Carl F. Pollard. Their encouragement and support are greatly appreciated as is the help of Stanley F. Hugenberg, Jr., a director of Churchill Downs, whose father was the heart its of operation. Jenan Dorman, along with Jay Ferguson and Candace Perry of the Kentucky Derby Museum's curatorial staff, read the manuscript, as did Tony Terry of Churchill Downs, and they offered much constructive criticism. Candace was also instrumental in assembling illustrations from the museum's collection.

Special thanks are in order to Jonelle Fisher of Midway, Kentucky. She made me aware of the role Central Kentuckians played in the early days of Churchill Downs. The likes of A. J. Alexander, Abe Buford, Dan Swigert, Hunt Reynolds, and the Harpers—their sleek horses and African-American trainers and jockeys made the track an instant success. Jo Fisher searched the files of the *Woodford Sun* and the *Blue Grass Clipper* and she escorted me to the old Nantura farm of the Harpers, next door to the Alexander family's farm, Woodburn. It was at Nantura that the incomparable Ten Broeck had been foaled and later stabled next to Longfellow, and where those two champions were buried, their grave markers the first in Kentucky dedicated to horses. Here Matt Winn had gazed with Frank Harper upon the Bluegrass's most prized horse flesh some 116 years before. We also went to Versailles to see the freshly polished Louisville Cup won by Ten Broeck at Churchill Downs in May 1876.

For additional research, the Keeneland Library was simply a delight in which to work. All libraries should have its dignified appearance and its professional staff. Cathy Schenck was particularly helpful and knowledgeable about its collections, as was Doris Waren, who is now retired. Theresa Fitzgerald, retired librarian of *The Bood-Horse*, patiently answered many questions. I would also like to acknowledge for their special assistance the reference area staff of the Louisville Free Public Library as well as the excellent staffs of The Filson Club and the University of Louisville's Photographic Archives. Dr. Thomas Owen, associate archivist of the University of Louisville, did yeoman's work to uncover bound newspapers in storage.

I deeply appreciate the late Warner L. Jones, chairman of the board of Churchill Downs from 1984-1992, for opening many doors and for his encouragement. It cannot be almost four decades ago that I met his vivacious twin daughters on the hill overlooking the steeplechase course of the Maryland Hunt Club. My family was relocating in Louisville and it was then I learned the accepted pronunciation of my adopted city's name. Over the next few years I would spend many delightful hours at Hermitage Farm, where Dark Star, the 1953 Derby winner, was bred. Warner Jones served on the Churchill Downs board for over fifty years, longer than anyone, including Matt Winn.

Finally, I would like to acknowledge William Butler. Following his preparation of *Churchill Downs: 100th Kentucky Derby*, Bill came to work at *The Courier-Journal* and *The Louisville Times* in our book publishing department. The newspapers' photographic files of the Derby were bulging, so we decided to feature that remarkable pictorial record. Working with Bill to bring out *They're Off: A Century of Kentucky Derby Coverage by The Courier-Journal and The Louisville Times* was good background for this project.

In preparing my research, I eagerly anticipated digging into the early corporate records at Churchill

Downs. I was surprised to find that despite having operated continuously for over 120 years, records existed for less than half that time — since 1937. (The first minute book does exist in private hands, and I would like to thank Ken Grayson of Lexington for allowing me to peruse it.) However, many of the changes at Churchill Downs were described over the years in local newspapers. It was management's preferred method of promoting the Derby—no expense spared in improvements to accommodate the racing patron. But all evidence of the internal decision-making is lost. Ironically, part, if not most, of the problem centered on Matt Winn. He was in control for so long that he simply told employees what to do and he told reporters what he wanted them to hear. He carried the record in his head. Then too, for much of its existence, Churchill Downs has been controlled by holding companies. Decisions of the Kentucky Jockey Club were made in Covington, Kentucky, and then approved by the Churchill Downs board. Meetings of the American Turf Association were held in Chicago and its decisions were later ratified in Louisville. And at the center of it all was Matt Winn.

Christened Martin Joseph Winn, this genial, ambitious, and astute, pudgy widower (his wife died in 1912) and father of ten children was raised in the Portland area of Louisville. His father Patrick ran a grocery store and saloon, above which his family lived, on Lytle Street west of Fifteenth. Martin began clerking for his father in 1879 when he was eighteen, and soon became a traveling agent, a drummer, for a series of wholesale grocers. Winn would later tell writer Henry Simmons that several years after the first Kentucky Derby, which he witnessed with his father, he was gathering grocery orders in Woodford County, near Midway, when he stopped at Nantura, the famous farm of the Harper family, then being run by Frank Harper. The nephew of the late John Harper asked Winn, so the story goes, if in his travels he had seen any better horses than those at Nantura. Winn said "he wouldn't go that far." Harper was naturally taken aback, as then on Nantura were the two best-known horses in Kentucky—Longfellow and Ten Broeck. Harper made certain that Winn was at Churchill Downs on July 4, 1878 when Ten Broeck took on Mollie McCarthy in one of the most famous match races of all times and the singular event which cemented the track's importance in racing. Winn said when he greeted Harper in the weighing room after

Ten Broeck had won, the owner yelled at him: "I'll never run my horse again. He satisfies me, and he ought to satisfy all." In any case, Ten Broeck, named for the famous turfman Richard Ten Broeck, the first American to race horses in England and France, ran many times thereafter, and was considered the greatest horse of his day.

One of Ten Broeck's few defeats, however, was to Aristides in the inaugural Kentucky Derby. Price McGrath's colt has always been considered a Kentucky product through and through, because he was foaled at McGrathiana in Lexington. But Aristides was bred on a farm quite familiar to me when I was growing up in Chestnut Hill on the outskirts of Philadelphia. Leamington, Aristides' sire was standing at Aristides Welch's Erdenheim Farm. When I knew the place, it was owned by George D. Widener.

Martin J. Winn continued to be interested in horses and to reside in Portland while working as a merchant tailor. In 1902, one of his clients, W. E. Applegate, asked him to become involved in the reorganization he was orchestrating of the management and ownership of Churchill Downs. Applegate then controlled over eighty percent of the New Louisville Jockey Club's stock, and he was disappointed in its financial performance. Winn came on board as vice president to run the catering operation as well as to put on summer entertainment. The sitting mayor of Louisville, Charles F. Grainger, was named president of the track, and Winn served in Grainger's administration on the board of public safety. He officially became Matt J. Winn, and a Kentucky Colonel, but he continued to be listed in the city directories as president of his tailoring operation until 1914. The next year he was listed as general manager of the New Louisville Jockey Club. Winn was forty-six. When he died at eighty-eight, both he and Churchill Downs were institutions, and he had managed to put his personal stamp on other race tracks as well.

It is surprising that considering its celebrity there are not more early photographs of Churchill Downs. The newspapers were not able to print photographs until the turn of the century and they were slow to bring on staff photographers, relying heavily on commercial firms like Royal Photo and Caufield & Shook. Both firms lasted for many years, but the early work of Royal Photo was removed from its glass plates to recover the silver, and Caufield & Shook lost its early years' negatives in the 1937 flood. However, some of

Royal's panoramic views exist at the Kentucky Derby Museum at Churchill Downs and in corporate offices, while Caufield & Shook's extensive pictorial record is kept separate from its overall collection at the University of Louisville Photographic Archives. Ina Duncan, widow of Caufield & Shook photographer and latter-day proprietor Dick Duncan, has been most helpful with the Derby collection, which is now part of the Kinetic Corporation.

Churchill Downs was photographed for thirty-two years by Henry Clay "Doc" Ashby, who died at the age of 64 in 1943. Unfortunately, however, his print collection, which reportedly numbered in the hundreds of thousands, could not be found. A few of his prints are in the Charles F. Price papers which have been recently donated to the Kentucky Derby Museum by his family.

There are no extant photographs of the first rather picayune grandstand, located where the backside is presently. An often reproduced 1889 photograph, thought to be of the original grandstand, shows, we now know, the elaborate additions incorporated by architect Charles Julian Clarke in 1882. It was the architectural firm of D. X. Murphy & Bro. which designed the familiar twin-spired grandstand in 1894, completed in time for the 1895 Derby. D.X. Murphy & Bro. later became known as Luckett and Farley, which today continues as Louisville's largest architectural firm. In its storage bowels are voluminous drawings which date to the firm's first work at Churchill Downs in 1894. President Dennis DeWitt made the files available. Those rolled sheets of drawings have been catalogued by Ramelle "Pat" Patterson, a volunteer at the Kentucky Derby Museum. Her work has been invaluable to this project. Gerald Baumgartle also was most helpful in retrieving the drawings at Luckett & Farley for inspection and copying.

I was first made aware of the architectural changes at Churchill Downs by the late Marjorie Rieser Weber, who shortly before she died in 1971, came to the attic in the Jefferson County Courthouse where I worked as the county archivist and requested the plans for the first clubhouse. Mrs. Weber had written her master's thesis at the University of Louisville in 1944 on horse racing in Kentucky and particularly in Jefferson County. Over the years, she had continued to write, mainly for the racing programs at Churchill Downs. Her assignment that day was to find the original plans so the clubhouse could be reproduced to house a new museum in time for the hundredth running of the Derby in 1974.

The county had never required nor kept such building plans, but it occurred to me that if the track had ever been sued by a contractor or architect, the plans might have been filed as an exhibit. A search of the various court indexes turned up numerous cases, and the last musty file from a box of those records requested from the state archives in Frankfort yielded paydirt. The plans were part of the official record of a Louisville Chancery Court case brought by a contractor over the sum of $455.60. The drawings were taken to Luckett & Farley and plans were made to reproduce the clubhouse for the museum, but its construction was never undertaken.

It seemed best to arrange the flow of this book chronologically and to allow an index to account for changes within subject headings. Few of the previous books have indexes and none have footnotes for reference or explanation. So many stories have been repeated without substantiation in the past that this feature of endnoting will provide a starting point for future researchers. Lastly, this book has had many authors and editors, as well as a corps of illustrators. Its words are mainly those of the journalists and others who recorded the changing times of horse racing and who saw the work at Churchill Downs in progress and expressed what they witnessed in the vernacular of the day. At times, it might sound strange or stilted, but for the most part it has a warmth and richness we have since excised from journalism. Sports writers were not reporters providing facts to be assembled by copy writers and editors. They were hired for their descriptive flair and were generally considered the newspapers' most creative writers. Horse racing was America's first real spectator sport. *The Turf, Field and Farm* referred to it on 16 May 1879 as "the Great National Pastime of the Country." As such, racing stories were page one material. This book is a compilation of that material along with explanatory narrative and over two hundred illustrations. What follows is the story of Churchill Downs, woven together and presented with a deep appreciation for the institution that has survived and been such a part of our community identity since 1875.

—Samuel W. Thomas, Louisville, January 1995

Tandems racing on the Louisville levee, 1871. Map (inset) shows location of Louisville's rare tracks.

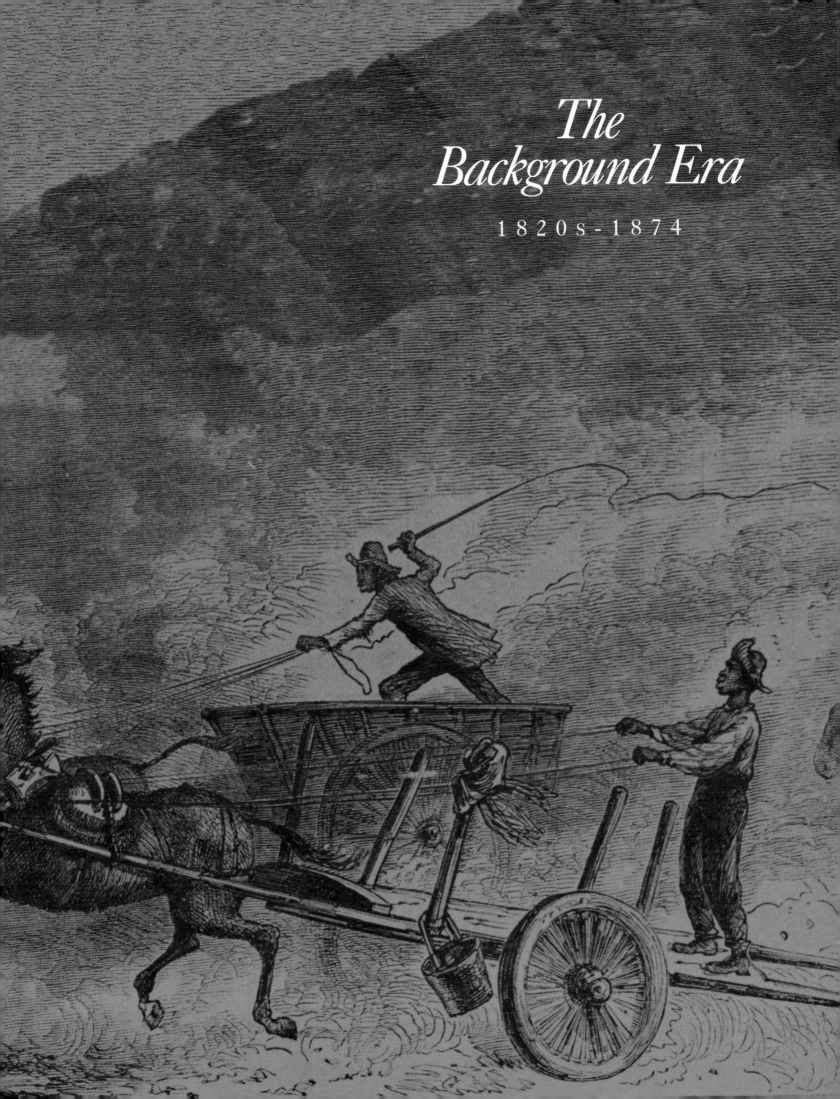

The Background Era

1 8 2 0 s - 1 8 7 4

Louisville was at a virtual standstill in November 1872. The country's fourteenth largest city with a burgeoning population of over 100,000 had been brought to its knees. The catastrophe was not the fault of the Ohio River overflowing its banks. Winds had been calm, and it had yet to snow. Workers were not on strike. Rather, the cause was the dreaded Epizootic, the horse influenza which had originated in Toronto, then spread to Boston and New York, before crippling Philadelphia, Baltimore and Washington, and Cleveland. Ironically, *The Courier-Journal* had tried to pacify its readers on November second by reporting that local veterinary surgeon Alexander Harthill was sure that the Canadian disease had not reached Louisville. "He thinks it improbable that it will do so." Certainly, he reasoned, "the pest" would first ravage nearby Cincinnati, Indianapolis, or St. Louis.[1]

But on the eleventh, *The Courier-Journal* had to announce that the "Canadian horse disease is among us." By the thirteenth, it had affected over five hundred horses; on the fourteenth, over a thousand were reported to be suffering from the disorder. "The hack stands are comparatively deserted, and vehicles of all kinds are scarce. For once aristocracy comes down to the level of the plebeian—the pavement—and the representatives of the two extremes wade through the mud of the streets side by side."

Although only some fifty animals died during the month-long onslaught, most of Jefferson County's 6,500 horses were made weak and useless.[2] All the street cars were "withdrawn," and every public stable in the city had been affected by the fifteenth. "The people therefore must travel," *The Courier-Journal* lamented, "from one extreme of the city to the other on foot. Goods from the stores in many cases are delivered by hand; freight is blockaded in the stores, warehouses and depots and is only removed by small lots at double price. The doctors visit their patients on foot...and, in short, general traffic has come to almost a standstill." On the sixteenth, the newspaper remarked: "The absence of the horse from the thoroughfares, the unusual silence of the street arising from the withdrawal of omnibuses, carriages, carts, drays, street cars, etc., from the public ways, formed a feature that could not be made at once familiar to the thousands who, for the first time in their lives, had no alternative but to walk." At each of the firehouses, locals were being enrolled "to turn out in force and pull the engine to the scene." It is not difficult to forget–if we were ever fully aware of–how reliant we once were upon the horse. No wonder organizations were created solely for the purpose of improving the breed. Before the steam engine was truly harnessed, man was dependent on the horse to perform the heavy tasks and lessen the load. As we do today with automobiles, it was only natural to determine whose horse could run the fastest. Eventually those casual contests became a sport.

In 1870, when Kentucky was the eighth largest state, the U. S. Census of Agriculture reported that the commonwealth possessed 317,034 horses and colts, out of a nationwide total of over seven million. The number of

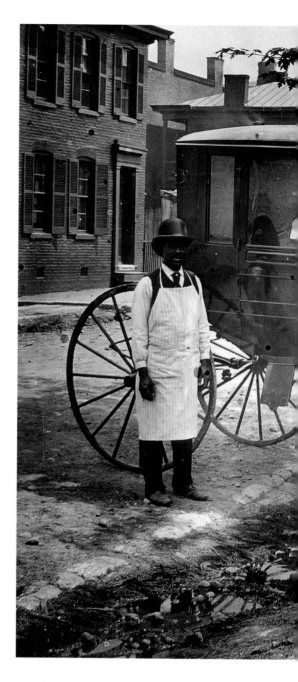

Jacob Street east of Second Street, *ca*. 1893.

Right: From "Treatment of Influenza," *Illustrated American Horse Book* (1878), p.156.

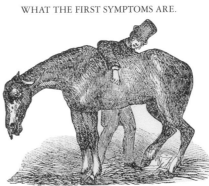

WHAT THE FIRST SYMPTOMS ARE.

TESTING FOR FATAL SYMPTOMS IN THIS DISEASE.

HOW TO TREAT IT SENSIBLY.

HOW TO CLOTHE THE HORSE.

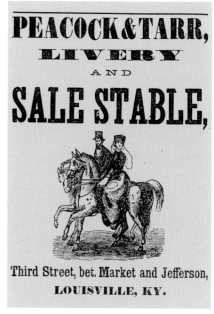

horses and colts in the country continued to increase to almost twenty million by 1920, afterward declining as mechanization spread.[3] But for those who lived in eras when horses were an everyday part of life, going to the track to enjoy contests of endurance and speed was as natural as a night at the speedway in the 1990s. Neither is the problem of confining fast driving to the race tracks a development of the automobile age. Just before the 1872 Epizootic scourge hit Louisville, the general council passed an ordinance prohibiting fast driving at street intersections. As a letter writer to *The Courier-Journal* then commented: "You never see an empty cart or dray driven at a walk, and generally, even when loaded, the driver is constantly cracking his whip to urge his horses or mules to a trot. The other day I saw several drays, each loaded with thirteen barrels of flour, and all driven at a sweeping trot." The writer was concerned that the ordinance simply prohibited driving beyond the speed of five miles an hour, and asked how that speed could be determined or documented in order to prosecute? Then he remarked: "Strange as it may seem, the city was better policed twenty or twenty-five years ago than it is now. Then no cart, dray, or wagon was driven faster than a walk, and no wheelbarrow was trundled on the sidewalks. Let these old regulations be restored and rigidly enforced...Let us have no more absurd ordinances, allowing speed of five or any other number of miles an hour."[4]

Just how fast could a horse run? What were its limits—not those imposed by ordinance? Everyone knew how fast a horse could walk. But how fast could it run, especially if endowed by breeding and improved by training? Those were the questions that ultimately became the *raison d' être* for the entire industry of horse breeding and the basis upon which the racing industry was created and sustained. In November 1872, when everyone was made aware of just how useful and necessary horses were, they also realized there needed to be a place where horses' speed could be tested and compared.

Left: Central Boarding and Livery Stable, 206 Guthrie Street, *ca.* 1895. Above: Advertisement, 1864 Louisville directory.

If not the greatest, certainly not the least of the good things for which Kentucky is famous is the blooded horse, bred and reared, in the "Bluegrass counties of the grand old Commonwealth." Wherever the racehorse is known, there the Kentucky thoroughbred is known and honored, for his claims to superiority have been gallantly upheld on both sides of the great water in many a hard-fought and spirited contest on the turf, and, whatever may have been his fortunes, never has his rival held him in contempt.

Though it is a fact that the strain of runners of the present day is largely of English blood, and that the first race horses were the produce of English sires and dams, until less than two generations ago, yet the American thoroughbred is distinguished for many good qualities not possessed by his British cousin. The wholesale importations of fashionable blood from the English isle, and the custom of breeding back to imported sires has obliterated much of the difference, but still the American race horse exists, and there are some old-fashioned turfmen who will contend that American long distance and heat races developed an animal superior to the best English blood.

Still credit is due to English-Americans, for the fact that the first blooded horses to reach American soil were imported by them. When the hardy pioneers of Virginia and the older Southern States, having acquired wealth sufficient to indulge in the luxuries of life, began naturally to long for the excitement of the turf, importations of blooded horses began. The best authorities agree that prior to 1800 some 160 thoroughbred sires and forty mares had been brought to America from England. Of these, about seventy horses and twenty mares were imported before 1776. These were bred to what was termed the work animals, or in some cases to what was termed the native horses, the descendants of Spanish stock, and excellent saddles resulted. In Virginia the blood was kept purer, and history states that with other Virginia celebrities, Governor Spotswood, Lord Fairfax and Gen. George Washington were fond of riding thoroughbreds. Tests of speed between favorite saddle horses became common, and the custom grew of meetings at certain places and times for the purpose of racing.

Explorations westward, to what was then Kentucky county of the Old Dominion, finally resulted in the settling of Kentucky, and after many hard-fought battles with crafty red men, two sections, which are now Lafayette and Jefferson counties, Kentucky, became indisputably the property of the pioneers. To these sections the great grasses of Kentucky were indigenous, in Fayette bluegrass and in Jefferson beargrass. The settlement of this State was accomplished about the time that racing had achieved great popularity as a sport in Virginia, but Kentucky was a country too new for anything of this kind. Breeding to thoroughbreds for the improvement of stock, not only for racing purposes but for the farm and road, had begun, and from the very beginning Kentucky was provided with good blood.

In Virginia, racing had taken on immense preparations. The rivalry between wealthy planters and breeders had grown to such an extent that racing circuits had begun to be recognized, and the desire to produce superior animals had led to numerous importations. Among the first of the noted sires to be introduced to American mares was Diomed, an English Derby winner, whose descendants number among them such noted animals as Sir Archie [also spelled Archy], Timoleson, Florizel, Boston and Lexington. Other English animals noted in the American stud are Glencoe, Margrave, Transby, Sarpedon, Saltram, Sir Harry, Arch Duke, John Bull and Spread Eagle, the last named five being also English Derby winners.

At the beginning of the Nineteenth century there appeared on the Virginia turf Col. William R. Johnson, who, with a number of kindred spirits, inaugurated the system of breeding to which the present race horse is due.[5] Races of one, two, three or four miles, and repeat were in vogue, and endurance was the first requisite of a first-class horse. Racing by this time had come to be a sport recognized and followed all over the South, and contests and matches in which much sectional feeling was involved, were of frequent occurrences. It was then that Kentucky swung into line, and that the Bluegrass region first came into prominence for the horses it produced. The sport was chiefly confined, however, to match races, then so popular, but the love of the turf was being developed, and the bone and blood given by the Bluegrass grown on limestone soil was gaining recognition. [Note: Before the first Kentucky Derby in 1875, *The Courier-Journal* remarked that "the first horse contest in the State was at Humble's Race Paths, near Harrodsburg. This was in April 1783. A month later, Haggins' Race Paths, near the same place, were thrown open to the public." From "The Kentucky Turf," *The Turf, Field and Farm*, 14 May 1875.]

The need of organization and of public acknowledgment of racing was also beginning to be felt, and efforts to establish a course near Bardstown were made somewhere about 1806. Races were run there, but further than that little is known. About Lexington, there were several tracks used for both training and racing. At various times between 1800 and 1825, there were tracks at Georgetown, Forks of Elkhorn, Versailles, Harrodsburg, Stanford, Lancaster, Danville, Crab Orchard, Nicholasville, Richmond, Winchester, Mt. Sterling, Paris, Cynthiana, Maysville, Covington, Newport, Augusta, and many other points in the State. In these early days, the race tracks were simply what the name implies. A course, surrounded by a single rail fence, open to the public, was all that was required, and the races were almost exclusively for stakes made up by the owners of the contesting horses, though occasionally a purse was made up by subscription. The running was for the sport it gave the owners and the people of the neighborhoods in which the races took place....

Until the time of the Civil war the American turfman indulged in only long distance and heat racing. For a horse who could simply run a mile or two miles, but who could not repeat, he had a supreme contempt, and such animals it was his desire to weed out. He bred for bottom and speed, and he demanded that his race horses have both, for bottom without speed was useless, and vice versa. To run four-mile heats and to run in good time was the test of a first-rate race horse, but to key a horse up to such a race required time. When the race was run he required time to be made fit for another go. Races, consequently, were not so common as in the present day, but when a great match or sweepstakes was arranged it attracted the attention of the nation, and public feeling ran high.

The war interfered with this, and from war times dated the decay of the old order of things. Some few four-mile heat races were run afterward, however, and heat racing was still popular until a year or so ago. It still is with the public, but owners refuse to put their horses to such severe trials, and it may be safely said that heat racing is now a thing of the past. But the demand for thoroughbred horses was never so great as at present, and the Kentucky Bluegrass still nourishes the best in the world.

Horse racing began in earnest in Louisville more than fifty years before the Kentucky Derby was conceived. As early as 1822, the Louisville Jockey Club publicized its three days of fall racing. "At that time the Jockey Club races were held on my father's place, on the head-waters of Beargrass, about eight miles from Louisville," wrote John Funk to the *Kentucky Live Stock Record* in 1879. The brick house owned by his father, Peter Funk, still stands on the northeast corner of Taylorsville Road and Hurstbourne Lane.[6] By 1827, the Hope Distillery Company grounds of a "hundred acres at the lower end of Main street, and immediately opposite the commencement of the Portland and Shippingport turnpike roads" had been converted into the Louisville Turf.[7] The meet was conducted "agreeably to the rules of the Lexington Jockey Club," which had come into being in 1809 when the twelve-year-old Kentucky Jockey Club was reorganized. It in turn was superseded in 1826 by the Kentucky Association for the Improvement of the Breeds of Stock.[8]

Evidently, the Louisville Jockey Club soon faded from existence and by 1831, racing was being sponsored by the Louisville Agricultural Society. Following the meet in October 1831, the Louisville Association for the Improvement of the Breed of Horses was established. A copy of its constitution as well as its rules and regulations, printed in 1832, is extant.[9] Fifty-two acres south of Magnolia Avenue and west of Seventh Street Road was subsequently purchased from Samuel Churchill and his brother Henry for a track, and the Oakland Race Course soon opened. Samuel Churchill would be one of its presidents.[10]

FROM "THE NEW LOUISVILLE JOCKEY CLUB," *SPIRIT OF THE TIMES*, 9 JUNE 1838
We learn that at a meeting of the Club, held, pursuant to notice, at the Galt House, on Saturday, the 18th May, 1838, Dr. Jas. C. Johnson was called to the chair, and Col. A. Tarlton appointed Secretary *pro tem*. It was resolved that this Association be called "The Louisville Jockey Club." Mr. Robert L. Ward was unanimously elected President, and Mr. A. Throckmorton, Esq., Dr. Jas. C. Johnson, H.B. Hill, Esq., and Col. Jas. Robertson, Vice Presidents; John G. Graham, Esq., Secretary, and Y. N. Oliver, Esq., Treasurer; James S. Irwin, Chas. Riddle, Geo. G. Presbury, Col. A. Tarlton, Mason Thompson, S. Hackell, and G. N. Patterson, Esqrs., Stewards. *Resolved,* That the President and Vice Presidents appoint a committee of five gentlemen to wait upon the Ladies.

FROM "SPORT IN KENTUCKY," *SPIRIT OF THE TIMES*, 11 MAY 1838
The Oakland Course is now probably one of the most complete in the country, in all its fixtures and appointments, and horses certainly run faster over it than they do any where else in the land. If they make any more quick time it will behoove Col. [Yelverton N.] Oliver, the proprietor, to have it measured again, although it has already been submitted to that process.

LOUISVILLE JOCKEY CLUB
RACES.

WILL commence on the first Wednesday in October next, on the Louisville Turf (at the Hope distillery) and continue 4 days, free for any horse, mare or gelding, agreeably to the rules of the Lexington Jockey Club.

First day, purse three mile beats, $120
Second do. two do. 80
Third do. one do. 50
Fourth do. three beats in 5 one mile and repeat, for the entrance money of the four days.
By order of the Club,
sept. 18 44 D. HEINSHON, Sec'ry.

BEARGRASS JOCKEY CLUB RACES,
WILL COMMENCE at the house of Major Peter Funk, on Wednesday, the 26th September, 1827, and continue for four days—free for any horse, mare or gelding, agreeable to the rules of said Club. The cash to be up for each day's race.
1st day's race, 3 mile heats, purse $100
2nd do. 2 do. 75
3d do. 1 do. 50
4th do. a sweepstake for 25
Entrance free for any untried two or three years old—the two years old to carry catches.
By order of the Club.
Jefferson county, Sept. 1 42—4t

LOUISVILLE RACES.

THE Louisville Agricultural Society Racing will commence on TUESDAY, 18th OCTOBER, 1831.
On Tuesday a purse of $100 with entrance, free for anything—one mile and repeat.
On Wednesdy, a purse of $600, 4 miles and repeat.
On Thursday, a purse of $200, 2 miles and repeat.
On Friday, a purse of $400, 3 miles and repeat.
On Saturday, preprietor's purse, bust three in five, mile beats.
There will be a Match Race on Tuesday for $500, 2 miles and repeat. august 6—td

Top: From *The Louisville Daily Focus,* 2 October 1827. Bottom: From *The Louisville Daily Focus,* October 1831. Opposite: Parole beating Ten Broeck at Baltimore. *The Spirit of the Times,* 22 December 1877.

We are told that there is a probability that the Cincinnati Course will pass into the hands of Oliver. He seems extremely well fitted for the re-arrangement of race courses, for he is sure in the first place to do that which of all things is most essential to their success–awake a general feeling among the gentlemen of the vicinity, which gives the thing a good "send-off." He may be said to have created all the courses in New Orleans, and he has lately done for the Louisville Course what we hope he may continue to do for as many others as possible–put up grand purses and induce breeders to go into numerous stakes.

FROM "ON DITS IN SPORTING CIRCLES," *THE SPIRIT OF THE TIMES*, 29 JUNE 1839

The Great Kentucky Stake, for all ages, we are desired to state, will come off over the Oakland Course, at Louisville, on the last day of September next. There are ten subscribers at $2000 each, half forfeit, Four mile heats. One of the subscribers writes us as follows:

   During the late races over the Oakland Course, Grey Eagle was sold to Mr. Shotwell, of Georgetown, for $6,250. Mr. S. takes his engagement, pays his forfeit, or puts up his stake. Tarlton, one of the nominations in the Great Stake broke down in the Four mile race. Muscdora, another nomination, won handily the first heat in 7:50—the track not so fast as I have seen it by several seconds. Mary Vaughan, a third nomination, was there, and ran a trial that convinced her owners she is invincible [at] four miles; they accordingly declined risking the chances of her breaking down or otherwise injuring herself in a race, before the great affair, so says report. It is now pretty certain that Muscdora, Hawk-eye, Mary Vaughan, and Grey Eagle, will start from Kentucky; if Wagner, Billy Townes, and Picton, can beat them, they can take Old Kentuck. There is the greatest possible excitement about the race; thousands are bet every day.

FROM *LOUISVILLE DAILY COURIER*, 14 OCTOBER 1853

Grey Eagle, the pride of Kentucky, and the renowned Wagner, the champion of the South, will be at the fair, and shown together in the ring. The sight of these two veteran champions of the turf would repay a man for a journey of a thousand miles. Grey Eagle is the property of J. P. Dobyns & Co., of Maysville, is now in his 18th year. He was by Woodpecker, dam Ophelius, by Eclipse. Old Wagner is the property of Mr. J. Campbell, who has owned him all his life. He is 19 years old, his dam Maria West, by Sir Charles, and notwithstanding all his hardships, and his great age, he is as active as ever, and as perfect, and unblemished as a colt.

   About 14 years ago, the great contest over the Oakland race track, four mile heats between Grey Eagle and Wagner took place, and the result is well remembered by every Kentuckian. Grey Eagle was beaten, after the first heat in 7:43–the best time ever made at that period. The second heat was run in 7:48, which was won by Wagner, and in the third heat the gallant Grey met with an accident on the third mile, and old Wagner was declared the champion, but from that day to this he has never won another race.

Engraving of Grey Eagle, from a painting by Edward Troye, in *American Turf Register* and *Sporting Magazine*, April 1843.

FROM "ON DITS IN SPORTING CIRCLES," *THE SPIRIT OF THE TIMES*, 29 JUNE 1839

   I wish you could have been at our late Spring Meeting. I never have seen so brilliant an affair. Our spirited stewards were all dressed in jockey style, that is, with fair top boots, buckskin small clothes, and Newmarket coats; then we had thousands of ladies, although the dust was almost suffocating. Won't you come out next Fall?

1840 oil painting of Oakland House and Race Course by Robert Brammer and Augustus A. Von Smith, Sr. The pear-shaped, one mile track took its name from old oaks in its infield.

FROM WALTER N. HALDEMAN, *PICTURE OF LOUISVILLE, DIRECTORY AND BUSINESS ADVERTISER OF 1844-1845.*

This beautiful and popular Course is reached, by going out Sixth or Seventh street. It is but little over a mile from the southern boundary of the city, and forms a pleasant drive to those who desire to breathe the pure atmosphere of the country during the sultry months of summer. This enclosure embraces 57 $\frac{1}{2}$ acres.

It is pronounced equal to any track on the continent, and since it has been in charge of the present proprietor, Col. Joseph Metcalfe, has revived a taste for the sports of the turf.

The area of the Course, is finely shaded by native oaks, so trimmed as not to obstruct the view. The Pavilion is very spacious, and is fitted up in good style. The Oakland House, kept by Col. Metcalfe, is a large and well arranged establishment, for the accommodation of visiters; and, especially, has attention been paid to having erected suitable buildings for the many stables of horses and their grooms, periodically brought on to contend for the liberal purses which the proprietor takes a pleasure in bestowing upon those who may win them. His stables will accommodate 120 horses.

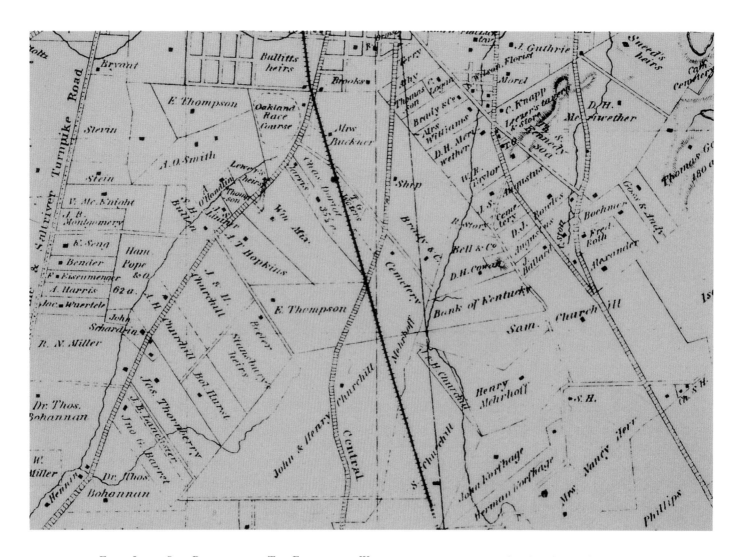

Section from 1858 *Map of Jefferson County, Kentucky,* by G.T. Bergmann, showing the Louisville and Nashville Railroad tracks running east of the defunct Oakland Race Course at top and future Churchill Downs property at bottom.

FROM JAMES SILK BUCKINGHAM, *THE EASTERN AND WESTERN STATES OF AMERICA* (LONDON, 1842).[11]

During the week that we remained at Louisville, there were various causes of excitement all in action at the same time. Horse-racing, in which the Kentuckians take great delight, had drawn together a great number of sportsmen, as they are called here. A large bazaar, or fancy fair, was holding in the city, to raise funds for an orphan asylum. Bargain-making and gallantry, philanthropy and coquetry, were here strangely mingled; and all the arts of the most worldly tradespeople were put in requisition to entrap inexperienced buyers, while pious frauds were justified in the eyes of the sellers by the gains realized for charitable purposes. The theatre and the circus were at the same time crowded every night, at the benefits of favorite actors and actresses; and concerts, given at the public ball-room were also well attended. After these, or rather contemporaneously with them, several religious meetings were held, connected with a great Baptist convention, which met here during this week, to hold its anniversary. To crown all, the city was said to be full of gamblers, this being the season at which they periodically ascend the river from New Orleans, and usually stop here for a month or two, before they scatter themselves among the fashionable watering-places, to allure their game. Many of the haunts of these gamblers were pointed out to me, and no pains were taken to conceal them. Their persons also are readily recognizable by the greater style of fashion and expensiveness in which they dress, and the air of dissipation by which they are marked from other men. Pistols and bowie-knives are carried by them all; while their numbers, their concentrated action, and their known ferocity and determination, make them so formidable that neither the community nor the public authorities seem willing to take any bold or decisive step against them; and while lottery offices abound in all the principal streets, under the sanction or sufferance of the public, it would be difficult to justify an interference with any other kind of gambling without suppressing this at the same time.

Even with pleasant accommodations, the Oakland Race Course did not survive long enough for the Louisville and Nashville Railroad to skirt the grounds in 1855. This was the first southern railroad system to have its northern terminus in Louisville, making the transportation of horses to race tracks in Tennessee much less difficult.

The Louisville, Cincinnati & Lexington Railroad had transported most of the huge crowds to the state fairs in Crescent Hill that began there in 1853, so when the National Race Course association undertook to provide for a suitable track site on which to reconstitute racing in the state's metropolitan area in the late 1850s, 150 acres was purchased between the railroad tracks and the Westport Road east of St. Matthews.

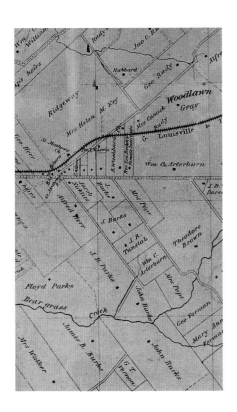

Section from 1858 map of Jefferson County showing St. Matthews area and Woodlawn property.

FROM "THE NATIONAL RACE COURSE," *LOUISVILLE DAILY COURIER*,
22 JUNE 1858

We have already referred to the proposition to establish the "National Race Course of America," in the vicinity of Louisville. In view of the contemplated enterprise, another meeting of stock-raisers and turfmen will take place today, at the Galt House, to determine finally whether the course shall be located here or elsewhere. The delegation from the "Blue Grass Region," and other parts of the State arrived last evening, to participate in the matter and further the object by substantial aid. Among them we notice Capt. A. Buford, Jas. K. Duke, R. Atchison [Aitcheson] Alexander, A. Keene Richards, Junius Ward, Jno. R. Viley, F. G. Murphy of Bardstown, and others who manifest an interest in sporting matters.

It is necessary to raise $50,000 by subscription of $500 per share, to be paid as may hereafter be prescribed. Many gentlemen from the interior of the State have signified their intention to subscribe liberally, but a similar liberality, we regret to say, has not yet been shown by the citizens of Louisville, who are mainly interested in its success.[12]

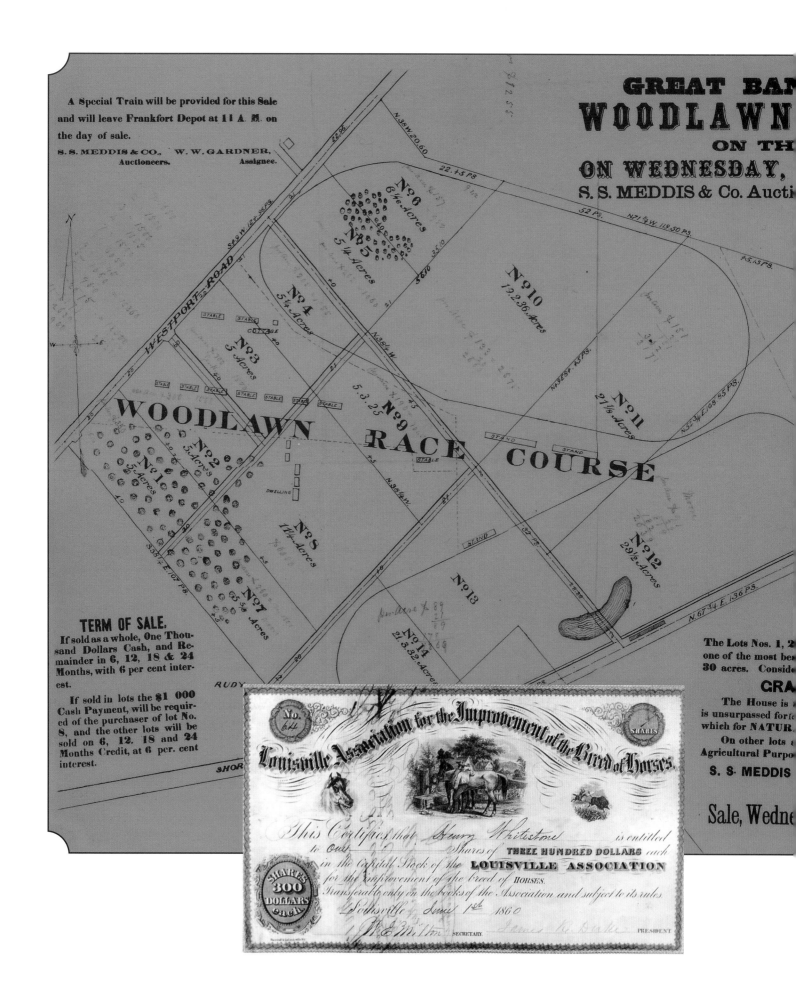

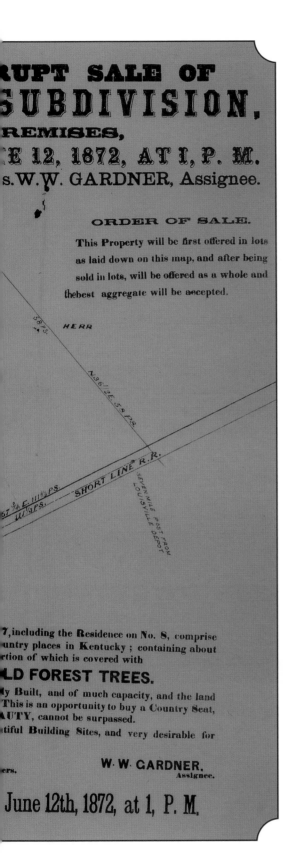

On 1 June 1860, stock was issued again in the name of the Louisville Association for the Improvement of the Breed of Horses. James K. Duke signed as president. Interestingly, the Yale law school graduate and charter member of the Kentucky Association in 1826 resided in Scott County.[13] The track soon was called Woodlawn, its name when George E. H. Gray owned the property.

FROM *LOUISVILLE DAILY COURIER*, 28 MAY 1860

We predicted yesterday that the four mile race over Woodlawn Course would be a great race. The event exceeded our expectation. About five thousand persons were present, and six hundred of these, at least, were ladies. The stand set apart for them was filled, and the members of the Club yielded half of their stand for their accommodation. At no race within twenty years have so many of the fair sex graced the stand of a Kentucky race course. The track was in fine condition, considering the weather for the past week, and the Superintendent, Mr. Carroll, is entitled to the highest praise for surmounting the disadvantages which would have disheartened one less energetic. The track was, however, a little stiff, and would not permit the fastest time, else the first heat would have been still lower in the forties.

In closing out our report of the Spring meeting, over Woodlawn Course, we must refer to the general management of its affairs. Whatever may have been the doubts of its permanency, the success of this year puts at rest all doubt. Every day the weather was unfavorable, yet thousands were there to witness the sport. And had the elements been more favorable, this would be remembered as the most brilliant of all the meetings on the race courses of Kentucky. The most perfect order and decorum were observed. Large purses brought together the finest race horses in the State. Woodlawn is yet in its infancy, but so long as it is conducted with the propriety that, so far, has been evident in its management, and so long as such men as Richard Atchison, Maj. Thomas H. Hunt, and their associates take an interest in its affairs, it will rank as it deserves to rank, with the first and best race courses in the world.[14]

Like the Oakland course, Woodlawn accommodated both Thoroughbreds and trotters.[15] In fact, Woodlawn had two separate tracks. The Civil War certainly compromised the track's success, and in an attempt to keep the operation afloat to support the horse breeders and owners, R. A. Alexander redeemed much of the stock. The proprietor of Woodburn farm at Spring Station, Woodford County, had shown various breeds of livestock at the state fairs in Crescent Hill. Then while in England, according to Thoroughbred historian Kent Hollingsworth, Alexander met Richard Ten Broeck who owned the fabled and nearly blind Lexington, which he had standing at W. F. Harper's farm near Woodburn. Alexander's purchase of the horse for $15,000 was rewarded when Lexington headed the American sire lists from 1861 until he died in 1875. Hollingsworth, editor of *The Bloodhorse*, claimed "Lexington sired more good horses than any other stallion before or since."[16] Lexington also put Spring Station on the map. Its name was derived, not from being a pioneer fort as was Spring Station in Jefferson County, but rather, it was on the Frankfort line that hooked up with the Louisville, Cincinnati & Lexington Railroad at LaGrange.

As *The Woodford Sun* would point out on 6 September 1889, "the first stock farm to attract widely extended notice" was Woodburn, then owned by R. A. Alexander's brother, A. J. Alexander. The "next in importance" locally was Nantura, owned by "celebrated turfman" F. B. Harper. Various other farms operations were mentioned, noting that "most of these stock breeders have clustered along the line of the L & N Railroad in the northeastern portion of the county, on account of the convenience of transportation, but completion of the Louisville Southern RR opens up a large territory of first class lands...[in] Fayette and Bourbon."

But the Civil War would interrupt all commerce; horse racing in Kentucky was no exception. Marauding bands invaded the horse farms in Central Kentucky and prize stock was taken. Writing in *Harper's New Monthly Magazine*'s 15 October 1883 issue, William Henry Bishop related the story of the abduction from Woodburn of Asteroid. The son of Lexington, foaled in 1861 along with Kentucky and Norfolk, would be undefeated in twelve starts.

> On the next occasion [of a guerrilla attack on 22 October 1864] it was the thorough-bred Asteroid that was run off. The artist [Edward] Troye was engaged in painting his portrait at the time, and his principal rage was at the interruption of his work. This portrait, in which the trainer, "Old Ansel," and the jockey, "Brown Dick," are introduced, though on a reduced scale, with a quaint idea of not detracting from the importance of the horse, was completed on the subsequent recovery of Asteroid, and hangs in the dining-room of Mr. L. Brodhead, the general manager of the estate; and Asteroid himself, long past his usefulness, now browses out a comfortable existence on the place, till he be overtaken by the usual lot of men and horses.

Edward Dudley Brown, known as Brown Dick, continued to ride for R. A. Alexander and then for Daniel Swigert, who married a cousin of Alexander's and who had become manager of Woodburn in 1862. When Swigert left Woodburn to establish his own operation, A. J. Alexander hired Swigert's brother-in-law, Lucas Brodhead, as manager. He also would become a director and a vice president of the Louisville Jockey Club.

After resumption of racing at Woodlawn following the Civil War, the spring meeting of 1866 was an unfortunate disaster, with many horses breaking down from "the severity of the Southern Campaign." Before the fall meeting, the course had been leased for five years by Abe Buford, A. H. Brand, and B. G. Bruce, all "experienced turfmen." General Buford would also later become a member of the Louisville Jockey Club's board of directors; Benjamin Gratz Bruce would become the club's secretary.[17]

Oil Painting of Asteroid, signed by Edward Troye, 11 December 1864, showing jockey Edward Brown at left and trainer Ansel Williamson at right. Brown would become a successful trainer and owner. Williamson would train for A. Keene Richards of Georgetown and later H. Price McGrath, for whom he would prepare Aristides for the first Kentucky Derby.

FROM "THE WOODLAWN PROGRAMME," *THE TURF, FIELD AND FARM,*
27 OCTOBER 1866

The turf is on a decline at Louisville. The people take no interest in racing, and it is thought that the beautiful Woodlawn will have to be abandoned. Last spring experienced gentlemen became the lessees of the course, and their names alone were a guarantee that racing would be conducted on the highest principles. They expended money with a lavish hand, offered an attractive program, and depended on the citizens of Louisville for their reward. They thought that the old love for turf institutions was strong with the people, and that they felt a pride in Woodlawn. But in this, it seems, they were mistaken. Notwithstanding the number of horses present, and the high principles upon which the fall races have been conducted, the meeting has been poorly attended, and the gate receipts are of the most beggarly character. In the face of such stubborn facts the lessees became disheartened, and on the evening of the 17th of October they surrendered the management of the course to the stockholders.

FROM "THE WOODLAWN PROGRAMME," *THE TURF, FIELD AND FARM*,
19 JANUARY 1867

In another column will be found the programme of the Spring Meeting over the Woodlawn Race Course. The turfmen of Kentucky are hopeful that they will be able to triumph over the failures of last year, and they are working with that energy which never fails to command success. It is believed that the prestige of Woodlawn will be restored before the frosts of another November settle down upon the earth, for when the June roses are in bloom the course will become the theatre of excitement. The liberal purses proposed will attract the horses, and the horses will draw the crowds. The merchants of Louisville seem to have awakened from their lethargic dream at last; and now that they have got their eyes open, they realize the importance of racing in a commercial point of view....

We are almost sorry that the management has not seen fit to introduce either a hurdle race or a steeple chase, for where a feeling of apathy prevails in regard to turf contests, the leaping races prove attractive cards, and stir the people up to the highest degree of enthusiasm. They excite the interest of the ladies especially, and wherever woman goes, man is sure to follow. It is true that there are few, if any, trained jumpers in the West; yet with good sized purses they could be attracted from the East and from Canada. Besides, in Kentucky, where the horse grows to perfection, they have the material for excellent leapers, and, with careful training, it would not be necessary to depend upon other sections for the magnets to draw the crowds and to give interest to the contests. These suggestions are made with the hope that they may prove beneficial in the future.

The Woodlawn Vase has been exhibited at the Kentucky Derby Museum.

Woodlawn's last vestige of support was lost when Robert Aitcheson Alexander died on 1 December 1867.[18] However, a piece of his legacy is very evident each spring. Since 1917, the winner of the Preakness Stakes at the Pimlico Race Course has been presented the Woodlawn Vase, created by Tiffany and Company in 1860. It was valued at $1,000 and the race for it, to be held both spring and fall, was to be a "dash of four miles." When Capt. T. G. Moore won the initial two races and appeared to have an odds on chance of winning it a third time, thereby retiring the silver trophy, R. A. Alexander intervened, paying $500 to obtain it for the Woodlawn Association. Alexander won it twice, and after he died, his brother and heir, A. J. Alexander, gave it to the Louisville Jockey Club. Referred to in *The Courier-Journal* as the Woodburn Challenge Vase, it was added to the winnings of the Great American Stallion Stake in the fall of 1878. The Dwyer Brothers won it with Bramble, and in 1881, they presented it to the Coney Island Jockey Club. It was also raced for at Jerome Park and Morris Park before being presented to the Maryland Jockey Club.[19]

Clubhouse at the Greenland Course, later part of Wilder Park, *ca.* 1890.

From "Racing at the Falls," *The Turf, Field and Farm*, 20 August 1869

There are places where the turf has flourished in which it flourishes no more. And it is safe to assert that where racing has been dethroned, the cause can be traced to stupidity or dishonesty on the part of the managers. For instance, we will go to Louisville, Kentucky. The natural beauty of the Woodlawn Course is not excelled in the world. The people of Louisville are descended from a stock that gloried in the excitements of the turf. The love of the horses, like the love of adventure, was bred in them. But lack of enterprise, and a want of tact in the management of the Woodlawn Course, crushed out all popular enthusiasm for the turf, and even gave to it other than a reputable name....

After Woodlawn had gone down, Greenland sprung up like a mushroom, but from its very start it never appealed to the love of the better classes. At an early period of its history it was made the theater of one of the most brutal displays that ever disgraced a civilized age, and the shock it then and there received was pregnant with the subtle poison of death. The subsequent career of Greenland has been one series of blunders, and, as a consequence, the turf stands lower than ever with the people of Louisville. And until a new association is formed, with the brains to understand the people, all attempts to revive racing at the Falls City must be spasmodic.

The 16 July 1869 issue of *The Turf, Field and Farm* carried the following announcement.

The Courier-Journal informs us that the beautiful race grounds at Louisville, Woodlawn, are to be sold at public auction. Is there not sufficient enterprise at Louisville to keep the grounds intact, or must they be despoiled by the vandal hand of civilization? Woodlawn is one of the very best racecourses in the country, and it should be preserved as a field where the game thoroughbred can write his name on the page of national renown. Surely a State that reaps so much profit from her breeding farms as Kentucky ought to be able to boast of a respectable racing park at her chief city.

Finally in 1872 "the celebrated race course" including "the trotting and running tracks" was sold and subdivided.[20] However a notation was made in the 9 May 1873 issue of *The Turf, Field and Farm* that "the trotting course, with its stands and stables, is still preserved, and will answer either for thoroughbreds or trotters." Sulkies were to be seen as late as 1876, but Woodlawn was soon after a memory.

View from the old water company reservoir above Mellwood Avenue, looking toward the river pumping station. Present site of the River Road Country Club. Section from 1873 map of Louisville with water company at top.

In the meantime, the Greenland Race Course opened after the Civil War on land that had also been in the Churchill family. Worden P. Hahn, who had been successful making bricks, purchased 184.5 acres along the National Turnpike Road (Southern Parkway) south of the House of Refuge in 1865. *The Louisville Daily Democrat* carried the following announcement on 30 June 1867:

The regular running races over the Greenland race-course will commence on Wednesday next, July 3d, and continue for four days. We visited the track yesterday afternoon, and finding a number of stables well represented, we can safely predict this will be a most interesting meeting, and that the various purses will be well contested for. Some changes have been made in the track so that it will compare favorably with any in the country, which, being but a pleasant drive from the city, it is easy of access. Mr. Hahn having built the track and having offered liberal purses to re-establish racing in our midst, is deserving of the support of our citizens. The track promises to be in fine condition and close races and fast time may be looked for. Omnibuses will leave Walker's daily for the track.

Like the other major tracks before it, Greenland also put on trotting meets and later it was used exclusively for that purpose. In 1872, Hahn sold out and it was eventually acquired by the Wilder family.[21] Three blocks west was Churchill Downs, almost too close for comfort. *The Live Stock Record* had noted on 12 November 1887 the possible formation of a new jockey club on the Wilder property. And again in 1890, in apparent opposition to the management of Churchill Downs, the old Greenland Race Course was leased by rival parties, but to no avail.[22] When subdivided as Wilder Park in 1892, the old clubhouse was at the northeast corner of Second and Kenton streets.

FROM *THE COURIER-JOURNAL* 20 MAY 1872

It has been for years a subject of remark that we have had no representative race-course. Oakland went down, Woodlawn followed, and it has been said that Louisville could not sustain a race-course. This is an error....We are glad to say another is about to come into existence...the proprietors of Villa Park have donated a hundred and odd acres for this purpose....It is, in a word, all that is wanted for the National Race-course of America. The proprietors are already laying out the track. They are too late for the stake races this fall, but they propose to offer such purses as will draw together the best horses in Kentucky and the South; and there is no question but what the Association will give the most exciting races that have occurred in the Western country....That will be done on the course of the Falls City Association. They have organized the club with Grandison Spratt, Esq. [proprietor of the Pickett Tobacco Warehouse] as President, one of the most popular gentlemen in the South and West.... What Jerome Park is to New York, and the grand Metairie to New Orleans, the new Association will be to Louisville.

Left: Masthead, Lexington, Ky.,
1 January 1876. Above: Published
in Baltimore, 1836.

Villa Park was the proposed feature of an expansive enterprise that got underway in the spring of 1872 on a 120-acre site overlooking Mellwood Avenue, west of the present grounds of the Veterans Administration Hospital. An exposition building and an amphitheater were also being planned in conjunction with the park, probably as a replacement for the fairgrounds in Crescent Hill that was outgrowing its grounds on either side of Crescent Avenue. In addition to the Grand Central Industrial Exposition and Villa Park, two race courses were being built in the river bottom west of the Louisville Water Company's pumping station. The smaller oval was located on 94 acres between River Road and the Ohio River. The larger track was for Thoroughbreds, and it was positioned between River Road and Reservoir (Mellwood) Avenue on 128 acres, with the Muddy Fork of Beargrass Creek meandering picturesquely through its middle. The site is now played over by golfers at the River Road Country Club.

M. G. Kern, who had laid out the St. Louis fairgrounds, was employed to lay out the exposition and park grounds, and in late June 1873, his plans were about to reach fruition with the introduction of water for fountains and lakes, and the roads were about to be made.[23] The Louisville, Westport and Harrods Creek steam railroad was under construction below the bluff, and mule cars ran out to the place, and of course, it was accessible by boat, by River Road, or a short walk from the train through Crescent Hill.[24] *The Courier-Journal* reported optimistically on 25 May 1872 that "laborers are already at work on the course, and the first meeting will be held in the fall."

Although the city Engineer's map, published with a date of January 1873, shows Villa Park's layout as well as that of the two race tracks, the project fell flat. The major cause was the economic panic of 1873 which precipitated a stifling downturn in the economy, forcing many local concerns to go out of business or to cut back.[25] But the fact that this well-publicized venture did not materialize could not have been anticipated by a young man on his way to Europe at the time. He had racing interest in his blood and his bride had been raised by her aunt, Pattie Anderson Ten Broeck, whose husband was the most celebrated American horseman of the period.

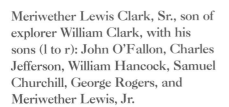
Meriwether Lewis Clark, Sr., son of explorer William Clark, with his sons (l to r): John O'Fallon, Charles Jefferson, William Hancock, Samuel Churchill, George Rogers, and Meriwether Lewis, Jr.

Meriwether Lewis Clark, Jr., was the son of a West Point graduate who fought in the Black Hawk war as well as the conflict in Mexico. General Meriwether Lewis Clark (1809-1881) was the son of William Clark, who had led the expedition to the Pacific with Meriwether Lewis. General Clark also served in the Confederate Army and was with Lee at the final surrender. His namesake was a son by his first wife, Abigail Prather Churchill (1817-1852), daughter of Samuel and Abigail Oldham Churchill, and sister of John and William Henry Churchill.[26]

Meriwether Lewis Clark, Jr., or Lutie as he was called, was born on 27 January 1846 at Spring Grove, the Churchill homestead, where his mother was visiting.[27] She died when Lutie was six and he was raised by his Churchill uncles who lived on Sixth Street between Walnut and Chestnut streets. He attended St. Joseph College in Bardstown before becoming a teller for Second National Bank.

On 26 April 1871, accompanied by his uncles, Lutie ventured across the river to Jeffersonville, Indiana, where he married Mary Martin Anderson, daughter of the late Orville Martin Anderson (1828-1857) and Caroline Scott Timberlake Anderson (1825-1855). Mary Anderson (1854-1934) had been raised by her aunts, Catherine Martin Anderson (Mrs. Thomas S.) Kennedy of Crescent Hill and Pattie Anderson (Mrs. Richard) Ten Broeck who resided at Hurstbourne on the Shelbyville road. Following the civil ceremony, according to the family Bible, the Clarks returned to Hurstbourne (a country club now incorporates the old house). Five days later, however, they were married again in the familiar confines of the St. Matthews Episcopal Church by the Rev. James Craik.

The church had been erected on Ridgeway property donated by Helen Scott Bullitt Massie Martin (1792-1872), widow of both Henry Massie and John Lewis Martin (1779-1854). Major Martin was secretary of the Lexington Jockey Club when it was formed in 1809. When Major Martin died, he was considered one of Louisville's wealthiest citizens. He was also the bride's great-grandfather, his grandson being Orville Martin Anderson. Mrs. Helen Bullitt Martin had been born and raised at Oxmoor, next door to the old John J. Jacob, Jr., place which Pattie and Richard Ten Broeck purchased in 1868. They had its name changed to Hurstbourne to honor his friend, the Duke of Portland, whose manor house bore that name.[28]

Richard Ten Broeck (1811-1892) was America's most celebrated horseman prior to the Civil War. The native of Albany, New York, would have known Meriwether Lewis Clark, Sr., at West Point. He soon got into racing in partnership with "the Napoleon of the Turf," William R. Johnson, whom Ten Broeck would later describe as "the best judge of horses I have ever known." He enjoyed reasonable success until he, Willa Viley, and others purchased Darley from Elisha Warfield, M.D., in 1853, changing his name to Lexington.[29] His four-mile heat races with Lecomte (which Ten Broeck later purchased too) are legendary. Ten Broeck eventually purchased full interest in Lexington, and when the horse's eyes began to fail, he was sold to R. A. Alexander of Woodburn. In 1856, Ten Broeck sold the Metairie Race Course in New Orleans and set sail for England, "the first man to race American thoroughbreds there.[30] Metairie had been formed to compete with Yelverton N. Oliver's Eclipse Course, which according to William H. P. Robertson's *The History of Thoroughbred Racing In America* (1964) had had its running surface improved by mixing the natural soil with sand. Metairie "was purchased outright by Richard Ten Broeck in 1851, and became the undisputed temple of American racing."

On 21 March 1857, the *Louisville Daily Courier* reported under the heading "Fast Horses and Matrimony" that: "Mr. Ten Broeck, the owner of the American horses now in England — Lecompte [usually spelled Lecomte], Prior and another Prioress — is now in Rome, where he is soon to be married to Miss Anderson, of Louisville. The marriage has been

John J. Jacob, Jr., house, renamed Hurstbourne by Richard Ten Broeck.

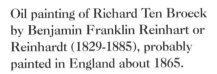

Oil painting of Richard Ten Broeck by Benjamin Franklin Reinhart or Reinhardt (1829-1885), probably painted in England about 1865.

postponed on account of the death of a brother of Miss Anderson, who died at Rome lately, very suddenly, of consumption."

Traveling to Europe after the death in childbirth of his young wife, Orville Martin Anderson had died in Rome on 12 February 1857. He was twenty-nine years old.[31] His only heir, Mary Martin Anderson, was to become very rich.

Although the *Louisville Daily Courier* soon retracted its statement about Ten Broeck's pending marriage based upon "the most undoubted authority," the couple was married in St. Mary's Church, Hants, England, on 16 June 1857.[32] It is presumed that Pattie Ten Broeck remained in Europe with her husband for about a decade before returning to Louisville and purchasing Hurstbourne, where she died on 27 March 1873.[33]

Lutie, accompanied by his wife, Mary, departed for Europe in the summer of 1872. "While abroad," *The Courier-Journal* recalled on 4 July 1878, "he bore in mind the idea of the establishment of the [Louisville Jockey] club, studied carefully and sought from such authorities as Admiral Rous, Earl of Portsmouth, Prince Batthyany, C. Alexander and others, leading gentlemen of the English Jockey Club, all the points of their racing and the arrangements of their stakes." Introductions to these gentlemen would have been supplied by Richard Ten Broeck, who knew them all, especially Henry John Rous (1795-1877). Upon his retirement from the Royal Navy in 1835 and until he died, Rous was a fixture on the English racing scene. His public handicapping of the Cesarewitch at Newmarket in 1857, whose participants included Ten Broeck's Prioress, produced one of the most exciting dead heats ever witnessed, which Prioress won in a run off.[34] "It was at Newmarket," Ten Broeck would recall, "that my intimacy with Admiral Rous began.... He was appointed Senior Steward of the Jockey Club, and acted in that capacity permanently without emolument, entirely from his passion for racing. The Admiral and I often attended the races together, canvassing in company the horses expected to run."[35]

Lewis and Mary Clark were in London when his uncle John Churchill and various Ballard cousins arrived in time to see Doncaster win the 1873 Derby at Epsom Downs. While in England Clark was asked by one of the leading horsemen, "why do you not start a jockey club at the metropolis of your state and have representative races? If your people appreciate them, others will do so. Give class races, and by your stakes compel the large establishments to breed for them." *The Courier-Journal* (4 July 1878) continued: "In France Vicompte Darn, the Vice President of the French Jockey Club afforded every facility for studying the rules and stakes of the French turf, so that when Col. Clark returned he had an object goal in view."[36]

The Clarks also visited Italy where he had a *carte de visite* made in Rome. They returned to Louisville in 1873 and were listed in the city directory residing at 8 Broadway, east of First Street. No profession was noted for Lutie.[37] He was twenty-seven years old, his wife was well connected and very rich, and he was looking ahead.

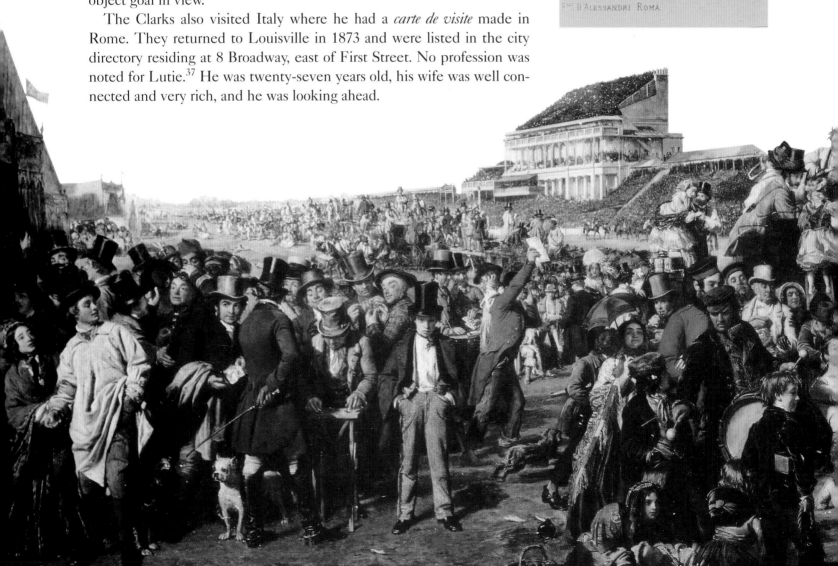

Opposite: *Carte de visite* of
Meriwether Lewis Clark, Jr., made
in Rome, *ca.* 1873. Right: Engraving
of Tattenham Corner, Epsom
Downs, during Derby, published by
Gustave Doré in *London a Pilgrimage,*
1872. Below: Derby Day at Epsom
Downs by W. P. Frith, 1857.

FROM "AN EXCELLENT ENTERPRISE. PROPOSED ORGANIZATION
OF A JOCKEY CLUB AND RUNNING PARK NEAR LOUISVILLE,"
THE COURIER-JOURNAL, 27 MAY 1874

Several gentlemen of this city have inaugurated a project, which has every promise of a successful fruition to establish near Louisville a running course, similar to that of the Jockey Club in New York and the Metairie Club in New Orleans. It is proposed to raise a stock subscription of 25,000 in $100 shares, $10,000 of which has already been pledged.

The grounds proposed to be selected are on the Third-street road extended, about three miles from the court-house and just beyond the city limits. They will embrace sixty-five acres of the old Churchill property, which seem admirably adapted in every respect to the purpose designed. The field is remarkably level, and the track can be made with but little filling or cutting, and with comparatively little cost. The soil is sandy clay, which readily absorbs moisture, and is said to be the very best possible for the purpose. The writer visited the place recently, after a heavy rain, and, while the adjoining roads and neighboring fields were wet and muddy, the moisture had almost disappeared from this. Nature could have done no better in preparing the spot for a running track. The place has been carefully surveyed by a competent engineer [probably W. H. McGonigale of Henning, McGonigale & Hobbs, surveyors], and a plan of the track and arrangements for visitors prepared. It is proposed to make a mile track–two stretches and two turns of a quarter of a mile each. Near the southeast corner will be placed the grand stand, from which an admirable view of the entire track may be had. The southeast corner has been set aside for the club-house and club-stand, around which will be made a delightful lawn, separated by a fence from the inside grounds. On the north side the stables will be built.

FROM *THE COURIER-JOURNAL*, 28 MAY 1874

The article in your paper of to-day [27 May] speaks of a "project inaugurated by several gentlemen, which promises successful fruition," to establish a running course near Louisville, &c.

Near Louisville! The grounds proposed are on Third-street road "extended." The number of acres, 65 – of the old "Churchill property." At first blush one would think that the old "Churchill property" was admirably adapted for the purposes.

Where will water be obtained, either for sprinkling track or streets? How will people get out to this old Churchill property? It may be that "Third street extended" makes the distance too far. The "Falls City grounds" are a mile nearer to the Court-house and more accessible, by railroad, river, street cars, and all sorts of streets, roads and avenues. And this "Falls City Association" was organized some time ago and with a view to promote the interests of Louisville, and not with any view of increasing the value of the "old Churchill property," or any other property.

FROM "AN EXCELLENT ENTERPRISE..."
THE COURIER-JOURNAL, 27 MAY 1874.

The subscription list is in the hands of gentlemen of means and energy, who will push the proposition to an entirely successful issue. It is proposed to make the club exclusive, in so far that persons of questionable character cannot obtain admission. It will embrace gentlemen of substance in the city, in business and in the professions, whose membership will make the club thoroughly respectable, and whose interest in its welfare will insure its success. A pleasant club-house with adjoining grounds, will make a delightful resting place at the end of the drive out the Third street road, and a grove at the spot set apart for this purpose will shelter the house and grounds from the heat and glare of the sun....

We propose hereafter to enlarge upon this subject, which strikes us as worthy of much attention and meanwhile it is sufficient to say that the project will be actively pressed and that the required subscription is expected to be made up within the next two weeks. The grounds can be placed in readiness for a meeting next fall, when purses sufficiently large will be made up to draw for the first races some of the best horses in the country.

FROM *THE COURIER-JOURNAL*, 28 MAY 1874

I feel glad that a "pleasant club-house, with adjoining grounds," will make a delightful resting place at the end of the extended drive out Third street, and that a "grove at the spot" set apart for this purpose will shelter the house and the grounds from the heat and the glare of the sun. Oh, most delightful grove! But what will shelter the faces of the people from the heat and glare of the sun in the evening? Going to the "Falls City Course," to the Grand Central Ground, the sun is at your back in the morning and at your back in the evening. [Signed] J. Richard Barret.[38]

FROM "THE PARK ASSOCIATION," *THE DAILY LOUISVILLE COMMERCIAL*,
7 JUNE 1874

It has seemed very strange to many visitors that a city as populous and prosperous as Louisville has no drive, and no place of resort where the owners of horseflesh could reap so much pleasurable enjoyment and at the same time promote various interests of the city....

Some persons discuss this question, having in view simply a race-track...Race-tracks have only two weeks in which to receive their revenues, and to give to their patrons the sought-for amusement. This park, like others which have been made by private enterprise, would have a track and all necessary adjuncts. If the association should deem it proper to lease it for a week in the spring and a week in the autumn to a jockey club, it would be very easy to form that entirely distinct association. Thus many persons, who would like to use a park for the whole year, and who do not approve of race-courses, could waive their rights for a limited period if the directors saw fit to encourage such undertakings....

The cost of such a park must not be underrated. To make it in every respect a success $40,000 should be raised for improvement, and annual dues of at least $10,000 to keep it in repair and perfect order. The club-house should be commodious and tasteful, combining a first-class restaurant, with first-class wines, together with a perfectly satisfactory department for the ladies to obtain their ices, fruits, &c.... If the scope of thought in Louisville has a boundary sufficiently wide to discern the wisdom of securing pleasure for the richer classes, with an ultimate view of benefiting their fellow-citizens who toil from morn till eve without hope of obtaining naught but moderate enjoyment. Here is a field for philanthropy at little cost, and one which it is to be hoped will soon be crowded with eager co-laborers.[39]

The list of likely supporters and contributors to the park concept included the names of several, in particular Meriwether Lewis Clark, who would soon be involved in developing the Churchill property into a race course, so it is most likely that the project was well along even when it was first discussed in *The Courier-Journal*. Three weeks after it was floated, there was no popping of the balloon. A meeting was set to initiate the formal process and create the organization that would build what is now referred to as America's most legendary race track.

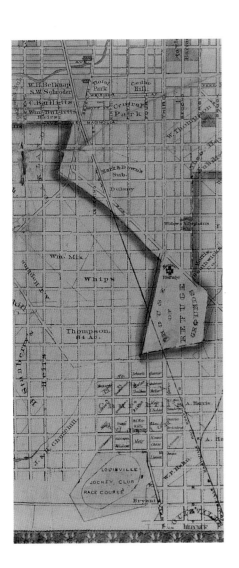

Section from Beers & Lanagan's *Atlas of Jefferson & Oldham Counties, Kentucky,* 1879. Louisville Jockey Club course is at the bottom.

PRESIDENT[1]
A. D. Hunt (1874); M. Lewis Clark, Jr. (1874-1894)

VICE PRESIDENT
St. John Boyle, Isaac Caldwell, E. H. Chase, M. L. Clark, Jr., E. H. Murray, J. W. Hunt Reynolds, Daniel Swigert, R. A. Johnson, Milton H. Smith, B. G. Thomas

TREASURER
Robert A. Newhouse; George C. Buchanan; Joel M. Womack; John R. Throckmorton; John Churchill

SECRETARY
Thomas J. Martin, Jr.; William Murphy; Darwin W. Johnson; W. N. Henderson; Benjamin Gratz Bruce; Joseph Swigert; Charles F. Price

DIRECTORS
Thomas Anderson, John M. Barbour, John S. Beecher, Luke P. Blackburn, A. W. Blakemore, Lee Bloom, Levi Bloom, Samuel S. Brown, Roman A. Browinski, George W. Bowen, St. John Boyle, J. Russ Butler, Isaac Caldwell, F. S. Carrington, Arthur Cary, E. H. Chase, John Churchill, W. H. Churchill, James Clark, M. Lewis Clark, Jr., J. P. Curd, A. V. du Pont, J. K. Faulkner, Nicholas Finzer, S. Van R. Fonda, J. William Gaulbert, James Graves, John E. Green, W. C. Hall, A. W. Hamilton, B. F. Harris, Joseph L. Harris, Norvin T. Harris, Warren N. Henderson, W. W. Hite, C. H. Hubbert, A. D. Hunt, R. P. Huntington, F. D. Hussey, Charles D. Jacob, Jilson P. Johnson, R. A. Johnson, W. P. Johnson, E. D. Lawrence, George J. Long, Thomas J. Martin, Jr., Amos G. McCampbell, J. G. McCulloch, E. H. Murray, H. Victor Newcomb, Robert A. Newhouse, Joseph S. Odiorne, C. Opdebeeck, W. G. Osborne, Frank Pragoff, W. R. Ray, J. W. Hunt Reynolds, C. C. Rufer, H. J. Scoggan, Milton H. Smith, A. B. Schell, Milton H. Smith, Grandison Spratt, Miller Stewart, Daniel Swigert, Manlius Taylor, B. G. Thomas, William H. Thomas, Isaac H. Tyler, G. C. Wharton, A. A. Wheeler, Joel M. Womack

"Louisville Derby Day."
The Graphic News (New York).
15 May 1886.

PART ONE

Louisville Jockey Club and Driving Park Association

1874-1894

FROM "PROPOSED RACING PARK," *THE DAILY LOUISVILLE COMMERCIAL*,
19 JUNE 1874

A number of gentlemen interested in the establishment of a new race-course within a short distance of the city met at the Galt House yesterday. A committee was appointed to prepare articles of incorporation and report at the next meeting.[2] Nearly $20,000 worth of stock has been subscribed, and everything indicates that Louisville will soon have a creditable racing park, controlled by gentlemen who will make it a success. Ground a short distance beyond the terminus of the Fourth-street railway will probably be selected, when preparations for making the track will immediately commence.

FROM "THE JOCKEY CLUB," *THE COURIER-JOURNAL*, 23 JUNE 1874

The gentlemen having the enterprise in hand have met with success from the beginning and are confident in the belief that the driving park and club house will be completed within a month or two and that the fall meeting over the running track will be held. The suggestion of the Turf, Field and Farm has been acted upon and the list of members shows that the business and solid interest of Louisville is largely represented, with just enough of the younger element to insure enterprise and success. It is intended to make this track an intersectional place of meeting and it is hoped that it will prove one of the most successful in the country.

FROM "THE JOCKEY CLUB," *THE DAILY LOUISVILLE COMMERCIAL*,
1 JULY 1874

A number of subscribers of the Jockey Club and Driving Park Association met at the Galt House last night and elected the following Directors: C. D. Jacob,[3] E. H. Chase, M. Lewis Clark, Jr., J. W. Hunt Reynolds, I. Caldwell, J. Womack, John E. Green, R. A. Newhouse, D. Swigert, H. V. Newcomb, T. J. Martin, Jr., C. C. Rufer, Dr. L. P. Blackburn, Major W. H. Thomas, A. D. Hunt, J. R. Butler, and General E. H. Murray.

FROM "LOUISVILLE JOCKEY CLUB AND DRIVING PARK ASSOCIATION,"
THE DAILY LOUISVILLE COMMERCIAL, 4 JULY 1874

The directors of this association met, pursuant to a call, at No. 29 Third street, for the purpose of electing officers. A full quorum being present the following named gentlemen were put in nomination and unanimously elected:

President: A. D. Hunt. Vice Presidents: E. H. Chase, M. L. Clark, Jr., General E. H. Murray. Treasurer: Robert A. Newhouse. Temporary Secretary: Thomas J. Martin, Jr. Executive Committee: E. H. Chase, M. L. Clark, Jr., Robert A. Newhouse, John E. Green, J. Womack.

The Executive Committee were instructed by the board to receive a proposal from the Messrs. Churchill for a lease on their grounds on Third street with a view of perfecting the lease, and proceeding at once to lay out the tracks, receive bids for the necessary fencing, club-house, stands, stables, &c., and proceeding without delay to make the improvements.

Sterling silver membership badge, engraved "1875" on back, with member's name in enameled letters.

FROM "THE JOCKEY CLUB AND DRIVING PARK," *THE COURIER-JOURNAL*, 27 JUNE 1874

The committee appointed to solicit subscriptions from the stock breeders at the sales of J. W. Hunt Reynolds, A. Keene Richards, and A. J. Alexander, met with signal success, the turfmen seeming to take great interest in the proposed improvement; and with such men as D. Swigert, A. J. Alexander, Gen. A. Buford, J. W. Hunt Reynolds, E. H. Taylor, Jr., H. C. McDowell, R. P. Pepper, and others, both Frankfort and Lexington will be represented, and Louisville can take her place as the point where thousands of strangers can come to see Kentucky's finest horses contest the liberal purses to be offered by the association.

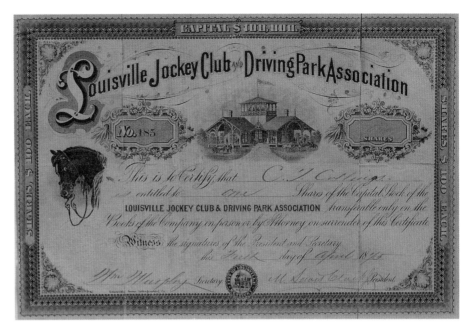

Above: Cipher of the Louisville Jockey Club, *ca.*1878. Right: Certificate issued 1 April 1875.

Abraham Dagworthy Hunt's election as president of the Louisville Jockey Club and Driving Park Association did not, for some undisclosed reason, meet with his approval, and the prominent banker's resignation was accepted by the board of directors on 2 October 1874. The position was then offered to General William Preston (1816-1887), a Louisville native with impressive credentials. He, however, "declined the honor," and on 23 October 1874, Meriwether Lewis Clark was elected club president. Interestingly, William Preston had written his friend John C. Breckinridge on 6 August 1867: "My kinsman, Mr. M. L. Clark is going in a fortnight to Europe, to remain for a few months, and I have given him this note of introduction to you, in the hopes that you may not have left Europe before he arrives. He is a young gentleman of high character and intelligence, for whom I have a strong regard..."[4]

FROM "THE LOUISVILLE JOCKEY CLUB," *THE TURF, FIELD AND FARM,*
10 JULY 1874

The proposition is to construct two tracks on the ground, one for running and the other for trotting purposes. This is well enough, but we trust that no effort will be made to combine the two branches of the turf in one programme. These hybrid affairs never give satisfaction. There is more or less jealousy between the breeders of trotters and the breeders of runners, and each will want to claim the precedence....

The effort to combine trotting and running at the old Woodlawn, it must not be forgotten, was a disastrous failure. We repeat that the proposition to construct two tracks in the new park is well enough, but we do not like the combination of Jockey Club and Driving Park. [Note: The Louisville Jockey Club did not drop the idea of mixing trotting with running until the fall meet of 1875. See *The Turf, Field and Farm,* 25 June 1875.]

FROM "JOCKEY CLUB — NOTICE TO CONTRACTORS,"
THE DAILY LOUISVILLE COMMERCIAL, 22 JULY 1874

The Executive Committee of the "Louisville Jockey Club and Driving Park Association" is now prepared to receive sealed proposals up to 12 m., Wednesday, July 22, 1874, to make a mile track on their grounds on Third street. The track to be made in accordance with plan and specifications, which with a profile of the grounds can be seen at the office of Robert A. Newhouse, No. 29 Third street, where proposals should be left. Usual rights reserved.

FROM "LETTER FROM LOUISVILLE," *THE TURF, FIELD AND FARM*, 21 AUGUST 1874

It can reasonably be expected that turf interests at Louisville will be revived by the establishment of the Louisville Jockey Club and Driving Park Association. Work on the grounds of the Association progresses rapidly, and the track is being made by Eli Leezer, the gentleman who made the old Metairie track at New Orleans, and who promises to this Association one of the best and fastest mile tracks on the continent. Grand stands, club house and stables of the handsomest design will follow the completion of the track.

FROM ELI F. LEEZER VS. THE LOUISVILLE JOCKEY CLUB
AND DRIVING PARK ASSOCIATION, 23 APRIL 1875,
JEFFERSON COURT OF COMMON PLEAS CASE 14860

Plaintiff states that he proceeded with the Construction of the said race-course under his said Contract, and had made Considerable progress with the work on the west side of the said race-course, it being that part of the track called the home-stretch in the plan submitted by defendant, when defendant made many and material changes in its original plan, changing the home stretch from the west side to the south east side, rendering worthless much of the work plaintiff had done, and requiring a great deal of labor and expenses to Conform to the new plan which was not included as necessary under the original plan.

With the racecourse under construction, work could proceed on the erection of an entrance gate, clubhouse, and stables. Architect John Andrewartha was selected to prepare the appropriate plans and specifications, and three contracts were awarded to builder and mechanic Jonathan Jacobs. At the time, John Andrewartha (1839-1916) was Louisville's most prolific architect. He had emigrated from England in 1865, and just before the Jockey Club work, he had completed Louisville City Hall as well as residences for James Bridgeford and Robert Elliott, and stone-front commercial buildings for Bamberger, Bloom & Co. and Samuel Thorner. His Courier-Journal Building at Fourth and Green (Liberty) streets was also getting underway. He introduced cast-iron architecture into Louisville with the Main Street building housing Kitts & Werne, Jewelers, which would later furnish some Louisville Jockey Club trophies.[5]

FROM "OUR NEW RACE COURSE,"
THE COURIER-JOURNAL, 28 OCTOBER 1874

The great breeders of our State have needed a track at Louisville as a place of resort for the Eastern and Southern buyers, and if they are not now satisfied they are hard to please. Louisville is the center or half-way point between the North and the South, and with her superb hotel accommodations and railroad facilities it has been a matter of surprise that a race course has not been well supported ere this, but the gentlemen having this new enterprise in hand, appreciating the reasons that caused the ruin of the Woodlawn Association, have secured a location which insures success beyond a doubt....

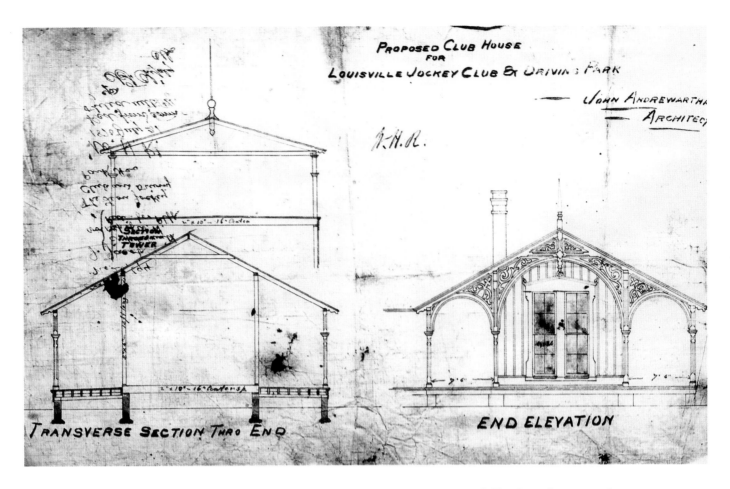

TRANSVERSE SECTION THRO END

END ELEVATION

From set of plans filed in Louisville Chancery Court, 1875.

FROM "A DESERVING ENTERPRISE," *THE DAILY LOUISVILLE COMMERCIAL*, 22 OCTOBER 1874

Work was commenced in July, and up to this time over $20,000 have been expended. The progress made has been rapid, and a vast deal of work has been accomplished. The grounds have been fenced in, the main track completed, and the inside or driving track only needs the finishing touches. A paling fence separates the two tracks. The porter's lodge, or entrance, and ticket offices have been built. The building, which is attractive in appearance, has been so constructed as to furnish accommodations for the Superintendent.

The club-house, which is a neat, cozy structure, and as attractive in appearance as can be found on any race-course in the country, is nearly completed. From the observatory of the club-house a fine view of the track is obtained.

Carpenter Jacobs submitted a bill of $8,595.60, dated 20 November 1874, for construction of the porter's lodge (entrance), clubhouse, and six stables. Jacobs, however, had a cost overrun because he could not build the clubhouse roof from the plans supplied by architect Andrewartha. The design had to be altered and the contractor sued for the additional cost — $455.60. Filed among the case papers was a set of Andrewartha's drawings for the clubhouse.[6] Only one good photograph, frequently reproduced, of

FROM "OUR NEW RACE COURSE,"
THE COURIER-JOURNAL, 28 OCTOBER 1874
The great event of the first running meeting will be the "Kentucky Derby" for three-year olds, a dash of a mile and one-half, and it is hoped that like the English Derby, the winner of this large stake will be *the horse* of the year.

FROM "THE LOUISVILLE JOCKEY CLUB," KENTUCKY LIVE STOCK RECORD, 9 APRIL 1875
Within the last ten days they have finished four new ten stall stables, and are now engaged in the erection of eight new six stall stables. The water from the city has been extended out to the Course, and is accessible for use to the Club House, Grand Stand and stables. The track has been widened some seventeen feet at the quarter pole, so that an abun-dance of room may be had in starting the horses for the Louisville Cup which promises to be one of the best races of the year.

The inner circle of the track has been graded and sown in blue and orchard grass, as have all the lots surrounding the stables and stands. They have commenced the building of the Grand Stand, which will be in keeping with the admirable improvements already finished.

Clubhouse scene. *The Courier-Journal,* 28 April 1901.

the original clubhouse is known to exist. It appeared in *The Courier-Journal* on 28 April 1901 and shows the structure in a dilapidated condition. Part of the board and batten exterior covering had been replaced by sheets of corrugated siding, and the paint, originally specified "with best material in fancy colors," had long since faded. The structure was either moved or destroyed after 1910.[7]

FROM "OUR NEW RACE COURSE," *THE COURIER-JOURNAL,*
28 OCTOBER 1874

Nothing could be better than this location, as Third street has long been the fashionable drive of our citizens, and the approach to the grounds is through the most beautiful part of our city, the broad Nicolson pavement reaching to the House of Refuge, from whence a turnpike, which has just been thoroughly graveled, with dirt road on both sides, leads to the gateway of the Park. [Note: Nicolson pavement was a short-lived experiment to avoid stone dust by substituting small wooden blocks covered by a mixture of hot coal tar, pitch, sand, and gravel.] The water pipes have been laid, along the drive, with sprinkling attachments every thousand feet, and in the spring both the road and the track will be thoroughly watered every day.

As soon as the lease was concluded the contracts for fences, track, gateway and lodge, club-house and stables were advertised and awarded, and this week will witness the completion of all.

The lodge is a very pretty little structure, with wide porches, having a ticket office below and a room for the superintendent above. The gateways are on each side and twenty feet wide. The Short-line [Louisville, Cincinnati and Lexington Railroad] Junction is distant about two hundred yards, and horses can be shipped from New Orleans, Nashville, Mobile, New York, St. Louis, or any other point to this junction without change of cars, an advantage not possessed by any other track in the country.

The tracks are two of the finest to be found anywhere, the outside one being the mile track, eighty feet on the home stretch and sixty on the back stretch and turns, the last being thrown up twenty-four inches on the outside. The inside one is similar to the other with the exception of being fifty feet on the home stretch and forty-five elsewhere.

The soil is all that horsemen could desire, being a springy, sandy clay, and the recent heavy rains have fully demonstrated to every one the perfect drainage of the track, and the elastic nature of the soil.

Six of the stables have been completed, and the race men pronounce them to be exactly what they desire. Accommodations will be provided very soon for one hundred horses. The stables that are not finished have six large stalls and a kitchen, while some of those to be erected will have stalls for ten to twelve, with kitchens, thereby suiting all.

The club-house is a perfect little gem, located at the beginning of the first turn of the track, fronting the home stretch to the side and back, and surrounded by beautiful shade trees. It is capped with an observatory from which the ladies can have a charming view of the course and the groves and fields bounded by the Ohio river, and it well repays one for the trouble. The whole house is encompassed or surrounded by porches, on which the members can enjoy themselves during the hot weather. Inside, one-half the house is set apart for the ladies, a dressing room, lunch-room and parlor comprising the suite devoted to that purpose, while the lords of creation take possession of the balance of the rooms.

The grandstand erected in the spring of 1875 may have also been designed by John Andrewartha, but perhaps not, since after the difficulties with his clubhouse roof, his relationship with the Louisville Jockey Club may have soured. The grandstand was a very simple arrangement of inclined seating covered by a roof sloping front and back, about 275 feet long by 45 feet wide with open seating in front on the terrace which was separated from the track by a picket fence.[8]

FROM "DERBY DAY," *THE DAILY LOUISVILLE COMMERCIAL*, 25 APRIL 1875

The inaugural meeting of the Louisville Jockey Club, commencing Monday, May 17, will mark an important event in the history of Louisville. As the metropolis of the State which has produced the finest and fastest horses that have ever stepped upon the turf, Louisville ought to take the lead of other cities in racing matters....

The "Kentucky Derby," to be run on the opening day, is destined to become the great race of this country, and it has been suggested that "Derby Day" be observed as a holiday. It is just the thing. For one day let us lay aside business cares, get away from the counting-room, and spend an afternoon in the cool, fresh air of the country. It will make us feel better and happier. St. Louis has her fair days, New Orleans and Memphis their Mardigras. Let Louisville have her "Derby Day." Inaugurate such a custom, and that day will see thousands of strangers in the city. In England "Derby Day" is the greatest of all days, and it can be made the same here if everybody will just say so.

FROM "THE COMING RACES," *THE COURIER-JOURNAL*, 27 APRIL 1875

Work was commenced yesterday toward grading Fourth street in preparation for extending the street railroad track out to the gate of the Jockey Club grounds. The work will be actively pushed forward, and by the beginning of the May meeting a single track, with side switches, will be completed to the very grounds of the club. The only question will be whether a single track will be sufficient to accommodate the throngs of people who will make use of this means of conveyance during the week.

Several gentlemen have leased the old Greenland Park, just the other [east] side of the Jockey Club grounds, and hold it exclusively for trotters. Mr. Robert Johnson is superintendent, and he has already accomplished wonders....There are a number of fast horses already on the track, preparing for the summer's campaign. The most noted of these is Lady Mac, owned by Mr. Johnson, and named for his sister, Mrs. Macauley.[9]

FROM "THE KENTUCKY DERBY"
THE COURIER-JOURNAL, 11 APRIL 1875

Appreciating these facts thoroughly, the gentlemen having the new enterprise in hand first sought for a suitable location for their course—one that would combine most facilities for the transportation of the horses to run as well as a cheap mode of transit for the spectators, and the result was the choice of the grounds on which they have erected their beautiful improvements....

There are two advantages which are peculiar to this track: The first, the fact that horses can be shipped to the grounds without change of cars, from any place in the Union; the second, the water pipes on these grounds, extended at the cost of the club, from the House of Refuge. The latter advantage all will appreciate, as the road will be watered every evening.

FROM "PARIS MUTUALS," *THE DAILY LOUISVILLE COMMERCIAL*, 1 MAY 1875

Mr. Ira E. Bride, who owns the Paris Mutuals pools, which will be used at the coming races, will exhibit his machine in the rotunda of the Galt House this morning between the hours of 11 and 1. As this system is something entirely new to many in this section, it will attract attention. It supersedes the old system of pool-selling, and is very simple when once understood.[10]

Pool-selling is a modern gambling device, is it?

Yes, it is about thirty years old. H. P. McGrath and Henry Perrit were the first men I ever saw selling pools, and that was at Lexington; they did their work gratuitously for the purpose of explaining the system.

Of the different systems of betting which do you prefer: that is, in their effect on the character of the turf?

Book-making, by all odds; it is conducted quietly, there are no commissions and not the same chance for dishonest practices.

–FROM AN INTERVIEW OF MAJOR BARAK G. THOMAS OF LEXINGTON, IN "TURF TALES," *THE COURIER-JOURNAL*, 10 SEPTEMBER 1882[11]

FROM "TURF TOPICS," *THE DAILY LOUISVILLE COMMERCIAL*, 18 APRIL 1875

The course over which these purses and stakes are to be run for is one of the finest and safest in the country. The turns and stretches are a quarter of a mile each, and are respectively sixty and eighty feet wide. On the inside of the rail is a training track, graded like the main track, and sixty feet wide all around. The soil is light and early, and the track is as near a water-level as can be, so the time made over it ought to be as good as that at Saratoga or Lexington.

In addition to the above facilities for working horses, there is, within a hundred yards or so of the new course, the old Greenland track, a full mile, and a good one, too; so Louisville will have the advantage that Saratoga possesses of two tracks.

The stabling is new and after the most approved plans. Water is brought in pipes from the city supply, so there is no chance of it ever giving out unless the Ohio river dries up. Arrangements have been made to accommodate any number of horses, and the rules adopted to prevent diseased animals being smuggled into the stables are very stringent.

FROM "THE COMING RACES," *THE COURIER-JOURNAL*, 9 MAY 1875

Commencing to-morrow morning, and continuing every night and morning thereafter during the week, Messrs. W. Scott Glore and Ira E. Bride will sell pools at the Galt House on the Lexington races. The sale of pools under what is known as the Paris Mutual system will then, for the first time in this city, be placed in operation, and the experience afforded by the sales on the Lexington races will fully familiarize the public with all the features of this plan, and enable these so desirous to intelligently patronize the pool department at the great meeting of the Louisville Jockey Club. To most of our readers the plan is entirely new, and therefore, whilst very simple, is novel.[12]

FROM "RACE MEETINGS," *THE DAILY LOUISVILLE COMMERCIAL*, 2 MAY 1875

Below is given the date of the running meetings that have fixed their time, to take place over the different courses during the spring and summer of 1875, and the number of days of each meeting:

May 4 — Nashville Blood Horse Association, Five days.
May 10 — Kentucky Association, Lexington, Ky. Six days.
May 17 — Louisville Jockey Club, Louisville, Ky. Six days.
May 25 — Maryland Jockey Club, Baltimore, Md. Four days.
June 5 — Jerome Park, Fordham, N.Y. June 5, June 12, and June 19.

FROM "OUR DERBY DAY," *THE COURIER-JOURNAL*, 16 MAY 1875

Lexington and Saratoga, Monmouth Park or Pimlico, each have advantages....but the advantages of all are blended in the course of the Louisville Jockey Club. The track is the broadest in the country, being ninety feet on the home stretch, and eighty on both curves and the back stretch, having quarter stretches and quarter curves. The soil is light and loamy, not too light, but with sufficient clay to give it the springy nature

Programme—First Day, Monday, May 17, 1875.

Compliments of M. J. Winn

NUMBERS MARKED (*) WILL PROBABLY START.

FIRST RACE—*ASSOCIATION PURSE, $300. Dash of 1¼ miles.*

NO.	OWNER.	NAME OF HORSE.	COLOR. AGE	PEDIGREE.	WEIGHT	DRESS OF RIDER.
*1	Wm. Cottrill	Bonaventure	ch f. 4 yrs.	Harry of the West out of Maggie G.	101	Red with White Sash.
*2	A. Buford	Kilburn	ch g. 4 yrs.	Ringmaster out of Ontario	101	Red, White Sash, Red, White Cap.
3	R. B. Cheatham	Vanderbilt	blk c. 4 yrs.	Vandal out of Melrose	14	Orange, Red Sleeves & Red Cap.
4	E. O. Elliot	Orphan Girl	ch m. 4 yrs.	Muggins dam by Wagner	101	White, Blue and Red Cap.
*5	F. Loyd	Capt. Hutchinson	b g. aged.	Voucher, dam by Zero	111	Green
6	A. B. Lewis & Co.	Bessie Lee	b m. 6 yrs.	Hunter's Lexington dam by Chorister	111	White Jacket and Lemon Cap.

SECOND RACE—*The Kentucky Derby for three year olds; $50, play or pay; Association to add $1000, second horse to have $200. Dash of 1½ miles and closed with the following entries.*

NO.	OWNER.	NAME OF HORSE.	COLOR. AGE	PEDIGREE.	WEIGHT	DRESS OF RIDER.
*1	Charles Pine		b c	Planet, out of Bayflower	100	Red and red.
2	J. W. Hunt Reynolds	Aniella	ch f	Australian, out of La Grand Duchess	97	Red, White Sleeves, Red and
*3	Charles A. Lewis	Verdigris	ch c	Versailes, out of Belle Brandon	100	Blue, with White Cap [white Cap
4	General A. Buford	McCreery	ch c	Enquirer, out of Ontario	100	Red, White Sash, Red & White Cap
*5	Stringfield & Clay	Enlister	gr c	Enquirer, out of Crinolet	100	Blue, Yellow Sash, Blue, Yel. Cap
6	Stringfield & Clay	Orel	b c	Enquirer, out dam of Charlie Walker	100	
7	Stringfield & Clay	Warsaw	ch c	War Dance, out of Sister of Charity	100	
8	John W. Miller	Maggie Miller	gr f	Lee Paul, dam dy Sovereign	97	
9	Withers & Bruce	Ettie Moore	b f	Lee Paul, dam by Joe Stoner	97	White, with Blue Sash,
*10	J. B. Rhodes	Searcher	b c	Enquirer, dam by Bonnie Scotland	100	Orange, and Black Stripes.
11	Shawhan & Bowen	War Call	b c	War Dance, dam by Knight St. George	100	
*12	General W. G. Harding	Camargo	ch c	Jack Malone, out of Vidette	104	Maroon.
13	General W. G. Harding	Ventilator	ch c	Vandal, out of Caroline	104	
*14	F. B. Harper	Ten Broeck	b c	Phaeton, out of Fanny Holton	100	Orange, with Red Cap.
15	H. P. McGrath	Chesapeake	b c	Lexington, out of Roxana	100	Green, with Orange Belt.
16	H. P. McGrath	Aristides	ch c	Leamington, out of Sarong	100	
17	A. Haskins	Aramis	b c	Phaeton, out of Nellie Gray	100	
*18	A. Keene Richards	Red Man	b c	War Dance, dam by Solferino	100	Silver-grey, and White Stripes.
*19	Samuel J. Salyers	Bill Bruce	br c	Enquirer, out of Au ora Raby	100	Orange, with Black Belt.
20	Samuel J. Salyers	Carrie Anderson	b f	Phaeton, out of Sallie Anderson	97	
21	James A. Grinstead	Gold Mine	ch f	Australian, out of Income	97	Green, with Red Cap
22	James A. Grinstead	Philti	b f	Phaeton, out of Lass of Sidney	97	
23	Williams & Owings	Playmate	ch c	Planet, out of Full Cry	100	Black, with Red Belt
*24	Allen Bushford		br c	Baywood, out of Lute	100	White, with Blue Sleeves.
*25	R anson, Morgan&Co	Bob Woolley	br c	Leamington, out of Item	100	Orange, with Black Stripes.
*26	A. B. Lewis & Co.	Vagabond	b c	Vandal, out of Gem	100	White, Lemon Cap
27	D. Swigert	Steinbok	ch c	Australian, out of Bonnet	100	Blue, with White Belt and Cap
28	D. Swigert	King Alfonso	b c	Phaeton, out of Capitola	100	
29	Jas. & A. C. Franklin	Montana	b f	Harry of the West, out of Waltz	97	Orange, Red Sleeves and Red Cap
30	Jas. & A. C. Franklin	Planiveo	ch c	Planet, out of Sallie Lewis	100	
31	Archer Cheatham	Vindicator	b c	Vandal, out of Hyacinth	100	
32	Geo. W. Darden	Vaterian	br f	Vandal, out of Nubia	97	
33	Geo. W. Darden	Grey Eagle	gr c	Vandal, out of Betty Martin	100	
*34	Jackson &Co	Van Dorn	b c	Vandal, out of Dewdrop	100	
35	James Davis	Demon	ch c	Jack Malone, out of Fannie Barrow	100	
36	R. B. Cheatham	Lady Bugg	ch f	Vandal, out of Fannie Ch-atham	97	Orange, Red Sleeves, Red Cap
37	R. B. Cheatham	Newbern	br c	Vandal, dam by Childe Harrold	100	
38	J. H. Morgan	Von Moltke	b c	Phaeton, out of Kate Anderson	100	
39	W. H. Gordon	Goth	b c	Vandal, out of Velvet	100	
40	John H. Stone	Pauline Sprague	ch f	Joe Johnson, out of Mollie Ingersol	97	
*41	Geo. H. Rice	Volcano	b c	Vandal, out of Iodine	100	Blue, with White Sleeves, Crescent
*42	Wm. Cottrill	Ascension	b f	Australian, out of Lilly Ward	97	Red, with White Sash [and Cap

THIRD RACE—*Association Purse, $600; Second Horse to have $100, mile heats.*

NO.	OWNER.	NAME OF HORSE.	COLOR. AGE	PEDIGREE.	WEIGHT	DRESS OF RIDER.
*1	J. H. Murphy	War Jig	b g 5 yrs.	War Dance, out of Dixie	111	Green & Green.
*2	Wm. Cottrill	Harry Felter	ch c 4 yrs.	Daniel Boone, out of Sigma	104	Red, with White Sash
*3	Williams & Owings	Fairplay	b c 4 yrs.	Virgil, out of Crucifix	104	Black, with Red Belt.
*4	B. G. Thomas	Vicksburg	ch c 3 yrs.	Vandal, out of Blondin	90	Blue, with Sun Belt & Scar-let Cap.
*5	F. Loyd	Mary L	ch m aged	Voucher, dam by Epsilon	111	Green

so essential for fast time....This is the only [grand] stand where every one can see the home stretch without once rising. The stand is second only in size to Saratoga and will seat 3,500 persons. The field stand is also very superior, and gives excellent opportunities for medium price class. The pools are so arranged that they are not in view of the ladies department.

The club house is a perfect little gem, with balconies all around it and a members' stand on top, but as the grand stand offers so much better facilities it has been concluded to use the club stand for the music. The ladies have the best portion of the grand stand allotted to them....The lodge and gateway are in the same style of architecture as the club house....The stables are separated from the track....for when the horses are too near the course they become what is called "track crazy."

FROM "OUR DERBY DAY," *THE COURIER-JOURNAL*, SUNDAY, 16 MAY 1875
The following gentlemen have been appointed a "ladies committee" for the races during the coming week. Their duties will be to attend to seating the ladies who may be present and to look after their comfort: Thomas J. Martin, Jr., chairman, Gen. E. H. Murray, A. Trigg Moss, Charles T. Ballard, John M. Ferguson, Henry Watterson, John S. Noyes, Wm. H. Henderson, John H. Moore, Ballard Smith.

FROM *PALL MALL GAZETTE* REPRINTED IN *THE COURIER-JOURNAL*, 12 NOVEMBER 1899
Now for the origin of the Derby. The eleventh Earl [of Derby] bequeathed the property to his grandson, Edward Smith Stanley, the twelfth Earl, who, on May 14, 1779, founded the famous Oaks Stakes for fillies, so named from his sylvan retreat at Woodmansterne, the first winner being Bridget, a bay mare, foaled in 1776, by King Herod, dam Jemina, the property of the noble founder himself. This success so pleased the Earl that in the following year he started the Derby stakes, so named out of compliment to him....[13]

FROM "KENTUCKY DERBY NOT OLDEST RACE," *THE COURIER-JOURNAL*, 6 MAY 1908
It was with considerable pride that the Kentuckians assert that this is the oldest turf classic run consecutively in this country. Strictly speaking, it is not the oldest race, but it has always been run as the Kentucky Derby since 1875....the Jerome Handicap was run....beginning in 1866....the first running of the Belmont was in 1867....the Nursery....in 1866....the Saratoga Cup....in 1865, and the Travers, oldest of all, run in 1864....both the Saratoga Cup and the Travers were discontinued for several years."

Aristides by Harry Lyman (1856-1933), dated 1881. Before 1940, publications issued by Churchill Downs incorrectly depicted Aristides with a blaze and conformation that resembled his sire, Leamington. Since then, Lyman's painting (above) has been used exclusively. A copy print of the painting was obtained in 1937, along with images of other early Derby winners, from the vast collection of Lexington horse photographer L.S. Sutcliffe.[14]

FROM AN INTERVIEW WITH MRS. ORVILLE ANDERSON TYLER, 15 APRIL 1994

Somewhere I have, but I cannot put my hands on it, a diary written by Meriwether Lewis Clark's wife, Mary, who was my husband's grandmother. She described how they were trying to hype the Derby up. She and her friends were riding around in carriages all dressed up. They were trying to promote the first one. They were not sure it was going to be successful. I am afraid the diary may be lost, but it was such a cute picture of how they tried to get people interested in the Derby. I am sure she had as much to do with it as he did.

Her mother died when she was a wee baby. Her father was Orville Anderson. He was quite a cotton broker. He had lots of money and several estates. We have letters from him. Unfortunately, he died two or three years after his wife did. She died just after having another child that died too. Orville Anderson went to Rome after his wife died, and he died of a fever over there. He was a horse person. He was riding over there. So this little child was left with all this money and no strings attached. She was raised by her aunt [Pattie Anderson Ten Broeck].[15]

The Derby came next, and fifteen finer or handsomer youngsters never faced a starter. McGrath's entries had the call in the betting and many thought he would win with Chesapeake, but Aristides, the son of Leamington, carried off the honors, and worthily earned a chaplet, one of the best three year olds ever stripped for a race in this country. It was extremely gratifying to the friends of the liberal Laird of McGrathiana, and will be doubly gratifying to Aristides Welch, the owner of Leamington, after whom the colt is christened. This is the best race at the weights ever run by three-year-olds in this country, and cannot fail to make Aristides a still stronger favorite for his Eastern engagements....

Aristides is a chestnut colt, with a star, and two white pasterns behind. He stands fifteen hands, one and three quarter inches high. He has a neat head and neck running into rather a straight shoulder, with great length, good barrel, excellent hips and stifles, sound feet and legs well under him. He has fine turn of speed, and from the way he finished up the Derby today gives every evidence of being a good stayer. He was bred by Mr. H. P. McGrath, at McGrathiana Stud Farm, near Lexington, Ky.[16]

"A Burgoo at McGrathiana means a day of rare enjoyment, and the gathering is one of the great events of the season," *The Turf, Field and Farm* would report in 1872. *The Courier-Journal* described in every detail the memorable feast at McGrathiana when Aristides was being prepared for his second match race with Ten Broeck at the Louisville Jockey Club. The list of visitors was a who's who of the racing world from all over the country. McGrath and his jockey, Bobby Swim, proudly extolled Aristides' merits, but unfortunately, because of an injury to the horse, the rematch did not take place. Bobby Swim was a jockey of note and had been in McGrath's employ for some time, so it is somewhat surprising that when Aristides won the Kentucky Derby, Oliver Lewis was in the irons, but perhaps Swim was not in good health. He died at age 32 and was buried in the Lexington Cemetery on 14 October 1878.[17] McGrath's right hand was Ansel Williamson, whose career included a stint as trainer for R. A. Alexander. The year before the first Derby, *The Daily Louisville Commercial* reported: "Everybody has heard of McGrath, the famous trainer of Kentucky, and Uncle Ansel and Bobby Swim are his right and left bowers. The former gets the horses ready to run and the latter pilots them to victory. Uncle Ansel is a grizzled, gray-haired old 'gentleman of color,' whose years number anything under a century, but who is as stout and hearty as an oak." When McGrath died on 5 July 1881, *The Courier-Journal* remarked that Ansel Williamson's recent death "seemed to depress the veteran turfman, and may have aggravated his illness." Williamson, who had also trained for R. A. Alexander, Abe Buford, and "his old master," A. Keene Richards, died on 18 June 1881.[18]

When the bugle calls the horses to the post in the fifty-fourth renewal of the Kentucky Derby Saturday, May 19, one of the most interested spectators at Churchill Downs will be Capt. J. T. Larkin, 926 Mary street, who witnessed the first Derby in 1875 and who has seen the winner crowned in each succeeding event.

When Aristides, carrying the colors of Price McGrath, won the inaugural Derby, persons destined to later become notable in the political life of Kentucky were present....

Henry Watterson was also there. After the first Derby had been run and the crown placed over the head of Aristides, these famous Kentuckians repaired to the pink cottage of Judge M. Lewis Clark, who made the Derby possible, and "Marse Henry" gave a toast to the owner of the winner and to Judge Clark, whose foresight was destined to make the Kentucky Derby the world's richest turf event.

"The day the first Derby was run the race track was in its infancy," Captain Larkin said. "The horses had to run over a wooden culvert and there was a creek in the center of the track. From the pink cottage to the site of the present grandstand was a great place to hunt crawfish. The creek ran past the door of the pink cottage, and the mint used in the juleps grew in a bed only a few feet from the door. Those were certainly the good old days in Kentucky."[19]

FROM "THE LOUISVILLE RACES," MRS. CHRISTINA JOHNSON GRUNDER'S LETTER
TO THE NEW YORK GRAPHIC, REPRINTED IN THE COURIER-JOURNAL, 28 MAY 1875[20]

The ladies were assured that the road to the grounds and the track itself would be kept so well watered that they could wear their best dresses without any fear of injury. Thus appealed to, the ladies graciously responded, and the result was that many wardrobes were left empty, while the display of dry goods was immense. But alas, for man's promises! 'Tis true the road was watered, but the fervent heat of the sun and the dry soil quickly absorbed the moisture, and the thousands of feet trampling for hours over the same line of march defied the best efforts to prevent clouds of suffocating dust. This not only damaged hats, ribbons, flowers, laces, silks, dainty fans and parasols, but it was no uncommon thing to see some of the most celebrated beauties with spots of dust, which had drifted through the vale, resting lovingly and securely upon a tip-tilted nose and each fair cheek. The fashion of a new powder for the hair seemed to have been suddenly adopted for this express occasion. It was not exactly blonde or tinged with gold, but seemed a favorite color that gentlemen as well as ladies wore it, and the entire audience bore a family resemblance. The ladies, however, were brave to the end. The afternoon sunshine flooded the grand stand and bathed every fair form in golden light. The strong glare of light revealed defects that many divinities were not suspected of possessing. Complexions and other valuable articles were utterly ruined. Still the ladies remained for six hours at least, enduring a crowd, heat and dust not only for love of the horse, but to oblige the gallant gentlemen who had done so much to give them pleasure and exhibit to the strangers that Louisville deserved the fame for which she is credited — of having the fairest daughters in the universe. The wildest imagination and the greatest stretch of gallantry and chivalry could not pronounce all the ladies handsome or elegant. The grand stand lost some of its interest from the large admixture of the country element. The rustics turned out in great numbers. Men stuck to their homespun, soiled shirts, and shocking hats. Many of these possess but one suit of clothes, not that they cannot afford another, but it is too much trouble to change one's clothes often or buy a second suit before the first is worn out. Sunday is clean-shirt day; and if the most fashionable race-day will come in the middle of the week, why that is the fault of those fellows who are "spiled by wearing biled shirts and kiver their hands with gloves," and they "hate all sich stuckupedness, and don't mean to inkirrage it" by the waste of an extra clean shirt.

FROM THE COURIER-JOURNAL,
18 DECEMBER 1922

Racing immediately took hold of the people of Louisville, for the promoters had followed the example set by Jerome Park and made a special bid for the ladies.[21]

There were twenty-two nominations for the first Louisville Cup race, the event Louisvillians claimed as their own. The favorite Ballankeel, winner of the Nashville Cup, prevailed in the two-and-a-quarter mile test. The magnificent Louisville Cup was delivered to the jockey club by F. G. B. Weihe, a young employee of the Fourth Street jewelers Cook & Sloss, and he witnessed the race from the judges' stand. Weihe kept a photograph of the cup, and years later his son sent a copy of the picture made by Wybrant's Studio to *The Courier-Journal*. It was published in the 10 May 1935 issue. Unfortunately, by that time, the cup was mistakenly considered to have been presented to Price McGrath for winning the Kentucky Derby, and the photograph was so captioned. The first trophy awarded to a winner of the Kentucky Derby was not until 1922, however.

FROM "THE FALL RACES," *THE COURIER-JOURNAL*, 8 SEPTEMBER 1875

All the improvements in track, stands, pool place, etc, that were suggested during the inaugural meeting, have been made, and will, when the fall races commence, lend additional attractiveness to the already beautiful course and its elegant appointments. Noticeable among these improvements will be an awning to hang from the top of the grand stand fifteen feet below. It will be neat and tasty in appearance, and will shade the many who may be in the stand from the afternoon sun. Another improvement to this part of the course will be a number of seats with backs, to tie in the ladies department, the managers having determined to do all that is necessary for the comfort of the fair sex, who are among its best friends.

The ground embraced by the railings around the tracks was barren last spring, but is now covered with bluegrass, the appearance of which is very beautiful, set off as it is by the bright whiteness of rails and fences.... [Note: In June 1874, a third track, in the form of a figure 8, was to be constructed in the infield for family carriages, according to the minutes of the board of directors.]

The first day will be St. Leger. This is in the fall meetings as Derby day is in spring. The St. Leger race was instituted in England in 1776, by Col. St. Leger, of Park Hill, near Doncaster. It was not called the "St. Leger," however, till two years subsequent, when the Marquis of Rockingham's horse "Allabeeutia" won the race. It has since been celebrated as the opening day of fall meetings, and will so be observed in Louisville at the coming races....

Mr. C. C. Rufer, the popular restaurateur, has been given charge of the clubhouse refreshments, and will, as he always does, dispense choice culinary articles to appreciative patrons. Mr. Rufer has increased the cooking facilities and made other improvements.[22]

FROM "THE LOUISVILLE CUP," *THE DAILY LOUISVILLE COMMERCIAL*, 16 MAY 1875

The show-window of Messrs. Cook & Sloss, jewelers, on Fourth street, for the past few days, are fairly ablaze with rich jewelry, diamonds, watches, and silverware, prominent among which was the "Louisville Cup," gotten up by this firm expressly for the Louisville Jockey Club races, from an entirely original design, at a cost of $1,000.

The "cup" is of solid sterling silver, weighing 270 3/4 ounces (troy), is eighteen inches high and twenty-two inches wide; the bowl is round; its diameter measures sixteen inches, and is gold lined; on either side, and forming the handles, are full carved solid heads of Longfellow, which will at once be recognized, being a very good likeness of one of Kentucky's favorite horses, and taken from a painting of the horse in his natural position; around the neck is a silver oxidized horseshoe, and drooping beneath are branches of laurel; there are two medallions of seven inches diameter; the one in front has a central figure of a horse and jockey-rider in bas relief running a hurdle; upon the four extremes of the medallion are horseshoes of small size in dark oxidized silver, and the circle forms a wreath of laurel between a margin of gold on each side; the opposite side contains simply the inscription, "Louisville Cup," on a burnished surface; branches of laurel gracefully droop from the medallions.

MADE BY THE WHITING M'F'G CO., N. Y.,
—FOR—
COOK & SLOSS, Louisville, Ky.

The "Gentleman's Cup"
(102 ounces 12 dwt. sterling silver)
To be awarded by the "Louisville Jockey Club" during the coming races. Furnished by KITTS & WERNE, Jewelers, 120 Main St.

Both: From *The Courier-Journal*, 20 May 1875.

<small>FROM "A REVIEW OF THE WEEK," *THE COURIER-JOURNAL*, 24 MAY 1875</small>
For the Gentleman's $250 cup, Major John H. Coster, of the American Jockey Club, and Mr. A. Trigg Moss, of the Louisville Jockey Club, started. The former rode Williams & Owings' Oxmore, and the latter A. Keene Richards' Misfortune. Mr. Moss won the cup by dint of good riding on a somewhat slow horse.[23]

<small>FROM "'LET 'EM GO!'" *THE COURIER-JOURNAL*, 13 MAY 1876</small>
The grounds surrounding the grand stand have been enlarged so as to afford more ample accommodation to the pool buyers and sellers than they have heretofore supplied. For this purpose, new awnings have been erected on the grounds, which will be amply sufficient to afford the sporting gentlemen and spectators all the protection they may desire from either rain or sunshine. Pool stands have also been erected that look so neat that they will not fail to attract a good crowd of the class that congregate around these places.

<small>FROM "'LADIES' DAY,'" *THE COURIER-JOURNAL*, 19 MAY 1876</small>
Yesterday was a star day for the Louisville Jockey Club. Never before during its history has this organization seen a day that has been a more brilliant success, both in point of attendance and elegance of sport....It being "Cup day," which has already properly become the day of the spring meeting, all the ladies that lay pretense to being among the fashionable were desirous of being on hand....It is fairly estimated that there were ten thousand people in attendance....

Pretty women have an intuitive knowledge of a horse's qualities. There has in Kentucky always been a kind of rivalry between the fair ones and the equine race, and though the ladies have felt and owned this, they have not been so liberal as to deny the ground for this rivalry. All over the United States the Bluegrass State is celebrated for its production of both pretty women and fine horses, and as celebrated for the one as for the other....

Ten Broeck has been so often described in this column, and is so well known to all turf men that further notice of him is needless here.[24]...The cup, which was manufactured by Cook & Sloss, was on exhibition, and attracted attention.[25] After the race it was formally presented to Mr. Harper.

Frank B. Harper (1824-1905) was proprietor of Nantura Farm on the Lexington and Frankfort Pike adjacent to the Alexander farm, Woodburn. Spring Station in Woodford County was the cradle of horse racing in Kentucky. Harpers had been on this land since Adam Harper first came to Kentucky about 1795. He had five children, four of which remained, unmarried, on the old homestead. Another son, William, married the granddaughter of pioneer Indian fighter William Whitley.[26] Ann Whitley Harper was Frank B. Harper's mother.[27] Uncle John (1803-1874) had been raising horses for decades before he made Nantura (and himself) celebrated as the home of Longfellow. When Longfellow died, a marker was erected in the graveyard in front of his stall carrying the apt eulogy "King of racers and king of stallions."[28] A son of Leamington, he was bred when his sire stood in 1866 at Bosque Bonita, Abe Buford's nearby farm.

In 1872, John Harper's mark on American racing was sealed when his mare Fanny Holton, sired by Lexington, out of Nantura, was bred to Phaeton, which was standing at Major Barak G. Thomas's Lexington farm. The foal was Ten Broeck, named for Richard Ten Broeck who, when he gave up racing in England and returned to America, had brought Phaeton as a three-year old to his Louisville farm. Phaeton stood at Hurstbourne (now a country club east of Louisville) for two years before being transferred to Major Thomas's operation. [29]

When Frank B. Harper died eighteen years later, he devised Nantura and his horses, household furniture, and silverware to his grandnephews, Frank Harper Hawkins and Clinton Hawkins, Jr., children of his niece. The inventory of his personal estate contained entries for various paintings of his horses and "1 silver punch bowl" valued at $150.[30]

Many years later the Hawkins brothers were interviewed for an article which appeared in *The Courier-Journal* in January 1939. Frank Hawkins related that his great-uncle Frank Harper had become owner of Ten Broeck after he protested to Uncle John about the colt possibly being gelded. As a part of the interview, the brothers were photographed with the "huge silver bowl," which they believed had been presented to Frank Harper for Ten Broeck's victory over Mollie McCarthy in the famous match race on 4 July 1878.[31]

Before that date, Ten Broeck had raced many times before appreciative crowds at the Louisville Jockey Club track. After being beaten soundly by Aristides in the Derby, he lost to his own half brother, King Alfonso, in the inaugural St. Leger that fall. He won a two-mile heat race, the Louisville Cup, and the Galt House Stake in the spring of 1876. In the fall meet he raced Add in the Post Stake, "a dash of three miles for all ages." His time of 5:26 1/4 was a record. Four days later on 27 September, closing day, Ten Broeck and Add again squared off, at four miles. Frank Harper asked for quiet, and "Billy Walker, the rider for Dan Swigert's stable," again pushed Ten Broeck to a new record.[32]

In the spring meet of 1877, Ten Broeck set two records against time. When he lowered the two-mile record of McWhirter and Courier by five seconds, *The Courier-Journal* reported:[33]

> President Clark then turned to the audience and announced that Ten Broeck had now made the fastest four miles, three miles, two miles, and one mile on record, and that Ten Broeck had run his last race and would now retire to the stud. Mr. Harper was introduced and he made his best bow to the applauding host. Ten Broeck's record now reads: For four miles, 7:15 3/4, September 27, 1876; for three miles, 5:26 1/2, September 23, 1876; for two miles, 3:27 1/2, May 29, 1877; for one mile, 1:39 3/4, [May 25, 1877].[34]

Frank Harper was presumptuous and probably greedy. In the fall, Ten Broeck raced again, only to be upset by Parole at Pimlico. Early in 1878, however, he defeated Aristides. The stage was then set for Mollie McCarthy to come from California for a duel of four-mile heats on the Fourth of July.[35]

I had the honor of an invitation to attend a banquet given by Mr. F. B. Harper at the old residence on the world-renowned Nantura Stock Farm, near Midway, Woodford Co., Ky., last Friday.... Invitations are only to the gentlemen on this occasion,

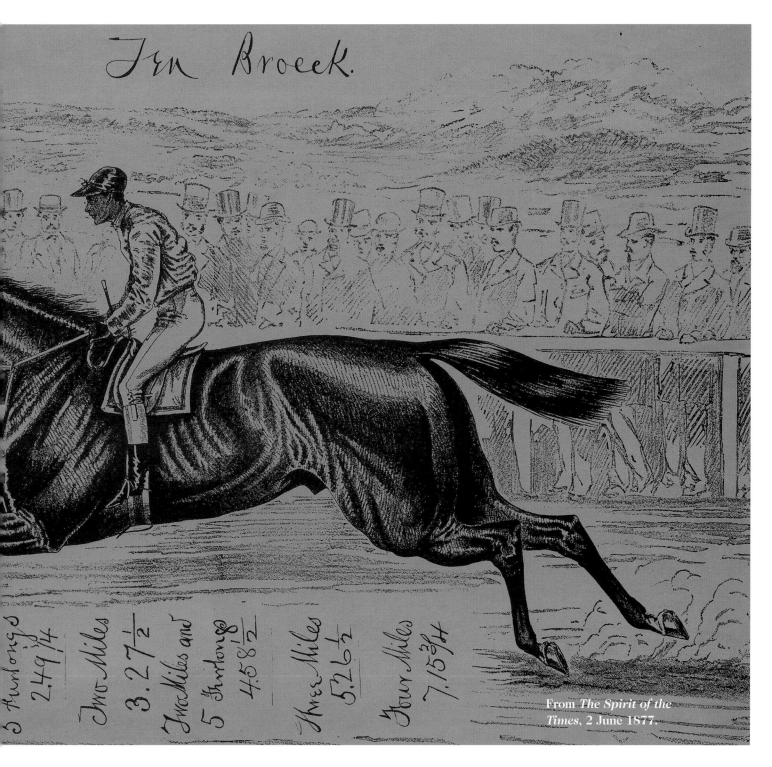

Ten Broeck.

3 Furlongs 2.49 3/4

Two Miles 3.27 1/2

Two Miles and 5 Furlongs 4.58 1/2

Three Miles 5.26 1/2

Four Miles 7.15 3/4

From *The Spirit of the Times*, 2 June 1877.

and they are having a glorious time, friends meeting friends, with the hospitality of Nantura flowing in that princely style that has always characterized Frank Harper's kind and generous heart on such occasions. Wines, liquors, cigars, and eggnog,

the latter in Ten Broeck's $1,000 cup, won at Louisville, Ky....The doors are thrown open and dinner is announced. All are eager to see the table, that is literally groaning with the good things of life, prepared by Aunt Susan, Frank Harper's cook,

who came from the Blackburn family, and has the reputation of being the best one in the country.[36]
–PHILIP C. KIDD, "MR. F. B. HARPER'S BIRTHDAY FEAST," *THE SPIRIT OF THE TIMES*, 19 FEBRUARY 1887.

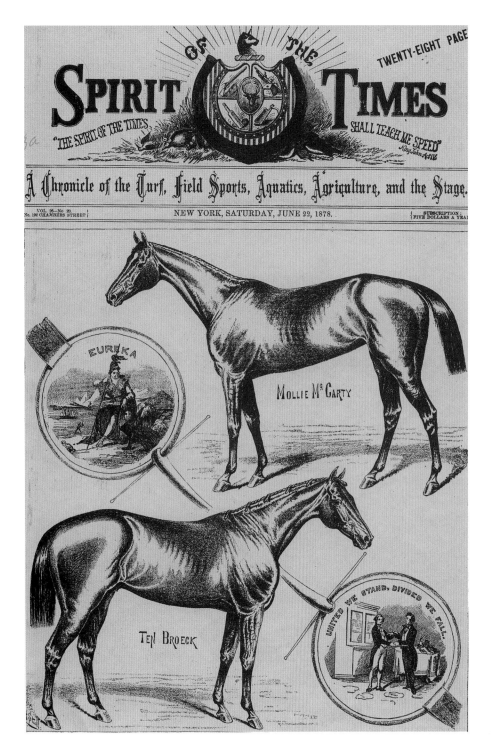

FROM "OBITUARY," *BLUE GRASS CLIPPER*,
4 OCTOBER 1883

Wesley James (known as "Jug") a colored boy of twenty-two years age, died some two weeks since, at the residence of Mr. F. B. Harper, in this vicinity. He was widely and well known as the breaker and jockey of the great Ten Broeck, whose well earned fame is world wide. Jug piloted him in some of his mighty contests. He had been in Mr. Harper's employ for many years before his death.

If a servant ever held confidential relations to his employer, this one did. There was no responsibility too great, no trust too important, for his fidelity. Trusted in all things, he was faithless in none. Amiable, polite, painstaking and honest, he was liked by all who knew him. If care, kindness and attention could have availed, he would have been saved. In death as during life, he was surrounded by friends, but the last drum tap has sounded for him, calling him to the start, over that course, where none are entered, save the spectre steed of death. Mr. Harper has sustained a heavy loss. He will not find it an easy task to replace this faithful, honest boy.

FROM *THE COURIER-JOURNAL*, 14 JUNE 1878

The Jockey Club is one of the several things which tell the outside world that Louisville still occupies a place on the globe. It is not run to make money, and its stockholders include some of the best people in Kentucky.

On Tuesday, Derby day, the field will present a sight never before witnessed in this country, for rich and poor, white and black, will be on the same footing there, and a general picnic and holiday is anticipated. It seems a pity to ruin so much beautiful grass, but the Club has determined to do the graceful thing and will do it. To preserve the order which has become a part of the Club, it must be remembered that this is but an experiment which will be a fixed fact for the future in case good order and feeling prevail.

There is nothing like a special attraction to bring out the good qualities of the Fourth of July. This the Ten Broeck-McCarthy race has done for Louisville. The mere fact that a mare of winged feet from California was to be boldly pitted against a horse who has made the quickest time on record in dashes of one, two, three and four miles was sufficient to excite public curiosity and to bring one of the largest crowds together ever assembled in this country. At eight o'clock yesterday morning the cars running to the races were crowded with eager, impatient persons. The streets of the city were alive with jostling forms and excited men. At half-past ten the Grand Stand was densely packed. Men in long night-gowns — like dusters — were hurrying over the grounds. In the Grand Stand were a number of Kentucky and other beauties. The belles of the Bluegrass region, with their animated faces and sprightly conversation, formed a pleasing part of the scene....

The bell called the horses from their stables. In an instant, the crowd as alive. The manifest tendency noticeable during the afternoon to cheer at the slightest pretext culminated in a glorious shout from the pent-up exhilaration of the perspiring mass. The police at once endeavored to assert themselves, but to little effect. The mounted officers charged and plunged about, the poolbuyers were shrieking, the drums of the invited militia were rolling, and on every hand there were clamor and bustle. Three of the stewards of the track dashed across the center field toward Ten Broeck's stable. Umbrellas were forgotten and fans ceased their motion. Watches were tried and field-glasses were put in order. The roofs of the outlying stables and of the lower stand were rapidly filled. The two trees in the pasture became black with men. The tops of vehicles bristled with humanity. Awning-posts were climbed, fences mounted and everything animated was on the *qui vive*. It took but a few moments for the horses to answer the signal. Ten Broeck was the first to make an appearance. The King was most royally received, and Billy Walker, his rider, was for the nonce the most important personage on the ground. His illustrious eminence was flanked and surrounded by an escort of mounted stewards, police and stable men, and the *entree* was attended with great *éclat*. Mr. Harper strolled along in the rear under a spreading umbrella, and the guard was so complete that even the breezes could scarcely reach him. When the horse was stripped he showed in most beautiful form, his satin coat gleaming in the sunlight and the brilliant rosettes of yellow and red knotted in his mane gave him the appearance of having just sprung from a milliner's bandbox. Shortly afterward Mollie McCarthy came in sight, and a shout arose hardly less long and loud than that which had saluted her opponent. When stripped she showed just as "pretty as a picture," and her training seemed to have been *perfect*, and while all this ceremony was attending Ten Broeck, Mollie, a short distance up the track, was sponged by Mr. Walsh, her trainer, with nobody near her save Howsen and a rubber. She was simply attired, and she arched her beautiful neck in proud consciousness that she, of all others, had been selected to cut the wings of the Kentucky conqueror. Both horses were somewhat restive, and demonstrated they were full of spirit for the fray. Ten Broeck cantered around the track, and Mollie stretched herself in a similar fashion, and then each came to the mark without any unnecessary delay. The judges were Col. M. Lewis Clark, the President of the club; Major Viley, of Lexington and Mr. Dan Swigert, of Woodford county....

Suddenly, and to the overwhelming astonishment of all, Ten Broeck's colors were seen to gleam in the advance, and the mare fell to the rear almost without a struggle. All this occurred in so short a period that when the second quarter-post was reached Ten Broeck led by as much as two lengths. Now the uproar began. The horse gradually lengthened out the intervening daylight. It was five lengths as they rounded the curve, and ten lengths as they went past the stand. Time, 5:53. Half way down the stretch *Mollie McCarthy was struck by the whip for the first time in her life!* It was now all over, so far as she was concerned. Mr. Harper, who was standing in the door of the weighing room, sprang forward as his horse came on, and shouted to Walker to run for his life. The confusion was now something terrific. McCarthy was seen to be out of the race entirely, and Walker ran to shut her out. The mare plunged slowly on, and did not give it up for half a mile. She had stopped entirely on the lower turn, just as Ten Broeck galloped slowly into the embrace of victory, winning the heat and race in 8:19 3/4.

The race was deemed a failure by the press, especially that of other cities eager to heap criticism.[37] Ten Broeck's slow time even caused *The Louisville Daily Commercial* of 6 July to ask "Was He Drugged?" The newspaper repeated reports of Ten Broeck having been drugged at Pimlico when defeated by Parole. His slow time and "sad condition" after defeating Mollie McCarthy could be explained by a dosing of morphine. "There are several things indicating that Ten Broeck was 'got at and fixed,'" *The Commercial* claimed. Jockey Billy Walker explained that Ten Broeck was just not put in condition.[38] *The Courier-Journal* on July 8th reflected: "For the first time in the course of her natural existence Louisville failed to satisfy the expectations of her guests." The blame was placed — "the middle men were the objects of distrust." "A lesson has been taught." It was a bitter pill for M. Lewis Clark. There would be only one other long distance race in Kentucky during the next thirty-three years.

Now, Major, if you will tell me about the Grey Eagle-Wagner race at Louisville a half century ago I will let you off. Do you remember it?

Oh, yes. In company with many others I went to Louisville on horseback to witness that contest, one of the most exciting turf events that has ever occurred. It was no Ten Broeck-Mollie McCarthy affair, but one which all the South, especially Kentucky and Virginia, witnessed.

–FROM AN INTERVIEW OF MAJOR BARAK G. THOMAS IN *THE COURIER-JOURNAL*, 10 SEPTEMBER 1882

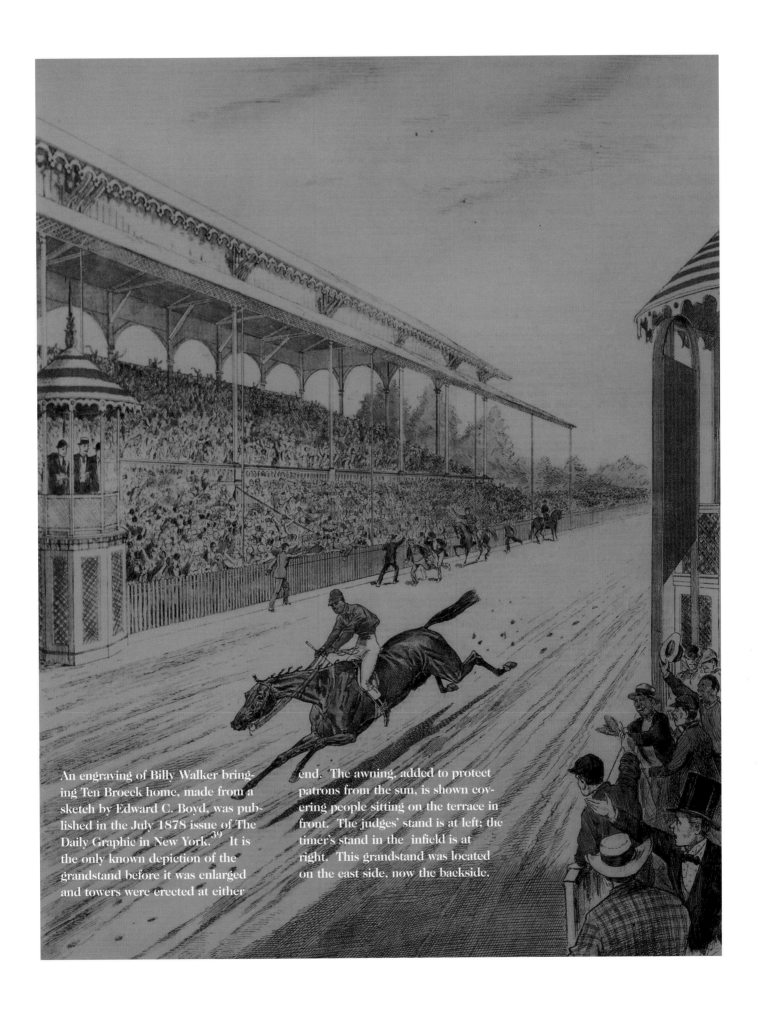

An engraving of Billy Walker bringing Ten Broeck home, made from a sketch by Edward C. Boyd, was published in the July 1878 issue of The Daily Graphic in New York.[39] It is the only known depiction of the grandstand before it was enlarged and towers were erected at either end. The awning, added to protect patrons from the sun, is shown covering people sitting on the terrace in front. The judges' stand is at left; the timer's stand in the infield is at right. This grandstand was located on the east side, now the backside.

The start had occurred directly in front of the grandstand and M. Lewis Clark had successfully gotten the contestants away fairly and "at the first venture" — "Mollie was just half a length in front as they went under the wire." The track being one mile in length, the start and finish for heat races were both directly in view. Finish calls were rarely contested, but starts were frequently criticized. There was no gate or stall to prevent horses from bolting or getting sideways or even backwards. False starts and recalls were common, especially with large fields.

FROM "THE LOUISVILLE SPRING MEETING," *THE TURF, FIELD AND FARM*, 16 MAY 1879

The interest taken by the American people in racing grows greater yearly, and now the raising and training of thoroughbred stock, and the attendance on the meetings given for the display of their performances may almost be called the Great National Pastime of the Country.

FROM *THE COURIER-JOURNAL*, 18 MAY 1878

The rapid growth of turf interests through the country, and the dissatisfaction in regards to starters, will bring about some invention to equalize all horses in the sound-off. The simplest and most perfect plan proposed is to have a moveable strong fence placed across the track, thirty feet back of the string, and place all the horses within this thirty-foot distance or area; as soon as all are in this area, the drum is tapped, and no animal will be left more than thirty feet in any event.

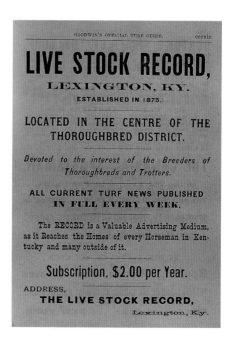

FROM "SPRING MEETING OF THE LOUISVILLE JOCKEY CLUB," *KENTUCKY LIVE STOCK RECORD*, 7 JUNE 1879

There was nothing to mar the harmony of the meeting, which was conducted in admirable style, and we cannot let the occasion pass to congratulate Col. W. H. Johnson, and his assistant, Mr. J. W. Wynn, on the uniform good starts made during the meeting with such large fields of horses. Col. Johnson adopted Mr. Wright's (of Catterick Bridge, England) system, which we advocated last winter, of drawing two parallel lines some twenty feet apart, and placing the horses between the lines, which makes it almost impossible to give a bad start without some bad behavior upon the part of the horse after the drum or flag falls.

It is not exactly clear how the early starts were prompted — by a drum beat or a flag drop or both. Newspapers relate that races at Churchill Downs were commenced by a bell calling the horses onto the track from the paddock to saddle up. There was a string stretched across the track between the judges' (starter's) stand and the timer's stand. Generally, about thirty yards behind this string, there was another line, scratched in the turf by the starter, that served as the initial assembly point. It was in this area that the jockeys received their assignments for position and the horses began their approach to the start. When the starter "tapped the drum," the race was underway. If the start was not deemed fair, the starter would initiate a recall by ringing a bell and having his assistants, positioned about 125 yards down the track, wave the horses off, and the process would start anew. The procedure could be repeated several times before the start was deemed fair. Newspaper accounts describing the start of local races noted "the tap of the drum" until 1880. Only the flag seemed to be mentioned after that time.[40]

OFFICE—NO. 37 PARK ROW.
VOLUME XXII.—NUMBER 1.

NEW YORK, FRIDAY, JANUARY 7, 1876.

SUBSCRIPTION
FIVE DOLLARS PER ANNUM

BRAMBLE:
Winner of Great American Stallion Stakes, Louisville.

Opposite and top: Dr. Benjamin Gratz Bruce, later secretary of the Louisville Jockey Club, was an editor of *The Turf, Field and Farm* in New York before returning to establish in 1875 the *Kentucky Live Stock Record*, later called *The Thoroughbred Record*. Above: Drawing by Henry Stull, *The Spirit of the Times*, 5 October 1878.

FROM "BRAMBLE THE VICTOR," *THE COURIER-JOURNAL*, 27 SEPTEMBER 1878

The event of the present meeting was the Great American Stallion Stake. Its richness and the uncertainty of result, attracted the attention of the entire sporting world. The value of the stake proper was $4,525 or with the Woodburn challenge vase, valued at $2,500 — $7,025.[41]

FROM "LOUISIVLLE JOCKEY CLUB," *THE TURF, FIELD AND FARM*,
20 DECEMBER 1878

This Association has removed its headquarters, heretofore located in the Galt House, to Walker's Exchange, on Third street, which is also the headquarters of the book-makers and pool-sellers, Messrs. J.R. Watts & Co. The Exchange has been long and favorably known as a resort for turf-men. It has been leased and fitted up by Messrs. Watts & Co., and a restaurant, under their control, is in the same building.

On 3 December 1878, Meriwether Lewis Clark became politically active. He was elected councilman representing the Fifth Ward in a special session of the general council. Louisville then had a bicameral system of councilmen and aldermen. *The Daily Louisville Commercial* on 14 March 1879 carried a synopsis of his report on the Louisville Gas Company to the general council. The inquiry was conducted with full disclosure of his "special interest" as a large stockholder in the gas company. He served on the common council until 18 December 1879, when he was replaced by Henry S. Jefferson, but he would use political connections, especially with four-term mayor and Louisville Jockey Club director Charles D. Jacob, to the track's advantage. The reason for Clark's leaving the common council may have been for recuperation.

Colonel Moore [Capt. Thomas G. Moore of Crab Orchard, Kentucky] and his son appeared in the rotunda of the Galt House, where Colonel Clark was sitting. Colonel Moore walked up to Colonel Clark and told him that he had insulted him on the track yesterday afternoon and that he demanded an apology. Colonel Clark replied that he had intended to offer no insult, but had simply been carrying out the rules of the association, but that if Colonel Moore felt insulted at what he had said he would apologize. Colonel Moore replied that he had been openly insulted in public and before turfmen on the race track, and the kind of apology which he demanded was a public apology and he would accept no other. Colonel Clark replied that he would not make an apology of that sort, and in order to try and avoid a difficulty he retired to a little private office in the rear of the counter at the Galt House. In a very few minutes Colonel Moore and his son followed Colonel Clark back to this office, and Colonel Moore said, "I intend to shoot you, you s-n of a b-h." At this remark Colonel Clark drew his pistol, and attempted to close the door opening into the rotunda with his foot, but only partially succeeded. Mr. William L. Murphy, clerk at the Galt House and Secretary of the Jockey Club, was the only person in the office with Colonel Clark at the time of the difficulty. When Colonel Clark drew his pistol young Moore handed his father a French six-shooter 42-caliber pistol, and Colonel Moore immediately fired at Colonel Clark through one of the windows of the door. The ball from the pistol entered the right side, just above the nipple, and lodged under the skin, the ball penetrating about five inches into the fleshy portion of his body. Drs. David Yandell and James Kellar were immediately summoned, and pronounced the wound a dangerous one.

M. Lewis Clark, Louisville Jockey Club president, *The Graphic News* (New York), 15 May 1886.

According to *The Courier-Journal* of 30 September 1879, Col. Clark was examined by "his kinsman, Gov. Blackburn," in consultation with Drs. Yandell and Kellar and a decision was made for him to remain at the Galt House. He recovered, and on 13 November 1879, Capt. Moore was ruled off the track for "his language and conduct on the track during the meeting." However, a year later he was reinstated by Clark.[42]

In May 1879, the Louisville Jockey Club advertised for bids for the sale of "Bar and Restaurant Privileges.... for the year 1879, for the two meetings, twelve days." Previous to that date, the privileges had been awarded to H. & W. Israel, but evidently the club had become dissatisfied with their operation. These privileges, along with those for pool selling, were a major source of income for the track.[43]

John Wesley Hunt Reynolds (1846-1880), a vice president and director of the Louisville Jockey Club, died unexpectedly on 22 September 1880. He was the son of William Bell Reynolds (1808-1862), a successful Louisville merchant, who had two stores built on the southwest corner of

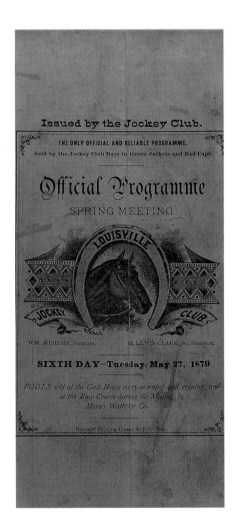

Sixth and Main streets that remain well preserved. His mother was Ann Hunt, daughter of John Wesley Hunt of Lexington, and sister of A.D. and Thomas Hunt and an aunt of John Hunt Morgan. Young Reynolds not only inherited a fortune from his father and grandfather, but from his aunt and uncle, Mr. and Mrs. John Hanna of Frankfort who adopted him after his mother died. He was educated in Germany, later developing Fleetwood Farm west of Frankfort on the Louisville Road, now the site of the Capital City Airport. He bred Falsetto, who was second in the 1879 Derby but won the Clark Handicap; his Felicia prevailed in the 1877 Kentucky Oaks. Reynold's black trainer, Eli Jordan, helped raise jockey Isaac Murphy, who frequently rode for Reynolds as well as for his widow. Meta Westfeldt Reynolds taught Murphy to read and write. After her husband's death, she continued to operate the farm. She later married Lew P. Tarlton who served as a judge for the Louisville Jockey Club.[44]

In 1881, Darwin Ward Johnson (1862-1936) became secretary of the Louisville Jockey Club, replacing William Murphy. His stepfather, Robert A. Johnson, was an influential member. Young Johnson had briefly worked in a tobacco warehouse, and would later serve as receiver for the Jefferson Circuit Court. In 1905 he co-founded the Commonwealth Life Insurance Company and was its president until his death. Late in life, Johnson recalled: "For my work as secretary, I was paid $100 a week. Now don't think that this was for each 52 weeks in the year. It was only while the meeting was in progress."[45]

FROM "OUR RACE COURSE," *THE EVENING POST*, 3 MAY 1882

The most decided improvements have been made out at the jockey club grounds. Visitors at former meetings will hardly know the place. The grand stand has been extended thirty-eight feet each way, making an increase of seventy-six feet. With this improvement the stand is 350 feet long, and about forty-five feet wide. It is one of the largest in the country, and by all odds, the most attractive in appearance. That assertion is the opinion of men who have been upon all the prominent race courses of the country. On either end of the grand stand and in the center, have been erected towers. Three towers are of rare architectural beauty, rise fully sixty feet from the ground, and give the place an imposing appearance. The entrance to the towers is from the ladies' stand; and the three are connected by a promenade extending along the roof. The extra space below has been judiciously utilized. At one end it has been turned into a dancing hall, at the other end into a fine saloon, furnished with chairs and tables, where people may avoid the crowd of the general saloon.

With the improvements made, the grand stand will probably seat eight or ten thousand people. In beautifying the stand the architect, Mr. Chas. Clarke, has shown good taste and judgment, nothing is overdone, yet nothing is lacking. The ornamental work is just sufficient to please the fancy of the year, and there is an absence of anything approaching gaudiness. Upon each of the towers are five poles, one upon every corner and one from the center. During the meet, a flag will fly from the poles. It is the intention of Colonel Clark to have the flags of all nations. The idea is a good one, and will give the place a far gayer appearance.

The public stand has also been improved, but not enlarged. Upon this stand there are also three towers. The pool place has not been removed, but considerably enlarged, and greatly improved. It is completely under cover, the roof being 120 by forty feet. All the arrangements are complete, and it is one of the largest, best arranged and most comfortable pooling stands in the country. The reporters' stand has been moved back across the track, and is now in front of the grand stand, to the left of the judges' stand. Such are the improvements that have been made about the grand stand. The result thus achieved is complimentary to the skill and merit of the designer, and the effect as noted from the center field picturesque and attractive.

The improvements about the grounds are most notable, and at once attract and please the eye. Everywhere are seen the good results of an effort to beautify the place. The board fence which ran along the back stretch has given way to a neat picket fence. The stables are now within the grounds proper, and the arrangements much more convenient for the men engaged in handling the horses. From the entrance gate up around the club-house is a wire fence, and a row of young cedars has been planted just inside. In this way the grounds have been thrown open without anything to oppose the view, and the effect is indeed pleasing. A new walk to the grand stand has been opened up through the club-house yard, by which pedestrians are saved considerable distance. It is the intention to arrange flower beds along through the club-house yard, which will greatly add to the attractiveness of the grounds....

Around the stables considerable improvement has also been made, and new stalls have been built, making the number now 310, yet the association will be crowded for room. There are 766 entries in the stake races, and when the meeting commences there will be more horses on the grounds than have ever been assembled at one time upon any other track in the country.

Grandstand architect Charles Julian Clarke (1836-1908) was a Frankfort native, educated at the universities of Kentucky and Louisville, and trained by architects Henry Whitestone and H. P. Bradshaw. Clarke was Bradshaw's partner when the latter died in 1877. Before the Louisville Jockey Club commission, he was responsible for the Second Presbyterian Church and the Main Street dry goods building which now serves as the Louisville Science Center. He was also working on the John N. Norton Memorial Infirmary in 1882, and later, with partner Arthur Loomis, was responsible for designing the Louisville Medical College and Levy Brothers clothing store.[46]

FROM "SPORTING," *THE COURIER-JOURNAL*, 14 MAY 1882

Yesterday the Grand Stand was completed entirely, and stands for strength and architectural beauty without a rival in this country. The structure itself, with its light, airy columns, so comfortable and attractive before, by the aid of the banners and walk on top, needs nothing to demonstrate a superiority evident to all.

Below: Clubhouse and grandstand, *Louisville Illustrated* (1889), part 7.

FROM "A FOUNDLING FOAL," *THE LOUISVILLE COMMERCIAL*, 17 MAY 1882

Over the field and down the lawn the fresh grass stretched away in a beautiful carpet, and on every side the white fences and pink stables, over which the racing colors floated, gave agreeable contrast to the natural green. The lawn has been dotted with flowers, and flags are planted everywhere....

Alongside these good-natured people, who follow with the wave of popular enthusiasm, are those who bet. They occupy the south side of the stand near the betting stalls, and in and out of the stand they rush between the races. Around the pool-seller's stand and before the bookmaker's and the French boxes is collected a solid mass of men, quiet but alert. There is a low hum through the crowd, over which the voice of the auctioneer rings like the trumpet over the whirring of the orchestra. There is little bidding. It is all done by a nod, or a wink, or a sign. The auctioneer knows where to look for his best bidder. It is almost invariably a professional gambler who buys the favorite. The bookmakers are busy with betting their own, squeezing odds against any horse you name, and

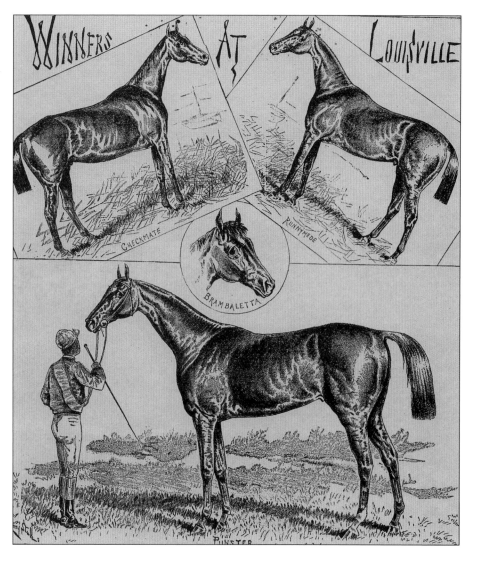

From *The Spirit of the Times*, 3 June 1882.

FROM "OUR RACE COURSE," *THE EVENING POST*, 3 MAY 1882

One of the most decided improvements is a steeple chase course. This is the first that has ever been arranged in Kentucky, or, in fact, anywhere in the Southwest. The lovers of this sport have always desired a steeple chase course, and the Louisville Jockey Club, while receiving the thanks of all, deserve credit for the enterprise that has filled this long felt want. There are at present sixteen steeple chase horses on the grounds and during the eleven days of the meeting there will be several races of this character. The course is in the center field and almost in the shape of a figure 8. The start is immediately opposite the grand stand, the horses going first away toward the head of the stretch and returning taking a water jump in front of the grand stand. The course then circles around the lower turn, then toward the center of the field, and entering the regular track at the half-mile pole, the race from that point to the finish being run on the level. The entire distance is about one mile and three-quarters, and there are ten jumps.

the French pool boxes are automatically counting the $5 bills that accumulate for division among those who name the winner. Then the bell rings, the auctioneer's voice ceases and the crowd melts away and into the grand stand. This side of the stand is marked from the other by that mute impassiveness that indicates the excitement of gambling.

FROM "APOLLO WINS," THE COURIER-JOURNAL, 17 MAY 1882

Fully 15,000 people found comfortable quarters within its gates. There was scarcely a vacant seat from one end of the Grand Stand to the other. The space about the pool boxes and the inclosure from the stables on the east of the track to the Club-house swarmed with expectant humans, while the visitors to the inner field thickened twenty feet deep at the timer's stand and tapered off along the fence, like a bended bow, to either end of the track. In the center of the field hundreds of horses were haltered, and the score of vehicles furnished reserved seats for those who had accepted the free and magnanimous invitation of the club. No Kentucky race course has ever before seen anything like it. It was simply an ovation to the spirit of the Jockey Club, a joyous outpouring of worshipers at the

Henry Stull painted Checkmate and jockey Isaac Murphy for owner James T. Williams. (See *The Courier-Journal*, 18 May 1882, below.) Eli Jordan, trainer for Williams and his partner Richard Owings, had first brought Murphy to Louisville in January 1875 when Churchill Downs was under construction. He rode in his first Derby in 1877 and thereafter ten times, winning in 1884, 1890, and 1891.

shrine of the thoroughbred. It was a perfect day. The sun cheerily assented to a repetition of the old performance, "Lew Clark's Luck," and shone with a generous warmth...and the sport was superb.

The ladies' side of the Grand Stand bloomed resplendent in many-hued bonnets that crowned a generous representation of the fairest women under the sun.

Wagering by women was not deemed socially acceptable, nor was it practiced. Ladies were seated in the grandstand opposite from the location of the betting shed, which was adjacent to the grandstand for the convenience of the gentlemen who would frequent it between races. The ladies were thus protected from viewing the crass sight of men haggling over bets. Such etiquette established the relative layout of the structures on the Louisville Jockey Club grounds, and most other tracks as well. Looking at the grandstand from the infield, the clubhouse frequented by the ladies was to the left, and the betting shed was invariably to the right along with the paddock. This same configuration would hold when the track was reoriented in 1894.

FROM *THE COURIER-JOURNAL*, 18 MAY 1882

Mr. Harry Stull, of the Spirit of the Times, famous for his delineation of horseflesh on canvas, is attending the races. Immediately after the Derby, Green Morris gave Mr. Stull an order to paint a portrait of the winner, Apollo. Mr. Stull has on exhibition at the Galt House lifelike paintings of the great Foxhall, Hindoo and his sire, Virgil, and an excellent likeness of Iroquois, the winner of the last English Derby. Mr. Stull intends remaining during the meeting. He will also produce Checkmate on canvas in racing trim, with Murphy, the smoked Englishman, on his back. The painting, when finished, will adorn the walls of Mr. [James T.] Williams' residence.[47]

Henry Stull (1851-1913) did paint Checkmate with Isaac Murphy aboard, and it did adorn the Williams' residence along with Stull's paintings of Virgil, Hindoo, and Foxhall, which Williams purchased at the Galt House exhibit.[48]

James T. Williams (1849-1921) owned three Kentucky Derby starters including Joe Cotton, the 1885 winner. His racing operation was then located in Eminence, Kentucky. In 1900, Williams purchased Stockwood Farm, once owned by Daniel Swigert, at Spring Station in Woodford County, where he died.[49] Even though Virgil was a very versatile horse, no one seemed to want him. Foaled in 1864, he first ran for R. A. Alexander and then Milton H. Sanford. Daniel Swigert raced him over hurdles and soon another owner used him for harness driving. Sanford bought him back, only to give the delicate black colt to B. G. Bruce. Bruce gave a half interest to J. T. Williams and Richard Owings for the horse's keep. When Vagrant won the renewal of the Kentucky Derby in 1876, the fortunes of his sire began to brighten. Sanford wanted his gift back, and Bruce complied for $2,000. When Swigert purchased Sanford's stud farm called Preakness in 1881, Virgil was the premier part of the package.[50] Williams' Hindoo, purchased by the Dwyer brothers, won the 1882 Derby; his Ben Ali would win in 1886. Only three other horses (Falsetto, *Sir Gallahad III, and Bull Lea) have sired three Derby winners.

When Brooklyn brothers Phil and Mike Dwyer returned to the Derby in 1883 with a coterie of their favorite bookies, a repeat of their victory with Hindoo was expected with the odds-on-favorite, Runnymede. The Dwyers had informed Col. Clark that their horses would not come to Louisville unless plenty of bookies were on hand, which allowed the betting brothers to bring along many of their compatriots.[51] Runnymede was upset, and Col. Clark must have been dismayed when, on 15 February 1888, he received a copy of an interview given by Capt. Samuel S. Brown in Pittsburgh, saying "that racing was governed by the interests of the bookmakers, and citing as an instance the Kentucky Derby of 1882, alleged to have been 'fixed' for the gamblers."[52] To make matters worse, Capt. Brown was not only a member of the Louisville Jockey Club, but also a director. He had even been a member of the executive committee at the time of the alleged fix. Clark immediately convened a "Court of Inquiry," comprised of the executive committee present which included himself, Col. John Churchill, Col. John M. Barbour, J.T. McCulloch, Lee Bloom and William Gaulbert. Affadavits that countered Brown's allegations were secured from Philip J. Dwyer, jockey James McLaughlin, trainer James Rowe, and various bookmakers.

When the executive committee met on 3 March 1888 to consider the matter, Capt. Brown, although expected to attend, was not to be found. The Louisville Jockey Club dropped the matter when Brown eventually "denied that he ever uttered any such charges."[53] But the overriding problems with gambling and bookmaking were not going to disappear.

Samuel S. Brown, *The Courier-Journal*, 12 December 1905.

From *The Courier-Journal*, 18 May 1882

The steeple-chase today, the fifth event on the card, will doubtless be a very interesting affair. It will be the first imitation of cross-country racing ever given in Kentucky. The field comprises some of the best steeple-chasers in the country. The Kentuckian is an admirer of pluck, and in this contest he will have displayed to his satisfaction the courage of his favorite animal at facing timber while running at no mean rate of speed. The steeple-chase is a feature of horse-racing in the East, and there is no reason why it should not be patronized in Kentucky.[54] The weights to be carried are light welter weights, which is twenty-eight pounds added to weight for age.

Samuel Smith Brown (1841-1905) would continue to race. His Proceeds was the Kentucky Derby favorite in 1904; his Agile won in 1905. His racing interests were supported by a steel mill fueled by his coal, hauled in his steamboats. When he died on 11 December 1905, his estate included stock in the Latonia track and the Memphis Jockey Club as well as ownership of the Kentucky Association track. His brother, Harry Brown, continued the racing stable. In 1903, Capt. Brown had purchased the old Creighton farm on the Iron Works Pike and established Senorita Stud. It is now the Kentucky Horse Park.[55]

FROM "HER CLEVER BOTTOM," *THE COURIER-JOURNAL*, 19 MAY 1882

The closing event of the day was the inaugural steeple-chase over the new course. This style of racing is a novelty here, and the audience will probably have to get used to it....The course, with numbers of hurdles, relieved here and there by "water jumps" and stone "walls" seemed fraught with dangers and of course added to the excitement.

Winner of the Grand National, *The Spirit of the Times*, 22 May 1886.

FROM "COL. CLARK AS A STARTER," *THE COURIER-JOURNAL*, 27 MAY 1882

The great cry and hue among a chronic set of kickers over the alleged bad starts of Col. Clark during the recent meeting has recoiled. Aside from a few unfortunate send-aways, there was no foundation for the severe criticisms; and, in justice to Col. Clark and the club he so ably represents, the Courier-Journal volunteers the following interviews with the leading turfmen who patronize the Louisville Jockey Club, and who are interested:...

Maj. B. G. Thomas was satisfied with Col. Clark, and would rather have him start his horses than any man he knew of. "Young man, you can't find any one who'll send them away head and head, and Col. Clark will act as fairly as any one. No professional starters for me, if you please."

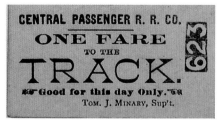

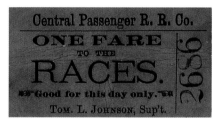

FROM "THE JOCKEY CLUB MEETING," *THE COURIER-JOURNAL*,
10 SEPTEMBER 1882

Strange to say the Second-street car line has rather helped the general look of the grounds by the fills made for their tracks, which are separated from the main grounds by a light picket fence, rendering the distance from the cars only about 100 feet from the grand stand, a convenience which must be seen and used to be thoroughly appreciated. The Fourth street and the Second-street lines have begun to wage war, and the rate on Tuesday will open at five cents each way, it is rumored.

FROM "THE LATE RACES," *LOUISVILLE COMMERCIAL*, 4 OCTOBER 1882

It has in certain circles passed into a current saying that races are demoralizing, and amongst the very sedate and somewhat straight-laced classes the idea of a race track is simply a focus around which gamblers, drunkards and thieves congregate. Now we have had here in Louisville ten days of this amusement, and it is doubtful whether in all the time and amongst the vast numbers in attendance there has been a single individual on the grounds grossly intoxicated. The absence of profanity was also a very striking feature.

FROM "AT THE TRACK," *THE COURIER-JOURNAL*, 15 MAY 1883

The general appearance of the entire grounds is much added to by the style of picket fencing being put up all around the grounds. The fence is white, with blue posts, and is very attractive. The grand stand has been improved by the continuance of the awning entirely around the south end, over the pooling shed; the ladies' end of the grand stand is being provided with handsome leather cushions. The pooling-shed has been

Left: Mule car going out Fourth Street, *ca.* 1875.

FROM *THE COURIER-JOURNAL*, 20 MAY 1882

Col. Clark's turnouts are becoming immense, and the crowd has now learned to watch for its appearance. That of yesterday quite took the cake from any of his previous efforts and caught the eye of the throng. A galaxy of beautiful ladies in rich costumes, piled on top of a tally-ho coach, like watermelons in a country wagon, is calculated to take the eye of anything. There were three of these in yesterday's turnout, each with a gracious distribution of feminine loveliness, and all came in behind fours (prancing steeds) and whirled around from the first quarter to the stand in a style that was electrical, judging from the way they were received by the crowd.[56]

lengthened sixty feet, and is now over two hundred feet long by seventy-five wide, and is the longest on any race track. North of the club room, Col. Clark is going to have erected a Turkish cafe about sixty by seventy feet, with a bay window opening out on the course, giving the occupants a chance to see the interior course. Numerous large improvements are in contemplation, and will be made right away. Col. Clark's plan is to buy west of the grounds some seventy acres, thus adding to the grounds a neat strip of woods and several open fields. This will be converted into a driving park. A lake will be constructed along a low, marshy portion of this land, and eyelets will be made at proper intervals in the forest strip. Thus, by adding a little on to nature, he will be able to make a most beautiful driving park.[57]...Numerous other improvements, such as ticket-offices, music stands, flower-beds etc., are being made, but the place must be seen to be appreciated.

FROM "AT THE TRACK," *THE COURIER-JOURNAL*, 1 MAY 1883

An additional force of men were put to work on the chute, and all of it is now completed save a little grading at the far end, which will require another day.

FROM "LEONATUS, NOBLE ROMAN," *LOUISVILLE COMMERCIAL*, 24 MAY 1883

The crowd in the grand stand sent out a volume of voice, and the crowd in the field took it up and carried it from boundary to boundary of Churchill Downs.

This may be the first published reference to the Louisville Jockey Club's grounds being termed Churchill Downs. Long-time racing secretary Charles F. Price credited Benjamin H. Ridgely (1859-1908) with the term, and in 1883, Ridgely was *The Commercial*'s city editor. He was a life-long friend of M. Lewis Clark, and became consul general to Mexico. Whether Ridgely was aware of the import his designation would have is not known. It may not have been picked up immediately. Matt J. Winn stated many years later that it was not until 1886 that a writer for *The Spirit of the Times* coined the term Churchill Downs and "the name caught public fancy."[58]

FROM "SPORTS OF THE SEASON," *LOUISVILLE COMMERCIAL*, 5 MAY 1883

The chute. It is completed and Col. Clark, President of the Jockey Club, is happy. So happy in fact that he pulled up pegs yesterday, drew a long breath and left on the midnight train for Nashville, where he will attend the races today. The chute is the new straight track at the Jockey Club grounds. Literally it is an extension of the home-stretch two furlongs west from the three-quarter pole, thus presenting an unbroken stretch of six furlongs, or three-quarters of a mile directly west from the grand stand. The work of building this new course has been in progress since the middle of last week, and the finishing touches were added yesterday. Nothing now is left to be done save to build a fence on either side of the chute, which is but the work of two days. Today the Jockey Club course is ahead of all race-tracks in America in safety for horses. Every race over it will be started on a straight track, thus avoiding the danger of a start on a turn. All three-quarter mile races will be started at the head of the chute and then end at the grand stand. In fact, all races, except at distances of a mile, a mile and a quarter, a mile and a sixteenth, two miles, two miles and a quarter, and three and four miles, will be started on the chute.

Until 1896, the Kentucky Derby was a race of a mile and a half; therefore, the start was begun at the half-mile pole until the straight chute was instituted. The 1883 Kentucky Derby (opening day) was postponed one day because of a wet track. The straight course, or chute, laid out for a three-quarter-mile dash, was reportedly the first six-furlong straight-away course in the country, but because spectators were disadvantaged by the viewing perspective, the dash concept was abandoned.[59] The present mile chute was built in the same location in the spring of 1920.

FROM "READY FOR THE DRUM," *LOUISVILLE COMMERCIAL*,
24 SEPTEMBER 1883

The management of the Louisville Jockey Club will have a grave and growing evil to contend with during the race meeting at Churchill Downs which is to be inaugurated today. The time has gone when it can be said that running races in Kentucky are not hedged about with fraud. It used [not] to be so, but within the past two years there has been a most disgraceful change. The world is full of rascals, and far too many of them are professional turfmen. Up to three or four years ago villainy on the turf was confined almost exclusively to the ranks of those sharkish and unscrupulous persons who travel the trotting circuits with a stable full of circus horses skillfully taught to trot or skip, to lose or win, as the betting may demand. Recently, however, this trotting horse rascality has become a belonging of the older, more exciting and far more respectable sport of the running course.... Last fall and last spring several races at Louisville were evidently the most brazen of "jobs," and from the best authority we have it that the recent meeting at Covington fairly bristled with outrages, such as pulling, and stuffing and "cutting down." Of course the same set of scamps will be here, and President Clark should be on the look out for

FROM "THE DERBY," THE COURIER-JOURNAL, 24 MAY 1883

Finally they all assembled at the half-mile on the regular track, the chute being too soft to use, and everybody waited in breathless silence the falling of the flag.

Left: "Three Quarters Shoot [Chute] and Lower Turn," *Louisville Illustrated* (1889), part 5. Below: Same view as inset, *The Graphic News* (New York), 15 May 1886.

FROM "THE CHUTE, AN UNPOPULAR IMPROVEMENT," *THE COURIER-JOURNAL*, 26 MAY 1883

"The only three-quarter straight course in this country" was undoubtedly intended to be a grand success — a startling innovation that would be....instantly adopted by every other racing association in the United States, but if the voice of the people counts anything, the managers of the Jockey Club were "off their base" in this particular, for nothing....was ever before more unceremoniously and unanimously condemned than the "chute."...On the straight course no one can tell whether his horse is first or sixteenth until they reach the distance stand, and then....the race is over.

them. The judges' stand should be filled at this meeting with observant and well informed turfmen, rather than with statesmen and other distinguished persons, who don't know the difference between a race horse and a Shetland pony.

Col. Clark's convention of the jockey clubs and leading breeders of America assembles at the office of the Jockey Club in the Courier-Journal building at 12 o'clock to-day. The Louisville, Lexington, Latonia, St. Louis, Washington and Driving Park, Chicago, Memphis, Nashville, New Orleans, Brighton Beach and Maryland clubs will be represented, and the organizer of the call has every reason to be proud of the hearty response which has been accorded his invitation.[60] The rumor is that a great blow will be struck at one of the greatest evils of the present day. If the clubs adopt a uniform scale of weights and rules a great work will have been accomplished.

The Louisville Jockey Club yesterday assumed charge of the pooling privileges at the track, and appointed as their agent Mr. Fred Bishop, who will conduct the pooling with the old employes who have become known to the habitues of the course. This change is due to the failure of the firm of Hughes & Cathcart, successors to J. R. Watts & Co., to comply with the terms of their contract for the pooling privilege. It is understood that on account of an alleged dissatisfaction with the programme, Maj. Hughes, a member of the firm, insisted on abrogating the contract. It is said that the other members of the firm were desirous of standing by it. The contract has still eight years to run.

Robert A. Johnson, 68, died in Knoxville on 15 March 1886. He was a vice president of the Louisville Jockey Club and he raced horses in partnership with John Churchill. In 1884, two of his horses, Loftin and Powhatan III, ran in the Kentucky Derby. Educated in Greek and Latin as well as law at the University of Virginia, he moved to Louisville and made a fortune as a commission merchant supplying cotton planters before participating in the Civil War. After the war, he retired to become a turfman.

The nephew of Richard Mentor Johnson, vice president of the United States, was married first to Cornelia Ruffin, and then as a widower, to Lucy Jacob Johnson, widow of his cousin, Darwin Ward Johnson. She was the sister of Louisville mayor Charles D. Jacob and mother of Darwin Ward Johnson, Jr., secretary of the Louisville Jockey Club.[61]

The track and grounds are simply perfect. Wm. Easton of the Horse Exchange was here last week, and from the club-house veranda, as he gazed upon the beautiful green sward and landscape, the reflection of the

From *Bird's-Eye View of Louisville...,*1883.

A remarkably well-informed firm of book-makers was observed to be making all the bets they could get on Freenight to beat Porter Ashe....The public has grown suspicious of most turfmen, however, and are tired of the in-and-out winning of their horses. It is time that bookmakers should be denied the privilege of running race horses, as this would take a great temptation out of the way.

green grass, hedges, and flowers, against whitewashed fences and the range of hills far in the distance, he said that he had "seen nothing to compare with the Louisville Jockey Club course in all America; that it looked like a race-course, delighting the eye and satisfying the taste at the same time." Then, to sit upon the porch, with a mint julep on the table beside you, and a score of the finest horses in the world doing their morning gallops, as if for your especial delectation, is calculated to make one appreciate what the Kentuckian loves so well. The inner field, so quiet and beautiful, too, now, with its emerald carpet, will soon be pressed by the feet of some thirty to forty thousand people on this, the people's day in Kentucky. What a study it is to the stranger! What good order and fellowship in the vast throng! Well do they appreciate the integrity and enterprise that has given them this source of pride and revenue to both the city and the State…The club has done away with steeplechases and hurdle races, the past in this country having fully demonstrated the almost impossibility of having these races run fairly. This interest should be centered in the steeplechase associations.

FROM "THE KENTUCKY DERBY," *THE SPIRIT OF THE TIMES*, 8 MAY 1886

In regard to the withholding of the entries to the stakes and purses by the Louisville Jockey Club, the gist of the matter is simply this: There is no desire to do other than simple justice. The parties owning the Turf Exchange broke their new contract with the Louisville Jockey Club, which gave the club $40,000 a year for the pooling privileges at the Spring and Fall Meetings, the payments being divided in equal parts, although the pooling in the spring is worth three times that in the fall. From 1877 to 1884 the Turf Exchange held, under an old verbal contract, for some $8,500 a year, and the last few years at $10,750 for six days in spring and six in fall. A vast amount of money was made during the lease, and the Jockey Club could have leased the privileges for many thousands per meeting more. Naturally the club declined to consider any proposition from the party breaking the contract; but, when a new firm was formed, received a bid of half the amount, which it declined, and awarded the pooling privileges for sixteen days, ten in the spring and six in the fall, to C. H. White, who also has the pooling at Lexington and Latonia. [Note: C. H. White & Co. had leased the Kentucky Association track in Lexington, retired its debt, and provided improvements including "a handsome new pooling shed." See *The Courier-Journal*, 19 November 1883.] Mr. White has requested the management to withhold the entries at night, unless the parties here will agree not to sell pools on them, and as the clubs derive their main revenue from him, it seems only right and just they should grant his request.

The Legislature of Kentucky passed a law prohibiting pool selling, except upon the race tracks and upon events and purses occurring there.[62] Such action will insure larger crowds and better betting at the courses, and as it applies to Kentucky, and [as] White has the pooling, it is about certain that the three clubs will act in concert. If men can bet over the coun-

FROM "RACING DAYS," *THE COURIER-JOURNAL*, 19 APRIL 1888

About twelve years ago the system of "Paris mutuals" got a foothold in this country, being introduced by a big pool concern in New York city. For a time it flourished, being a means by which the small bettor could invest. But it was generally mismanaged and the public was becoming extremely tired of such a form of investment when about 1880 the English system of book-making raised its head.

Its progress was slow for a time, as its manipulators made an "iron-clad" book and the people were loath to stand such a great percentage. But year by year, as competition forced a lengthening of the odds, book-making gained in popular favor, and it may be said that in no section where the system has ever taken root can it be supplanted by any other. Its advantages over auction pools are many.

With book-making one can back the favorite with a $5 note and know just what he stands to win, which is not the case with a mutual ticket; he can lay $5 or $500 without disclosing his identity, (impossible in the auction); he can get his money on more quickly and get the odds (impossible, as either the auction or mutual), and winning, cashes his ticket in one-quarter the time required by the other systems.

"Ben Ali" winner of Kentucky Derby.

try they do not care to see the track or races, and the pool rooms over the country only eat up in a very short time, if kept open during the season, all the money the bettors have to wager. The jockey clubs throughout the country will be quick to appreciate the increased attendance and enhanced value of the privileges when the profits are centered in one place, and that the source of the amusement and interest. The many inducements to fraud and rascality are materially lessened by this action, and the cause of grievance of so many people who have cause to remember the evils of an open pool room removed.

EDWARD CORRIGAN.

Top: Drawing by Henry Stull, *The Spirit of the Times,* 22 May 1886. Above: Edward Corrigan, *The Courier-Journal,* 13 May 1887. Opposite: Churchill Downs barn used by J.B. Haggin, *The Graphic News* (New York), 15 May 1886.

FROM "HAGGIN NOT SATISFIED," *THE COURIER-JOURNAL,* 15 MAY 1886

Mr. J. B. Haggin, the well-known California turfman who carried away the Derby Stake yesterday, was met in the lobby of the Galt House last evening by a Courier-Journal reporter, and, in answer to a question, said: "Yes, I did say that if the bookmakers did not make some satisfactory arrangement and commence operations on the track I would take my stable away. I mean it, too. It is not because I care for the bookmakers or the man that has the privilege of the betting at the track, but for the reason that I desire to back my horses, and I can't do it unless there are bookmakers at the track. I have won the Derby, and will pack up and get out unless this matter is arranged to-morrow."

Mr. Haggin vainly endeavored yesterday to get money on Ben Ali. There was only one place to bet, and that was in the auction betting. The French pools were in operation, but it was impossible to get near them to place money. The moment Mr. Haggin made his appearance and began backing his horse, Ben Ali at once became a great favorite, and the odds became too insignificant to engage him in further efforts to back the colt.

Mr. Ed. Corrigan, whose stable is always the center of interest, on account of his fine lot of flyers, also expressed his intention of leaving

FROM *THE COURIER-JOURNAL*, 26 SEPTEMBER 1886

The twentieth anniversary of the founding of the American Jockey Club, which has done much for the advancement of the best interests of the turf, was celebrated this evening [September 25th] by a dinner at Delmonico's, at which about one hundred racing men and others were present....August Belmont, President of the American Jockey Club, presided. On his right sat Col. M. Lewis Clark, President of the Louisville Jockey Club....

Mr. Belmont began the speaking, and was followed by Col. Clark, who spoke of the importance of establishing one set of racing rules and one scale of weights for all the great American Jockey Clubs.

FROM "DERBY DAY," *THE COURIER-JOURNAL*, 11 MAY 1887

The following straight tip comes from Washington: "A gang of counterfeiters loaded down with bogus silver dollars, half-dollars and quarters are following the races. Some of them have gone to Louisville."

unless matters were adjusted.[63]   All horse owners are in favor of book-makers being on the track, as there are few, if any, who do not back their starters.

James Ben Ali Haggin (1821-1914) was born in Harrodsburg. He went to California as a lawyer, and his acquisition of gold, silver, and copper mines made him rich. His horse, Ben Ali, had been bred by Daniel Swigert at Elmendorf, the third colt by Virgil to win the Kentucky Derby. In 1897, Haggin married Pearl Voorhies from Versailles and bought Elmendorf from the bookmaker, Cornelius J. Enright, who had purchased it from Swigert in 1891.[64] Enright and W. E. Applegate, a large stockholder in Churchill Downs, had become proprietors of the Suburban Pool Room with "orders solicited by telegraph," sometime in 1889. Haggin built a huge classical revival mansion at Elmendorf which he called Green Hills. It was acquired in 1923 by Joseph E. and George D. Widener of Philadelphia, and all but the four Corinthian columns of the front portico was razed.

Although it has been said Haggin pulled his stable out of Churchill Downs in protest and led a boycott of the track by eastern owners that lasted for two more decades, his absence from the track was more likely due to the fact that his breeding operation, although the largest in the world, began to "concentrate on breeding for the market," according to William H. P. Robertson.[65]

FROM *THE COURIER-JOURNAL*, 15 MAY 1886

The book-makers and Mr. C. H. White are still at variance, but there is a prospect of a reconciliation and a possibility that the book-makers will go on the track today. Mr. White has reduced his charge for the booking privilege to $2,300 per day, but the book-makers still refuse to pay over what they offered at the start.

Last night an offer of $18,000 for the privilege for the remainder of the Louisville meeting was made by several representative book-makers to Mr. White. They argue that his charges are extraordinary and entirely out of proportion to the profits arising from the privilege.

Mr. White paid $30,600 for the entire pooling privilege of the spring and fall meeting. His charge to the book-makers was $100 per day for each of them, and as thirty expected to go on in the ten days of the spring meeting he would have received $30,000 or only $600 less than he himself paid for the privilege for the year. This would have left him with only $600 to make up at this meeting, and all the fall meeting would have been clear profit.

The book-makers emphatically declare that they will leave Louisville for good before they will submit to such extortion.

FROM "FIGHTING THE BOOKIES," *THE COURIER-JOURNAL*, 24 APRIL 1888

The difference existing between the Louisville Jockey Club and the Western Book-makers' Association has attracted a great deal of attention in the South and West, and the other racing Associations are watching for the result with great interest. Few of the jockey clubs have dared to stand against the bookmakers' combination, as the sale of the pooling privileges is one of the largest items in their receipts, and the pencilers have on that account gained an ascendancy which has alarmed even the most liberal of the clubs. A great deal, therefore, depends on the issue of the fight the Louisville club proposes to make. Yesterday, when asked about his plan, Col. Clark said:

My terms were $34,000 and the auction pools. The bookmakers offered $26,000 and the auction pools. Last year the bookmakers gave $30,000.[66] This year the club gives $4,000 more money in stakes than ever before, and if we accepted the bookmakers' terms it would thus make a difference to us of $8,000. It has been reported that last year Waddell & Co. lost $6,000 on the privilege, but the books alone took in $27,800, which left a deficit of only $2,200, which was very much more than covered by their pooling in town. If they had not had the privilege, of course, the club could have withheld the entries.

We have secured ten French pool boxes and will sell $2, $5 and $25 French pool tickets. We will also have auction pools. I believe we can make more money this way than we could by selling the privilege. If the book-makers could dictate to us and compel us to take $26,000, they could force us to take $260.

Apparently the associations are going to make a square stand against the book-makers. It has been announced from New York that Jerome Park and Coney Island will take exactly the same position assumed by the Louisville Jockey Club and will sell only French and auction pools, and it is said that Lexington will do the same thing.

FROM AN UNIDENTIFIED STOCKHOLDER IN "A NEW RACE COURSE,"
THE CRITIC, 9 FEBRUARY 1890

I have no feeling against Col. M. Lewis Clark. The Jockey Club is a closed corporation and he runs it to suit himself. He may be satisfied, no doubt he is entirely pleased, with his method of conducting the club, but I am free to say that I don't think the public is at all satisfied. Any ordinary observer can see that racing at the Jockey Club course has been deteriorating year by year, until there is nothing left but the Derby to attract people. The fall meeting is getting worse every year, until it would be a favor to horsemen and the public to shut up shop altogether during that season. Louisville is the metropolis of the greatest stock-raising State in the Union. It ought to have a broad-gauge Jockey Club run on business principles, with liberal purses that will make this city a Mecca twice a year for the thousands of people who love good racing and are willing to pay for it.

I understand a movement is now on foot to start such a race course, not to compete with the Jockey Club, but to give Louisville a first-class institution, that will properly represent the great thoroughbred interest of the State. [67]

Ban Box, *The Graphic News* (New York), 15 May 1886.

FROM *THE COURIER-JOURNAL*, 4 JULY 1887

Lexington, July 3. — Mr. Gus Strauss, of this city, has received a letter from Mr. Frank B. Harper, the owner of the famous Ten Broeck, who died the other day. In it he gives an account of the funeral of this celebrated horse and tells how he was buried and where. He says: "All are sad over the death of Ten Broeck.... We laid him to rest in a nice coffin and buried him in front of his stable door. His grave is still decorated with flowers. We are going to erect a nice monument over his last resting place, and enclose it with a fence. The stables are all draped in mourning as is also the front gate."

Thus is one of the greatest race-horses the world ever produced, put away after his races are all run, and for him the bell has tapped for the last time. This short letter of Mr. Harper shows how much the true Kentuckian thinks of that noble and faithful animal—the horse. [68]

FROM "RACING DAYS," *THE COURIER-JOURNAL,* 19 APRIL 1888

Silver-tongued Bob [Cathcart], as he was called, was a man of striking presence. Not above the medium height, his well-knit figure gave expression to a most singular grace of manner. His rich baritone voice, resonant and clear, pleased all within its range....The night before the Kentucky Derby he would stroll leisurely into the basement of the Galt House, Louisville, and between the puffs of his cigar say "How d'ye" to almost every man of the large assemblage, which was composed mainly of the prominent breeders, owners and turf notables. Then vaulting lightly over the rail of the pool stand Bob would take up a piece of chalk and proceed to mark upon the blackboard the names and weights of the racers of the following day.

Before taking a bid for first choice Cathcart would give an elaborate description — pedigree, performance, etc.—of each horse entered in the race. "Silver-tongued Bob" passed away two years ago, and his place is yet unfilled. With him seemed to wane the day of the auction pool as an adjunct of racing. True, on each of the tracks to-day there is an effort made to perpetuate the system, but the financial transactions are very small compared to the business done by the book-makers.[69]

FROM "TOPICS OF THE TURF," *THE COURIER-JOURNAL,* 10 FEBRUARY 1890

Col. M. Lewis Clark was asked by a Courier-Journal reporter if he had seen an article in one of the Sunday papers criticizing the management of the Louisville Jockey Club, and what he had to say about it. He said:

The animus of the attack is very plain. The Widner [Wilder] park track has been recently leased by parties, who desire to try the experiment of a rival race-course, and, of course, the destruction of the Louisville Jockey Club would facilitate that desire. To keep up a jockey club in Louisville, with its population, small as compared to Chicago, St. Louis and Cincinnati, giving as liberal stakes, etc., as those cities do, and with the receipts from attendance and privileges so much below those of the cities above named, has been and will continue to be a very difficult problem, and that this has been accomplished for sixteen years speaks for itself as to the judicious management of our club.

As to the criticism that there has been no shareholders' meeting for some years, the affairs of the club are managed by an Executive Committee, and this committee has met whenever they thought occasion required. That the stockholders' annual meeting have not been recently held is simply owing to the fact that the stockholders did not attend; as the stock is scattered mostly in single shares, with the exception of some five or six owners, and the holders of a single share of $100 each did not attach sufficient interest to attend the meetings, unless there was something of unusual interest....

As to the criticism upon my salary as President, I gave my services to the club for nothing from its beginning in 1874, until 1884, and in 1884, at a stockholders' meeting, at which I believe nearly all of the stock of the club was represented, a full and detailed statement was made, and the stockholders, in recognition of the value they fixed upon my services voted a salary of $5,000 per year for the future. That the club has not been carried on with a view to my salary is shown from the fact that its income has been applied to its outside debts, and that my salary, although an operative expense, that should ordinarily be first paid has not been paid at all, the club owing me salary for about two years.

FROM "LIVELY AT THE DOWNS," *LOUISVILLE COMMERCIAL,* 17 FEBRUARY 1890

Col. Clark has come to the conclusion that the chute is a failure. The public does not like it. It is contrary to the principles that made a circular track. The people want to see a race from start to finish.

FROM "A MEASLY $100,000," *THE CRITIC,* 23 MARCH 1890

When Col. M. Lewis Clark was appointed "Park Commissioner"—a position, by the way, which an investigating committee of the Council has decided that the Mayor had no right to create—it was a matter of surprise that he should volunteer to do the arduous work required of him for nothing.[70] To go back to the purchase of "Burnt Knob," it will be remembered that the suggestion of this land [now Iroquois Park] for park purposes was made by Col. Clark to the Mayor. Mr. Jacob, with customary gullibility, swallowed bait, hook, line and all. He bought the land without consulting the Council, and then posed as the very personification of the modern spirit of progress.

Col. M. Lewis Clark was delighted. His uncles, the Messrs. Churchill, own the Jockey Club grounds and a large body of land adjoining, and the purchase of "Burnt Knob" and the certainty that a costly boulevard would pass within a stone's throw of their property, meant an increase of thousands of dollars in values to them. The Critic is informed that the present plan is to divert the Third-street boulevard, so that it will pass right in front of the Jockey Club grounds.

But the bulk of Colonel John Churchill's property lies west of the Third-street boulevard. Something must be done to improve that. Colonel M. Lewis Clark, Colonel Churchill's enterprising nephew, as Park Commissioner, comes to the rescue. He gets the Mayor's consent to extend a branch road known as "Taylor's Boulevard," across from Third street just north of the Jockey Club grounds over to the Seventh-street road and out that road to the park.[71]

Manlius Taylor, superintendent of Churchill Downs, *The Graphic News* (New York), 15 May 1886.

FROM "COLONEL CLARK'S EAGLE EYE," *LOUISVILLE COMMERCIAL*,
15 APRIL 1890

M. Lewis Clark went to Frankfort to read the proposed charter of the Falls City Running and the Trotting Association being incorporated by the Legislature. It gave the company the privilege of opening an office in Louisville like Latonia Club's charter which Clark believed was "a franchise to open a pool-room in the city." In 1883-84 the Louisville Jockey Club had tried to get a new charter passed with the same provision, and it was denied. Clark visited the governor and was assured the charter would be amended.[72]

FROM "THE DERBY TO BE DOUBLED," *LOUISVILLE COMMERCIAL*, 26 MAY 1890
With all these natural advantages there is only one thing needed to place Churchill Downs at once in its old position as the greatest race course west of the Alleghenies....Make the Kentucky Derby worth $10,000 to the winner....

FROM "FIGHTING THE POOL-ROOMS," *THE COURIER-JOURNAL*,
4 SEPTEMBER 1890

The owners of five different pool-rooms in the city will be summoned by City Court....It is claimed by those making the fight that the selling of pools upon horse racing is as much a species of gambling as oontz or poker playing....They were issued as follows: Bourlier & Co., Turf Exchange; Waddell & Burt, The Newmarket; Payne & Co., The Climax; Enright & Co., The Suburban; and Bollinger & Wehmhoff, the Ascot.[73]

FROM "HOW THE WINNERS WON,"
LOUISVILLE COMMERCIAL, 16 MAY 1888
The sport was marred, however, in a great measure by Col. Clark's persistent disregard of the wishes of a great majority of his patrons in starting most of the races from the chute....If the track is to be given over entirely to the betting contingent let the chute stand, but if the voice of the lovers of true sport may be heard, Col. Clark will sow his chute in potatoes and run the races at Churchill Downs as in the good old times of yore.

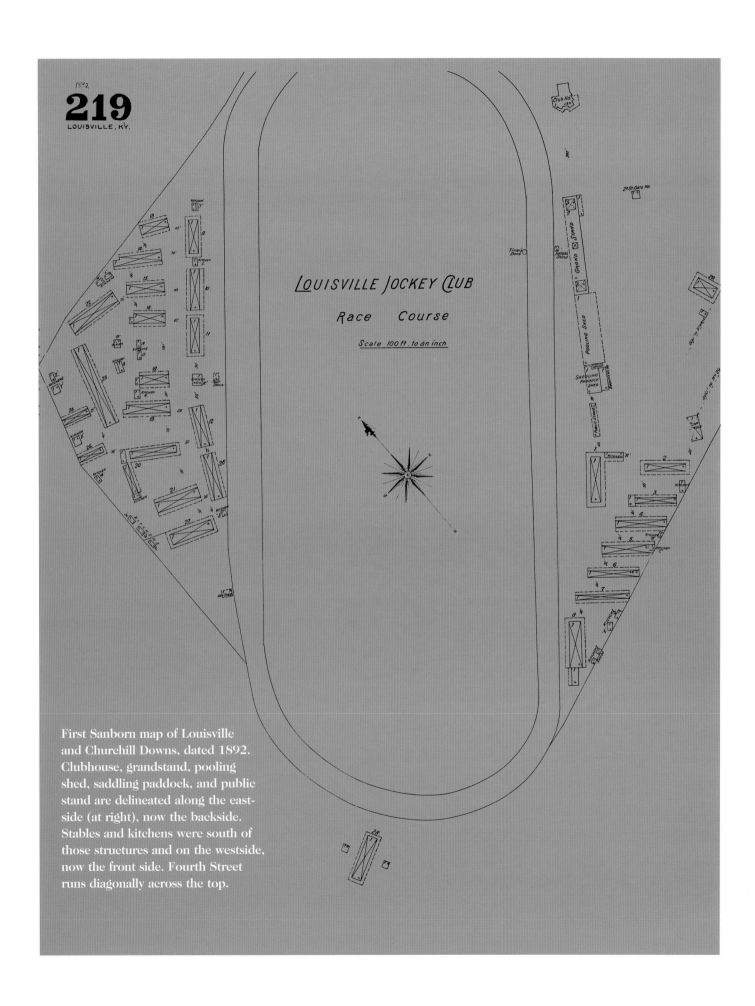

219
LOUISVILLE, KY.

LOUISVILLE JOCKEY CLUB

Race Course

Scale 100 ft. to an inch

First Sanborn map of Louisville and Churchill Downs, dated 1892. Clubhouse, grandstand, pooling shed, saddling paddock, and public stand are delineated along the east-side (at right), now the backside. Stables and kitchens were south of those structures and on the westside, now the front side. Fourth Street runs diagonally across the top.

There are touts and touts, and they range from the commonest sort to the ones who wear $200-split-second watches and hide behind fences to watch fast trials and afterward carry the information to their employers, the bookmakers. All are nuisances on the race track alike. Owners hate them, trainers abhor them, the public is worried by them, and for years the officials have been puzzling their brains to find a way to bar them out.

Col. Clark thinks he has found this way, and will put an original idea into effect next week. When the meeting opens three roomy stands will be placed on the lawn beyond the new betting shed. Into these stands every tout must go, willy-nilly, if he expects to remain on the grounds. A regularly drawn-up license to tout will be issued to them, and any one found pursuing the honorable vocation without his license or outside the three stands will be promptly ejected from the grounds. The touting privilege has been fixed at $5 a day. This will entitle them to seats in the tout boxes and the freedom of the inclosure, provided no unfair advantage is taken of competitors by work outside of the stands....

Another reformation will be directed against the jockeys' valets.[74] "If a boy cannot carry his own saddle, he can ride at some other track," says Colonel Clark. This season the riders will weigh in at the new saddling paddock and weigh out in the old place, under the judges' stand. From there a path inclosed by neat iron fences leads to the jockeys' room under the grand stand, and up this walk they will have to saunter alone, without the support of the burly black touts who call themselves valets. These fellows are not wanted here, and if they desire to see the races it will have to be from the whitewashed stand at the lower end of the grounds.

Colonel William Henry Churchill, brother of John Churchill, died on 27 December 1891 at the family residence, 633 Sixth street. He was 77 years old. According to his obituary:

> In 1840 they formed a partnership for the purpose of farming, and through fifty-one years carried on their business together without a disagreement....Colonel John Churchill....remained his partner, companion and friend to the last. Together they farmed what is known as Churchill Downs, where the Louisville Jockey Club stands. Until 1863 the Downs were farmed. In that year Colonel Churchill moved into the city and into the house, 633 Sixth Street, where he died....His familiar figure was always seen at the fall and spring meetings of the Jockey Club. Few men took greater interest in thoroughbred stock and enjoyed racing more. To him and his brother much of the success of the track is due.[75]

Richard "Dick" Ten Broeck, about 83, died on 1 August 1892 at his ranch in Menlo Park, California. His exploits as a turfman were well known and his reminiscences had appeared in the 27 December 1890 issue of *The Spirit of the Times*. He had been the first American owner-trainer to race American-bred horses in England, and in 1868 he returned to the United

THE GAUDY BOOKMAKER.

From *The Courier-Journal*, 10 May 1889.

As long as Colonel Clark is in authority at Churchill Downs there will be no steeplechases. According to Clark, "it's hard enough to prevent crookedness on the flat; it can't be done when the rider can safely roll off and thereby lose!" Cannot something be done to revive the sport without bringing to life the former attendant evil? It is true now that comparatively few attend races as mere spectators, but if the races could be made more exciting, the good people would once again "go to the races" in numbers as great as of old.

States and established his stable at Hurstbourne on the Shelbyville Road east of Louisville. There he brought Phaeton, the sire of Ten Broeck, from Europe. After his first wife, Pattie Anderson Ten Broeck, the aunt of Mrs. M. Lewis Clark, died, Richard Ten Broeck married Mary Cornelia Newcomb, the widow of Horatio Dalton Newcomb, once the president of the L & N Railroad. They moved to England but returned about 1887 when Ten Broeck retired and began to show signs of mental instability.[76]

Dr. Benjamin Gratz Bruce, 63, secretary of the Louisville Jockey Club, died at his home in Lexington on 23 September 1892. After graduating from medical school at Transylvania University, he went into the wholesale grocery business and then moved to New York where he and his brother, Sanders Dewees Bruce, started the journal, *The Turf, Field and Farm*, in 1865. Dr. Bruce later returned to Lexington to start up the *Kentucky Live Stock Record*, which became *The Thoroughbred Record*. He assisted his brother with the first two volumes of the American Stud Book. The rights to the set of six volumes of pedigrees were purchased by the American Jockey Club and became the basis of its registry. His library was perhaps the best in the country on turf subjects. He had served at various times as president, vice-president, and secretary of the Kentucky Association, and was also secretary of the American Turf Congress. Dr. Bruce had advised R. A. Alexander to purchase Lexington and not to import a stallion. However, he twice went to England to select horses to import for others. His sister was married to John Hunt Morgan.

The interim secretary, Joseph Swigert, was replaced by Charles F. Price, who had been touted by Daniel E. O'Sullivan.[77]

Benjamin Gratz Bruce, *The Graphic News* (New York), 15 May 1886.

FROM *THE COURIER-JOURNAL*, 1 SEPTEMBER 1890

New roofs have been put upon some of the stables and all of them have been newly painted and white-washed. The chute has been closed up and the grass in it testifies that it has seen its last days.

FROM "RIOT AT GARFIELD," *THE COURIER-JOURNAL*, 6 SEPTEMBER 1892

Chicago, Sept. 5 — Two hundred officers, commanded by Inspector Lewis, Captains Manney and Bletner, raided Garfield Park track this afternoon and arrested 160 people. The police in fourteen patrol wagons made their appearance at the gates during the progress of the third race. They were denied admittance, the gates shut in their faces and messengers were sent scudding to warn the judges and bookmakers that the police were coming. The officers lost no time in smashing in the gates, and before many of the bookmakers could pack up their money and get away the heavily loaded patrol wagons came down the homestretch and a ring of officers was around the betting ring. Twenty-five bookmakers and nearly as many jockeys were taken into custody.

Col. Clark, presiding judge; George V. Hankins, president of the track, and Harry Varnell, one of the stockholders, were also arrested. Col. Clark, who weighs [well] over 200 pounds, declined to get into the patrol wagon, and asked for a carriage in which to ride to the police station. Several officers seized him in front, more "boosted" from behind, and the portly Kentuckian was tossed into the wagon before he could draw a long breath. The crowd in the grand stand hooted and jeered the police, but no attention was paid to it, until a chair was hurled at one of the officers.

A part owner of Garfield Park, Chicago turfman B. J. Johnson took particular delight with Churchill Downs where he kept some of his stable. M. Lewis Clark was well compensated for his role as presiding judge at Garfield Park, and as such for putting on fair racing. However because of his prominence he was being bombarded by the "silk stockings" at Washington Park who were being supported by Chicago Mayor Washbourne. Fanning the fire was Ed Corrigan, who had run Garfield Park previously for several years, and who had built and opened nearby Hawthorne in 1891. The confrontations between police and patrons of Garfield Park escalated, resulting in several deaths by gunfire, including prominent horse owner J. M. Brown. As a result, Garfield Park shut down for good, and its ownership moved across the state line to nearby Roby, Indiana, where a new track was proposed "on the plan of Washington Park." The grandstand was to be enclosed by glass and heated by steam for winter racing.[78]

FROM "LOOKOUT," *LOUISVILLE COMMERCIAL*, 11 MAY 1893

The "books," however, were not in for any big business. It is a matter of record that it was the lightest betting Derby ever run....That 20,000 people formed the crowd is putting it low. They had come in all sorts of conveyances, were of all colors and nationalities.

FROM "ARISTIDES DEAD," *THE COURIER-JOURNAL*, 22 JUNE 1893

St. Louis, Mo., June 21, — (Special.) — The noted race horse and stallion, Aristides, by imported Leamington, dam Sarony [Sarong], by Lexington, the property of J. J. Tompkins, of Chicago, died here to-day. He was twenty-one years old and greatly noted as a race horse, being the

FROM *THE CRITIC*, 25 DECEMBER 1892

Colonel M. Lewis Clark will preside at the Pendennis Club for the balance of the winter. He refused to have his salary, as Judge at Roby [Indiana] race track, near Chicago, cut from $125 to $90 a day. The whole Kentucky contingent was frozen out by the gamblers who are running that track solely for profit. Colonel Clark is one of the greatest judges in America, and he is a terror to dishonest jockeys and rascally owners. While it paid the Colonel very handsomely to sit up in his glass cage and watch the skates go round at both Garfield and Roby Park, it did not help his reputation any. The people who control racing in Chicago are such tough characters that no man who has a care for his good name ought to associate with them.[79]

winner of the first Kentucky Derby. Later his defeat of the record-breaking Ten Broeck gave him national fame. As a sire he was not a great success, and like many of his predecessors, his closing days thus ended under a cloud.

Opposite: Statue of Aristides in the grandstand garden by Carl William Regutti, dedicated in 1987.

FROM "A CAKE WALK," *LOUISVILLE COMMERCIAL*, 16 MAY 1894

There have been worse races than the twentieth Kentucky Derby—there are always others—but luckily for the turf, contests of less interest have been few in number. A fair horse, fit to run in stakes where the company is not of aristocratic caste, finished first. This was Chant. Between him and the point where Tom Elmore lingered, on the dim horizon, were selling platers, three in number, toiling home at intervals of an eighth of a mile. When Chant won there was a cheer. There is always greeting for the horse that takes a place in the glorious line that Aristides heads. But in the cheer of yesterday there was much of derision. The memory of the public is not long, and there is little reverence for greatness in decay.

Still there were many among the 15,000 perspiring people in the field and grand stand whose mind pictures were vivid in color, and they looked back to other days. They saw Lord Murphy falling to his knees, then staggering back to his stride to catch and beat his rivals; they saw Hindoo, the peerless, romp in with the blue ribbon; Apollo, the despised outsider, they saw too, saving the bookmakers a fortune by his half length victory over the talent's idol, Runnymede; they saw Buchanan prove that the rogue's badge he wore was not his by right; Ben Ali's battle with Blue Wing came into their view, as did the grand struggle of the two giant chestnuts on that May day in 1889 when Proctor Knott's colors were lowered by Spokane, the Montana champion; they looked back to the gloomy drizzle in which only three horses started, and to the subsequent duel of Azra and Huron, which transformed a chilled handful of people into a collection of howling maniacs.

TIME FOR A CHANGE....

When the Kentucky Derby degenerates into a bench-show—a contest of dogs—it is time to alter its conditions. Men no longer race for glory in this country. Owners will no longer enter good colts and trainers will not race them a mile and a half in early May for the money that the Louisville Jockey Club can afford to offer.

Reluctantly the warning is given that the cut in the Derby distance must be made to keep the contest above contempt. The old days of the Southern turf are ended and could a word come from the spirit lips of the gentlemen of Kentucky, Virginia, Tennessee, and the Carolinas, the men who raced for honor only and thereby laid the foundation in honesty for the American turf of today, that word would be an admonition to the man who is the present embodiment of their ideas—M. Lewis Clark—to conform to modern methods just so far as to be able to extend the influence of his heritage from them.

Racing is no longer a sport. It is a business. The Derby should be made a mile and a quarter.

New Louisville Jockey Club
(1894-1919)[1]

PRESIDENT
William F. Schulte (1894-1902);
Charles F. Grainger (1902-1919)

VICE PRESIDENT
Emile Bourlier; W. E. Applegate;
Matt J. Winn

TREASURER
Henry Wehmhoff; Charles F.
Bollinger; J. C. Boardman;
H. C. Applegate

DIRECTORS
H. C. Applegate, W. E. Applegate,
J. C. Boardman, Charles Bollinger,
Emile Bourlier, Harry M. Brennan,
Samuel S. Brown, Charles P.
Dehler, Walter E. Glover, Charles F.
Grainger, Saunders P. Jones,
W. G. Osborne, Charles F. Price,
J. B. Respess, W. F. Schulte, Louis
Seelbach, Andrew Vennie, Henry
Wehmhoff, Matt J. Winn

Louisville Racing Association
(A holding company controlling
Churchill Downs and Douglas
Park, 1907-1912)[2]

PRESIDENT
Charles F. Grainger

VICE PRESIDENT AND
GENERAL MANAGER
Matt J. Winn

SECRETARY
Hamilton C. Applegate

TREASURER
John Hachmeister

DIRECTORS
Hamilton C. Applegate, Louis A.
Cella, Charles F. Grainger, John
Hachmeister, Matt J. Winn

Churchill Downs just after
construction of clubhouse at left,
ca. 1903.

PART TWO

New Louisville Jockey Club

1894-1919

The fortieth race meeting under the auspices of the Louisville Jockey Club closed yesterday. Financially it was unfortunate and the club will figure from $3,000 to $5,000 on the distressing side of the ledger. Pelting rain and the cutting cold snap which developed Friday evening had much to do with the finances and the morning shower Derby Day materially curtailed the expected paid attendance. Yet the club charges its heaviest loss to the diminished number of bookmakers, the receipts from this source falling nearly $1,000 less a day than was anticipated.

Under present conditions a fall meeting is not looked for by the knowing ones, and the impression is growing that a spring meeting, if at all, will be consummated by some enterprising syndicate securing the privileges and assuming the risks.

The Louisville Evening Post thinks the prospects of a fall running meeting in the Falls City very good, and a spring meeting practically assured. Turfmen all over the country will join The Record in the hope that the Post's predictions will come true. That paper on 25 July 1894 says:...

Col. Clark came over from Chicago the first of the week, and since then several meetings have been held. The Evening Post's informant stated that the plan was to organize an entirely new company, which will be represented by several of the present stockholders and purchase Churchill Downs.

Whether the course will be used exclusively for runners, or whether it will be a combination for trotters, is not definitely known, although it was intimated by a gentleman in a position to know that an effort is being made in that direction. A number of lovers of trotters have been making an effort to establish a driving association here, and they may be asked to combine with the new club and hold trots annually.

Among those who are taking an active part in the re-organization of the club or the formation of a new one, as the case may be, are Emile Bourlier, W. E. Applegate and Billy Boardman.[3]

That the movement is on foot there is not the shadow of a doubt, although several of the leaders persist in disclaiming all knowledge of it. The report is that the old jockey club grounds will be abandoned. That there will be no fall meeting it has been announced officially, and it is understood Mr. Churchill, the owner, wishes to cut it up and sell it as town lots. He is not anxious to have racing continued there, and hence will offer no inducements in the way of terms to those desiring a re-organization of the old or the organization of a new club.

It is therefore probable that there will never be another meeting at Churchill Downs.

The plans of those behind the new organization is to purchase ground just back of the present Jockey Club grounds.[4] The work of regrading and improving this track for running races has been going on

From *The Courier-Journal*, 13 May 1897.

for some time, and plans are now being considered for the erection of a pretentious grand stand which will be erected very soon.

The only thing in doubt concerning this just now is the exact location of the stand, which has not been decided on. The erection of the grand stand will, it is said, be proceeded with at once, and Louisville may yet have a fall meeting under the auspices of the new club. If this is done the fixed events of the old club will probably be run off on the new track.

The men who are behind the scheme mean business and the probability that their scheme will be carried through is very strong.

The new track [on land owned by E.V. Thompson, Sr.] is easily accessible to the Iroquois car lines, and is but little farther from the city than the old track.

FROM "A NEW DEAL," *THE COURIER-JOURNAL*, 7 AUGUST 1894

Shortly before 5 o'clock yesterday afternoon Col. M. Lewis Clark and Mr. William G. Osborne appeared in County Clerk Webb's office and filed a deed of assignment of the Louisville Jockey Club. The deed converts to William G. Osborne all the rights, privileges and franchises that are transferable together with the lease of the grounds and improvements of the club, south of the city.[5]....

This assignment has been anticipated for some time, and a movement for the reorganization of the club was started some time ago. There is little doubt that a syndicate headed by Mr. Emile Bourlier and Mr. Edward Applegate will bid on the club improvements, privileges, etc., at a price that will suffice to pay all of the club indebtedness save Col. Clark's salary, which has been unpaid for more than two years and which he has voluntarily sacrificed. It is said that Mr. Henry Wehmhoff[6] and Mr. William Boardman will be in the syndicate...

"The action taken to-day," said Mr. Chas. F. Price, the Secretary of the Jockey Club, last night, "is more in the nature of a liquidation and reorganization than an assignment. The Jockey Club's liabilities are $21,331, but every creditor save one will be paid in full. The only sufferer will be Col. Clark. The club owes him over $11,000 in salary, besides $2,800 that came out of his pocket to cover the loss of the last fall meeting. He may get a part or all of his personal debt due him, but he will lose all of his salary for the past two years and more. This is purely a self-sacrifice on his part, and is done to protect the other or outside creditors of the Jockey Club. Under the bankruptcy law Col. Clark is entitled to as much consideration as any other creditor, but it has been his determination for years that when the Louisville Jockey Club passed out of existence it would owe no man a cent. Outside of Col. Clark's salary the club owes about $10,000. All of this will be paid out of the sum derived from a sale of improvements, the lease franchise and other assets of the club."

In reply to a question as to the direct cause of the bankrupted condition of the Jockey Club, Mr. Price said it was due to bad weather and lack of support on the part of the hotels, street railway and other business interests...They lose sight of the fact that the Louisville Jockey Club has done more not only to advertise the city, but to bring visitors who spend money here, than probably any other institution or enterprise in existence...

The Churchill Downs property has been held by the Jockey Club through a lease from Mr. John Churchill, who ranks second to Col. Clark as the largest holder of club stock. There are 198 stockholders, but Col. Clark and Mr. Churchill have what is equivalent to a controlling interest.

At the time this track was started, racing was at a low ebb in Kentucky and in the country. Yearlings that then sold for $200 now bring prices up in the thousands. Col. Clark brought about a meeting of race breeders and this Jockey Club was projected. Col. Clark at that time predicted that the winner of the Kentucky Derby would sell for more than the value of the farm where he was raised, and that the get of the Kentucky Derby winner would bring more than his dam and grand dam combined. This prediction proved true as to Hindoo and other noted winners.

M. Lewis Clark, president of the Louisville Jockey Club. From *The Courier-Journal*, 2 September 1894.

FROM "JOCKEY CLUB PLANS," *THE COURIER-JOURNAL*, 8 AUGUST 1894

Louisville will have a spring race meeting of not less than two weeks and it will be under the auspices of the New Louisville Jockey Club, with Messrs. Emile Bourlier, Edward Applegate, Henry Wehmhoff, J. C. Boardman and two or three others as the moving spirits.[7]

Mr. Bourlier yesterday closed with Mr. John Churchill a contract for leasing the Churchill Downs track for a period of fifteen years.[8] This leaves no doubt about the purchase of the track and privileges by the Bourlier and Applegate syndicate. Assignee W. G. Osborne will receive bids up to 10 o'clock on Saturday morning, and, of course, desires offers, but those well informed realize that the deal with Messrs. Bourlier and others has reached a point where outside interference seems to be improbable....

Mr. Bourlier says that they will spend from $20,000 to $30,000 in thoroughly fitting up the track and buildings for a spring meeting. The grand stand will be effectively renovated, but will not be rebuilt entirely in time for the first meeting under the new management. This will be done, however. One of the first arrangements will be for a long meeting. Nothing less than two weeks will be considered, and, no effort will be spared to make it a week longer. Race-horse owners have long had an objection to the short meeting, when they could pass through Louisville from the South with their stables to tracks having about thirty days of racing. With a long meeting here the best of horses from Little Rock, New Orleans and Nashville would stop over.

There will be an increase in the amount of purses sufficient to make this attractive to horse-owners. Another change will be in reducing the Derby route from a mile and a half to a mile and a quarter, which is now the Clark Stakes distance, and the cut in the Clark Stakes to a mile and one-eighth, or possibly a mile. The cut of the Derby route is a certainty. It has long been agitated. The argument of those who favored it has been

FROM "A NEW DEAL," *THE COURIER-JOURNAL*, 7 AUGUST 1894

"I could not go on longer shouldering the burden," said Col. Clark last night. "The stockholders and merchants would not support the enterprise and I have become discouraged and almost disgusted. My time is wanted elsewhere at bigger figures than I was supposed to receive here and the pay is certain. I can not afford to lose more than I have lost for the club. I could wish nothing worse for my worst enemy than that he should become my successor and contend with all that I have contended with. I may get back the $4,000 I borrowed for the club, but nothing more. I believe that the people of Louisville will realize, when too late, what they have lost by failing to assist the Jockey Club.

North elevation of proposed grandstand by architectural firm D. X.
Murphy & Bro., 1894. The betting
shed roof is outlined on the grandstand wall. The doorway led from
the shed into the restaurant and
bar area on the first floor of the
grandstand.

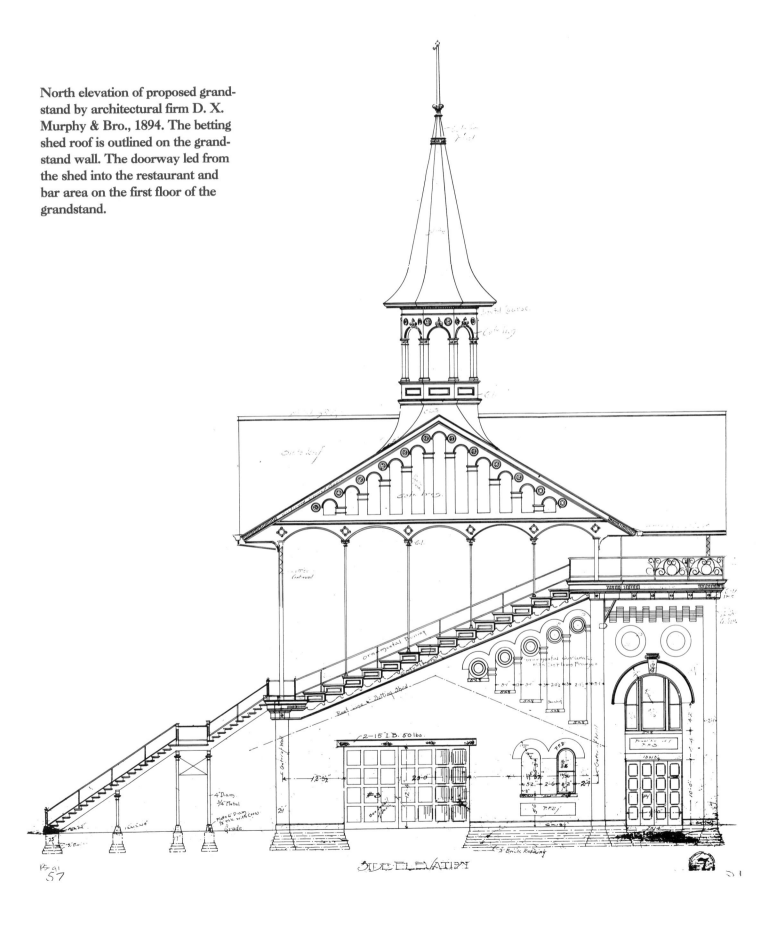

SIDE ELEVATION

that the Derby came too early in the spring to enable trainers to get three-year-olds up to a mile and a half bruising race. On the other hand, those who opposed a change said that the reduction of the distance meant a disgraceful falling back from the old turf standard when the stamina of horses was tested at longer distances, and in heat races at that.

FROM "JOCKEY CLUB ORGANIZED," *THE COURIER-JOURNAL*, 2 SEPTEMBER 1894

A meeting of the stockholders was held yesterday morning and the new Louisville Jockey Club was organized with the following officers: President, William F. Schulte; Vice President, Emile Bourlier; Presiding Judge, Col. M. Lewis Clark; Secretary, Charles F. Price; Treasurer, Henry Wehmhoff; Directors, W. E. Applegate, Henry Wehmhoff, Emile Bourlier, W. F. Schulte and W. G. Osborne.

A few years ago Mr. Schulte was a successful broker on Main street, and it was about five years ago that he took an active interest in racing....He has an interest in the Newmarket poolroom, and is qualified to judiciously consider the joint interests of horsemen and bookmakers.

Mr. Emile Bourlier is widely known as a city official, active politician and successful, progressive business man. He has become familiar with turf matters by a long connection with the Turf Exchange poolroom....

Treasurer Wehmhoff is one of the most progressive of those associated with the new club. He believes in spending money to make the track attractive, and will insist upon conducting the enterprise upon the strictest of business lines. Though still a young man, Mr. Wehmhoff is regarded as one of the coolest and most reliable of business men in figuring upon ventures that call for the risk or outlay of a large amount of money. He has a large interest in the Turf Exchange, and is said to be worth about $75,000, all of which he has made himself.

Mr. Applegate is one of the prominent breeders in Kentucky, and is favorably known in business circles, being of the firm of Applegate Bros., whisky dealers. Perhaps he is more widely known as a bookmaker.

Mr. Osborne, who was the assignee of the old club and materially aided the negotiations, is a Main-street broker. Like Mr. Price, he was formerly a newspaper man.

Work has already been commenced in improving stables and buildings at Churchill Downs. Some of the buildings will be torn down entirely and supplanted by new ones. The grand stand will be remodeled and a new one will be built next year, probably on the opposite side of the track so as to avoid the glare of an afternoon sun.

FROM "TROTTERS," *LOUISVILLE COMMERCIAL*, 20 OCTOBER 1894

All day yesterday Churchill Downs presented a scene of activity which the old course has not shown for several months. The old fixtures were being renovated and placed in readiness for the reception of the large crowds which will doubtless swarm the grounds during the first day's meeting next week.

Capt. John Welch, who has charge of the horses and grounds, was hard

William F. Schulte, president of the New Louisville Jockey Club. From *The Courier-Journal*, 2 September 1894.

FROM "JOCKEY CLUB PLANS," *THE COURIER-JOURNAL*, 8 AUGUST 1894

The trotting association which has just been organized will experience no difficulty in securing the Churchill Downs for a fall trotting meeting. Mr. Bourlier says that they can secure the grounds at an exceedingly low rate, and that the New Louisville Jockey Club will give their hearty support.

1895 construction scene of the grandstand and betting shed (above) at the Louisville Driving and Fair Association, which became known as Douglas Park.

at work, arranging the many details so necessary to the comfort of those attending the races. Numerous scrapers, sprinklers and rollers were engaged in putting the track in the best possible condition. The track at Churchill Downs was built for runners and it is, therefore, hardly to be expected that the phenomenally fast time made upon tracks especially prepared for trotters will be excelled; but at the worst it is a fast running track and with the amount of work being expended on it, it should be in splendid condition and furnish rare sport.

FROM "SUNDAY AT CHURCHILL DOWNS," *LOUISVILLE COMMERCIAL*, 22 OCTOBER 1894

It is a well-known fact that for years the Jockey Club has almost totally neglected the track, and it had gotten into such bad shape as to be the subject of comment among horsemen bringing their stables here for the races. When it was decided to hold a trotting meeting it was of course too late in the season to think of building a track and grand stand, so the Driving Association had but Hobson's choice left, which, in this instance, was Churchill Downs.

The trotting horse organization known as the Louisville Driving and Fair Association was permanently formed on 6 August 1894 at the Galt House, with Paul Jones elected president and J. J. Douglas and John E. Green vice presidents.[9] Concern was voiced about the availability of Churchill Downs for a fall meet, and the following year a trotting track was constructed southeast of Churchill Downs by "the expert track builder," Seth Griffin. Tracks in Boston and Peoria were being modeled after his design for Louisville — "mile circles with shorter stretches and longer, more gentle curves than have heretofore been attempted." Its grandstand had almost the same seating capacity as the new facility at Churchill Downs. The functions under the grandstand were below grade, "where the temperature is delightful on the hottest days and is made more grateful by wetting the asphalt floors."[10]

Distiller Paul Jones died just before the track opened in September 1895, and the operation became the domain of Col. James J. Douglas.[11] The track was converted to running when the Douglas Park Jockey Club was incorporated in 1901. The facility was in weeds by 1906 when taken over and materially improved for competition with Churchill Downs.[12] Head to head racing was averted, and in 1918, the Kentucky Jockey Club, which controlled Churchill Downs, purchased the 123-acre site for a training track. The last of the property was sold off in 1958.[13]

FROM "A SPLENDID STRUCTURE," *THE COURIER-JOURNAL*, 4 FEBRUARY 1895

The thousands who will pass through the gates at Churchill Downs on Derby Day next will see one of the handsomest and best equipped race tracks in the country. Over $80,000 worth of improvements have been contracted for, and by the time the last nail is driven and the finishing touches are made the promoters of the New Louisville Jockey Club will probably have expended an even $100,000. Everything has been planned on a magnificent scale, from the $42,000 grand stand down to the twenty or more new stables, each of which will accommodate twenty horses. These, with the old stables, all of which have been overhauled and improved, will give an aggregate stable capacity of 750 horses.

The new grand stand, fifteen feet of the walls of which are already up, will be the handsomest structure of the kind west of the Alleghenies. It will be 250 feet long and will be made of vitrified [glazed] brick, stone and steel. The back wall, or what is known architecturally as the "front" of the grand stand as you pass through the new entrance, is the most attractive, being thirty-one feet high and very imposing. With its monogram, keystone and other ornate architecture, it will compare favorably with any of the most pretentious office buildings or business structures on the prominent thoroughfares.

FROM "A SPLENDID STRUCTURE," *THE COURIER-JOURNAL*, 4 FEBRUARY 1895

D. X. Murphy & Bro., of this city, are the architects who designed the grand stand, and the contracts were awarded as follows: Brickwork, Fred Hoertz; cut stone, Peter & Burghard; cast and wrought iron and steel, the Snead & Co., Iron Works; carpenters' and joiners' work, John Fitchner; slate, copper and galvanized iron work, Bourlier Cornice and Roofing Company; contractor for stables and betting-shed, J. N. Struck. From this it will be seen that all the contracts were given to local firms, the Jockey Club people claiming that, while they received a number of favorable bids from outside concerns, they preferred to spend their money in Louisville.[14]

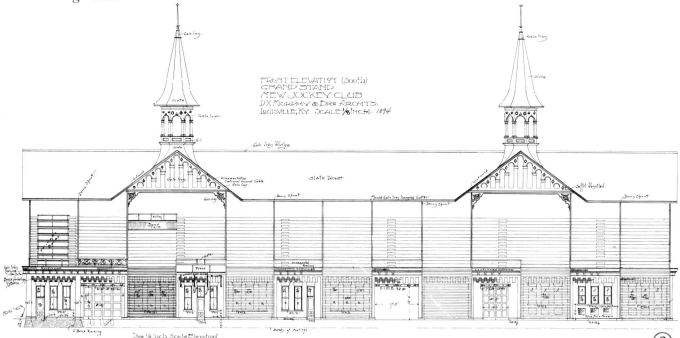

Opposite: Shaded areas at the first
level were the six flights of stairs.
The only private boxes were at the
left end. Right: Spire and gable framing section looking north to south.
Track-side gable at left. Below:
South part of rear elevation with
Victorian Romanesque window
sashes. Ornate grillwork at right surrounded private boxes.

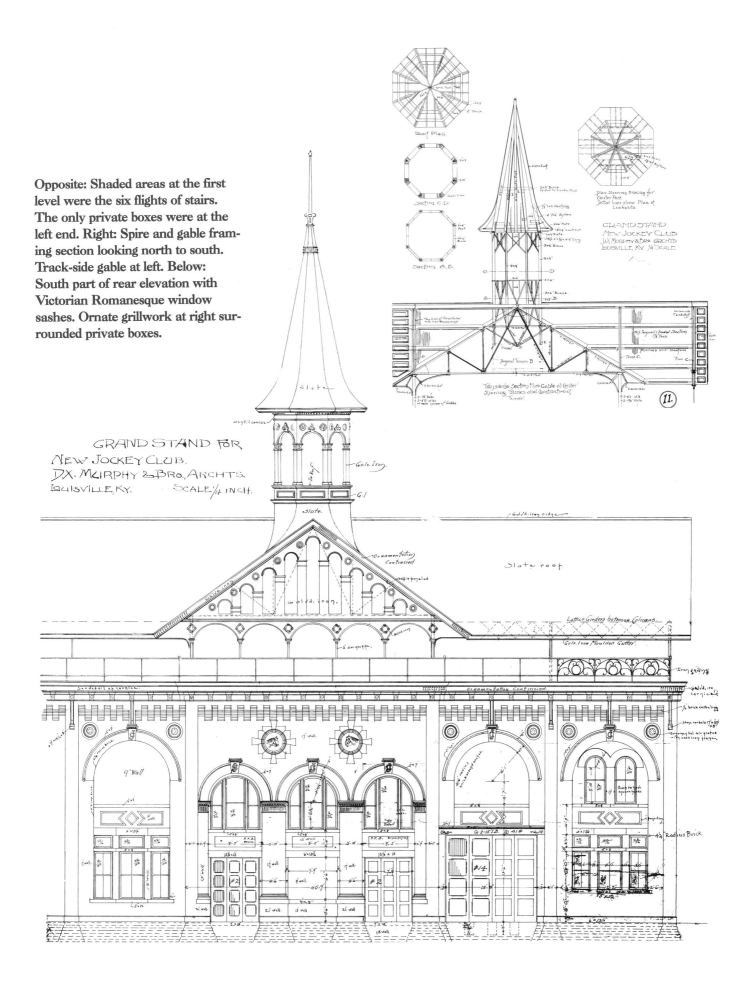

The view presented in the accompanying illustration is from the center field or track side. The wall here is over fifteen feet high, making the lowest seat in the new grand stand higher than the highest seat in the old one. This will give the spectators an opportunity to watch every movement of the horses in a race, the feet of the runners being visible from every point. Six flights of wide and roomy steps lead up to the stand, the capacity of which alone is estimated at 1,500 people. This plan was copied from the old Garfield track at Chicago.[15] Three-fifths of the visitors to the race track, or at least the male portion of them, seldom sit down or occupy a seat during the entire day's racing. They usually stay in the betting ring, or on the lawn until the gong announces "They're off!" Then they make a rush for the most advantageous point of view. That is the idea of the steps. They can be easily and quickly reached and afford an excellent view of the race. The seating capacity of the grand stand is about 4,500, which, with the steps, will accommodate in all 6,000 people.

In the lower or under part of the stand below the seats will be the bar, restaurant, toilet-rooms, offices for the Secretary and other officials, telegraph office, barber-shop, and under the ladies' part of the stand, the paddock. The appointments will be modern and handsome in every way. The bar will have costly fixtures, the toilet-rooms will be finished in marble, and the entire effect generally one not only of comfort and completeness, but of comparative elegance. The ladies' part of the stand will be provided with opera chairs, while comfortable settees or chairs will be placed in the part allotted to the male portion. The betting-shed adjoins the grand stand, affording easy and convenient access both for bettor and spectator. The betting-shed will have stone foundations supporting its columns, and the structure will be three feet higher than before, giving ample light and ventilation....

No better stables are to be seen on any race track in the country than the new ones being put up at Churchill Downs. Already a dozen of them have been completed, and as many more will be erected as soon as time and the weather will permit. Each stable has twenty stalls, besides three rooms on the end for the trainer and stable boys. In addition to this each stable has a four-room kitchen adjoining, giving more accommodations to turfmen than prevail on any other track. The stalls in each of the stables are lined with oak, and have doors of the same material. Each stall has also a window-transom and a ventilator leading up to and through the roof. A twelve-foot loft gives ample room for hay, etc., at the same time affording protection to the horses from the heat of midsummer. Every turfman who has seen them says they are the best stables he has ever seen on a race track.

It is not known when the decision to reconfigure the race track was made, but most probably it was done after the architects had evaluated the existing structure and determined it would not be feasible to upgrade it in time for the spring meet. Such deliberations would not have taken place until late in the fall of 1894, after the new ownership group had secured a

FROM "A SPLENDID STRUCTURE," THE COURIER-JOURNAL, 4 FEBRUARY 1895

As already stated all these improvements will cost in the aggregate nearly $100,000. This is a great deal of money to expend before a cent is received in return, but the promoters of the New Louisville Jockey Club are confident that racing here will be re-established to its former glory or prestige and are willing to make the trial or investment.

I started out as an office boy in the summertime for D. X. Murphy & Bro. in 1926. My job was cleaning rust off of steel tapes and things like that. When I got out of college in 1933, I went right into their office. Mr. Murphy gave me three shares of stock, and I kept on going until I owned it all.

We always had something to do with Churchill Downs. We did a little bit every year. They always had a long list of things they'd like to do, but they didn't have the money to do it. As the money developed, then they would do some of it.

When I was first in the office, D. X. was still there, and Mr. Winn was still living. D. X. would spend every afternoon at Churchill Downs playing poker or something with Mr. Winn. J. C. Murphy, D. X.'s brother, was still there too. He said he did the twin spires, and Mr. Baldez said he did the twin spires. J. C. could have come in and told Baldez, "this is what I want you to draw." That is probably what happened.

—FROM AN INTERVIEW WITH ARCHITECT THOMAS DADE LUCKETT II, 20 OCTOBER 1993

lease on the property and had formally incorporated. If the weather did not cooperate, the contractors might not have had enough time to make substantial improvements to the existing grandstand in time for the opening day of the 1895 spring meet. That prospect would have been disastrous to the new organization trying to demonstrate it could operate a track. More importantly, however, the group wanted to provide a new image. So, instead of tearing down the old grandstand, betting shed, and clubhouse, and rebuilding on those sites, the prudent scheme was to reconfigure the track — flip it — and erect a new grandstand and betting shed on the opposite (west) side. If for any reason construction was not completed by Derby day, the old structures would provide an alternative. In putting the grandstand on the west side, the patrons would be spared the sun's glare; and moving the stables to the east side must have taken advantage of the prevailing breezes from the west.

What made the relocation feasible, twenty years after the initial positioning of the structures, was the spread of the street railway system. The east side of the track was the favored destination point in 1874. By 1894, people could be brought as easily to the west side of the track. Reconfiguration of the track was, all in all, a sound solution.

Plans for the grandstand were drawn by Joseph Dominic Baldez (1870-1957), a draftsman in the D. X. Murphy & Bro. firm. Baldez (pronounced Bal-deez), the son of a carpenter, went to work in 1889 as a draftsman for the firm of Wehle & Dodd, which became Maury & Dodd. In 1893 he was a draftsman for Drach & Thomas, and sometime in 1894 he became a draftsman for D. X. Murphy & Bro., the firm retained to design the new grandstand. Baldez is credited with the design for the decorative twin spires, which were popular architectural elements at the time. His inspiration may very well have been similar spires designed for buildings under construction at the Central Asylum for the Insane at Lakeland whose architects were Drach, Thomas & Bohne, the firm he had just departed.[16] He may also have been influenced by spires on the landmark residence of Charles H. Mantle, built about 1880 on the northeast corner of Fourth and Oak streets and called, appropriately, The Towers. Additionally, the grandstand for the bicycle track at Fontaine Ferry Park in Louisville's west end had a similar pediment and tower arrangement in the middle of the roof, flanked by smaller towers at the ends.

FROM *LOUISVILLE COMMERCIAL*, 5 MAY 1895

Everything is in readiness for the dropping of the flag, the tap of the drum and the blast of the bugle. The grand stand is in fine condition, and all of the furniture has been moved into it. Mr. [James S.] Green, the Superintendent, has all of the grounds sodded nicely, and deserves a nice compliment from the club for the excellent service he has rendered.[17] He has been busy night and day working on the stables, assigning quarters and keeping the track in condition. Tomorrow morning he will harrow the track, and leave the little inside track for the exercising of horses. If there is no rain on it the track will be of the cardboard order, and it is pretty safe to say some records will be broken, because all of the best horses in the world are gathered here.

The new grand stand is simply a thing of beauty, with its two tall, tapering spires, its flying colors and its freshly painted surroundings. It was built at a cost of $60,000, and is made so substantially that it will last for years without any improvements. The construction is so arranged that everybody, from the top to the bottom row of seats, may see clearly the hoofs of the horses across the track. There can not be a trick played but it may be plainly seen, and the people as well as the judges will be able to tell whether the best horse has won. The seats, too, are like those of theaters, and everything bears the appearance of neatness that is attractive of itself. Mr. Schulte and Mr. Price, assisted by Superintendent Green, have done everything in their power to make it a splendid piece of architecture, and it will not be their fault if the public does not approve of it. The grand stand to be seen at its best has to be viewed from the outside of the track or from the half-post. While the side facing the track looks well, it is nothing in comparison to the other view. That it is an improvement on the location of the old one is apparent to everybody, and there is a surprise in store for those who will see it for the first time this year. Then all the stables are neatly whitewashed, the fences painted, and the Four Hundred of the equine society are gathered there. On the first floor are the bar, lunch counter, the Secretary's office, the paddock and the betting stand. All of them are neatly paved, and there are drains that at once carry off all the sloppy water that may accumulate. When it is raining outside the people will not have to go out in the wet to get to the betting stand, and under the roof of the grand stand the people will be as dry and comfortable as can be.... There is nothing left unprovided for, and on the top are toilet rooms for the ladies. The orchestra will be right under the roof, where everybody may hear the music.

What was missing, however, was a new clubhouse. The twenty-year-old structure that reportedly also had served as a part-time residence for M. Lewis Clark was no longer convenient to the grandstand. But the new owners were not socially prominent in Louisville. They all had their roots in gaming — pool selling — and their interest was in providing the straightest line to the betting shed.

The old clubhouse stood for at least a decade after M. Lewis Clark committed suicide in Memphis in 1899. The most frequently reproduced photograph of the frame structure was published in *The Courier-Journal* on 28 April 1901. A caption of the 1889 photograph of the grandstand and clubhouse, reprinted in *The Louisville Times* on 1 May 1934, pointed out that "the old clubhouse was razed and Lyman Davis, then secretary, now superintendent of greenhouses had his residence there."[18]

"Clark Lived In Downs Clubhouse," was the headline of an article in *The Courier-Journal* on 6 May 1937 that briefly recounted the evolution of

Clubhouse. From *The Graphic News* (New York), 15 May 1886.

[M. Lewis Clark] also worried over the destruction of the little Swiss cottage at Churchill Downs, which served as a clubhouse and where he kept bachelor's hall for so many years. This happened after the syndicate of sporting men became the holders of the stock and organized the new jockey club.

FROM "ISAAC MURPHY DEAD," *THE COURIER-JOURNAL*, 13 FEBRUARY 1896

Lexington, Ky., Feb. 12 — (Special.) — Isaac Murphy, the colored jockey, died at his home here to-day of pneumonia. He has been in bad health for several years, which caused his retirement from the saddle after a long and famous career. Recently Murphy entered a few horses of his own. He was thirty-two years of age, and leaves a wife. Murphy's winnings enabled him to save considerable money, and he also left some property....

"Honest Isaac" he was, indeed, and "the colored Archer," too, though the great English jockey [Fred Archer] might as well have been called "the white Murphy." He was the finest judge of pace ever seen in a saddle on our tracks. His seat was good and his hands perfect. Invariably he saved his mount and so seemed frequently a less strong finisher than he really was. By "drawing it too fine" at the wire he lost some races, but he stole ten times as many on inferior horses by superior horsemanship. During his best years [James] McLaughlin was the Eastern idol, but Murphy was his master and proved it when they met.

At one time Murphy's yearly pay ranged from $10,000 to $15,000. He never bet, never gambled, and, living quietly with his family, amassed a small fortune, which he invested in Lexington real estate. Nearly all went, however, in the last few years, during which Murphy, to the regret of his thousands of admirers, yielded to a fondness for wine, which hastened his retirement from the saddle and in every way marred his life.

Murphy was born and brought up on the estate of the late Hunt Reynolds, near [Frankfort], and began riding at an early age, having mounts on the horses belonging to the Fleetwood Stock Farm, Maj. B. G. Thomas and other Kentucky owners, his riding even then attracting the attention of the critics. Mrs. Reynolds taught him to read and write, and it is to the refining influences of her household that Murphy owed his good breeding and his fine moral character. He was almost raised on horseback, and rode some of the Hunt Reynolds horses when he could hardly walk.[19] Murphy was always very grateful to his bene-

Tintype of jockey Isaac Murphy (1861-1896), three-time winner of the Kentucky Derby, *ca.* 1890.

factress, and in all his contracts specified that whenever she needed him to ride any of her horses he must be allowed to go....

At Churchill Downs Murphy had scores of victories to his credit, including three Kentucky Derbies, he having had the mounts on Buchanan in 1884, Riley in 1890 and Kingman in 1891.

HERE IS BEN BRUSH, THE DERBY FAVORITE

Photographed Just Outside His Boudoir at the Track by the Times Special Artist.

"This is the best and truest newspaper picture of a race horse I ever saw," according to secretary Charles F. Price. From *The Louisville Times*, 6 May 1896.

FROM *THE COURIER-JOURNAL*, 7 MAY 1896

Col. Clark received the visits of a number of friends in the judges' stand. He shows but little trace of his recent severe illness.

FROM A 1933 ARTICLE BY CLEM MCCARTHY IN THE CHARLES F. PRICE PAPERS

Of all the stirring, blood-tingling Kentucky Derby struggles Judge Price has witnessed, the finish of the 1896 running stands out in his memory. "The nose finish in that race," he avers, "was an equine battle that would have thrilled a sphinx. It was a gruelling race the entire length of the homestretch, with the determined Ben Brush, urged on with hand and heel as only that great colored jockey, Willie Simms, could drive a horse, poking his nose ahead of the game Ben Eder in the very last stride.

"That was a race one cannot forget, but one never can tell: the next Kentucky Derby always holds forth the hope of bringing out a more bitterly fought contest than any of its predecessors."

the structure. While these accounts refer to Col. Clark residing in the clubhouse, Captain J. T. Larkin recalled Clark's entertaining in the "pink cottage."[20] Perhaps the buildings were one and the same.

FROM "DERBY NOTES," *LOUISVILLE COMMERCIAL*, 7 MAY 1896

The street-car tracks from Fourth to Seventh street were lined on both sides with stands for lunches, cider, pop, lemonade and peanuts, with little strips of canvas for the operation of crap games. Most of these affairs were run by negroes, and they were a sadly disappointed lot when they learned for certain that there would be no free field.[21] For, as a consequence, they lost heavily on their investments, their various catch-penny schemes being practically not patronized.

FROM "BEN BRUSH," *LOUISVILLE COMMERCIAL*, 7 MAY 1896

The old grand stand loomed up across the race track, neglected and deserted, save for a few negroes who sat there and took in the races from there....Although the colored man and brother was not as much in evidence as if there had been a free field, still there was quite a respectable number of negroes in the grand stand and around the "bookies."

Although the time-honored but highly imperfect starting technique of simply dropping a flag was again employed in the 1896 Kentucky Derby, starter Jack Chinn was experimenting in other races at Churchill Downs with a starting "machine" of sorts.[23] A barrier to prevent the horses from breaking away down the track was needed. Webbing like a volleyball net was stretched across the track, fastened to arms at either end that had been attached to posts put in the ground. To begin the race, the starter would cause the arms to fly up taking the webbing out of the horses' way. The machine, invented by Louisvillian W. H. Dill, was being tried at Churchill Downs, but there were other versions in use.[24]

The Thoroughbred Record on 21 March 1896 had described the features of three such machines, including one in use at New Orleans, "the invention of 'Curly' Brown, well-known as a starter." It had been described in detail in the previous issue. Curly Brown was using his machine at Newport when he learned of Dill's installation at Churchill Downs and he responded quickly that it was "an infringement on his idea."[25]

Starter Jack Chinn and the new machine. From *The Louisville Times*, 9 May 1896.

FROM *THE COURIER-JOURNAL*, 13 MAY 1897

It lacks eight minutes of 4 o'clock when the six colts line up. Ornament begins to dance a little, and the jockeying of the boys on the other starters causes a wait. Typhoon does not relish the delay, and prances back of the field. In a few minutes they move up and break, but Typhoon whirls around and the flag does not fall. A minute later, when they have been at the post only six minutes, they break once again. Down go the red and yellow squares. There is a roar from the crowded grand stand, and the twenty-third Kentucky Derby is begun.[22]

FROM "CAUGHT AT THE COURSE," *THE COURIER-JOURNAL*, 7 MAY 1896
Ben Brush was presented with a very beautiful collar by Charles Reimers. It was of white roses and pink and was tied with white and magenta ribbon. The jockey was also presented with bouquets from Mrs. W. F. Schulte and Charles Reimers.[26] The crowd cheered heartily as the winner was led away adorned with the pretty flowers.

The 1896 Kentucky Derby carries special significance. As promised by the new owners, the race distance was reduced from a mile and a half to the present mile and a quarter. A larger purse ($4,850) was an added incentive, and for the first time a "collar" of roses was presented to the winner. Mrs. Belle Overton Schulte, wife of the president of the New Louisville Jockey Club, handed a bouquet to the winning jockey, Willie Simms.[27]

The phrase, "Run for the Roses," was not coined until 1925 by sports writer Bill Corum, who later became president of Churchill Downs. But the tradition was started by Charles William Reimers, who had his nursery and greenhouses at the end of Hite Avenue overlooking Brownsboro Road in Crescent Hill, where he had been a florist for more than twenty years when he died in 1912.

FROM "JOHN CHURCHILL PASSES AWAY," *THE COURIER-JOURNAL*, 22 MARCH 1897
Mr. John Churchill, one of the pioneer residents of Louisville and widely-known in Kentucky, Virginia and the South, died last night at 9:05 o'clock at his residence, 1114 Fourth avenue....

At the death of Armistead Churchill his property fell into the possession of Samuel Churchill, his son. The latter resided during a part of his life on the Spring Grove estate, and it was there that John Churchill was born, March 20, 1819. He received his education at Bardstown, Ky., but practically spent all of his life in and about Louisville. In 1857 Mr. Churchill married Mrs. Selina Lawrence, who survived the marriage day but a year, dying childless. Mr. Churchill remained a widower over thirty years. In 1890 he married Miss Tina Nicholas, of this city. A wife and one child, John Churchill, Jr., survive the deceased.

On account of the great wealth which Mr. Churchill inherited from his father he was never actively engaged in any business venture. Only once did he become a party to a large business enterprise, having purchased, in partnership with Messrs. Albert and Thos. Johnson, the street railway franchise of Indianapolis. They sold their interest several years ago, after having realized handsomely on their investment....

He was one of the few surviving children of Samuel Churchill, and there were seventeen in all. Those still living are ex-Gov. T. J. Churchill, of Arkansas, Mrs. Hampton Zane and Mrs. Blackburn, widow of ex.-Gov. Luke P. Blackburn. W. H. Churchill, one of the sons, died about six years ago. The two brothers were inseparable and were familiar figures on the streets of Louisville, both being over six feet in height and as straight as arrows. When Henry Churchill died he left to his brother John the greatest part of his share of the great estate, which in its entirety, is valued at about $750,000.

FROM "IN DEATH COL. M. LEWIS CLARK FINDS RELIEF,"
THE COURIER-JOURNAL, 23 APRIL 1899

Memphis Tenn., April 22 - [Special] — Col. M. Lewis Clark, of Louisville, prominent in turf circles throughout the United States, killed himself this morning in his room at Gaston's Hotel.[28] With a revolver he sent a bullet through his head as he lay on his bed. He was alone. When found life was extinct. The remains will be conveyed to Louisville to-morrow night reaching that city Monday morning. They will be escorted by a party of friends from this city and Louisville.[29] Failing health is supposed to be at the bottom of the tragedy. That his health was bad is well known. As to his finances there is considerable uncertainty. People here who claim to know, among them the Messrs. Caldwell, bankers, say his finances were never in better shape, that he was in receipt of a regular income, was not a spendthrift, and also recently inherited a considerable income.

Col. Clark came to Memphis to act as presiding judge of the races on April 8. He went to Gaston's where he usually stopped, and was assigned to room 26. When he came to Memphis it was noticed by his friends that his spirits seemed very much depressed....

It was hardly a year ago that Col. Clark figured in an exciting episode that attracted wide attention at the time and contributed to the conviction that the Colonel was a fearless sort of fellow. It was at the meeting of the Turf Congress at Cincinnati, that Turfman Corrigan bobbed up with a

Above: "Lieut. Gibson Wins the Twenty-sixth Kentucky Derby," *The Courier-Journal*, 4 May 1900. Opposite: John Pope Rowan Churchill, instrumental in the beginning of Churchill Downs. From *The Courier-Journal*, 22 March 1897.

WINS THE TWENTY=SIXTH KENTUCKY DERBY.

wordy attack on Col. Clark for upholding the claims of the Harlem [now the Chicago suburb of River Forest] track to official sanction. The latter was quick to resent. Col. Clark covered his opponent with a gun and made him back down in complete style.

FROM *THE COURIER-JOURNAL*, 4 MAY 1899

Viewed from any standpoint other than the Chicago one, the racing industry of the country appears to be on a stronger and more sportsmanlike plane than has obtained since the panic of '93, when the breeding and running of thoroughbreds in sympathy with every other line of legitimate business were given a set-back which the lapse of half a dozen years has scarcely fully restored.

From one point of view the depression in the value of bloodstock was immense help to the sport, as it froze out a number of small and ignorant breeders who were flooding the country with a lot of cheap-bred and badly mated stock, the aggregate value of which did not amount to the historical tinker's dam. The best men in the breeding business had to get together for mutual preservation, while the heart-breaking decline in the thoroughbred market made it possible to bring capitalists of former Secretary of the Navy [William C.] Whitney's caliber into the game on a purely business basis. The subtle influences of race horse ownership did the rest and converts of three years' standing are to-day the most enthusiastic and generous patrons of the turf.

Another matter of congratulation among ardent lovers of racing is the evolution which has taken place in the personnel of the organizations in control of the tracks. Half a dozen years ago the Corrigans, Condons, Ullmans and Walbaums appeared to be pretty nearly the whole thing in the racing game. In place of these old-timers, the Belmonts, Pagets, Lawrences and Whitneys are to-day at the head of turf affairs in the East, while the Schultes, Montgomerys, Aulls and Maffits control the situation in the West.[30]

Charles F. Price. From *The Courier-Journal*, 1 May 1900.

FROM "PRICE OUT," *THE COURIER-JOURNAL*, 1 MAY 1900

Mr. Charles F. Price, Secretary of the New Louisville Jockey Club, resigned his position yesterday afternoon to take effect at once, and the Louisville Club on the eve of its big spring meeting is without a secretary, one of its most important officers....

Early yesterday morning a certain stockholder in the Louisville Jockey Club received a letter from Col. W. E. Applegate, in which the latter stated that Mr. W. F. Schulte would be the presiding judge at the coming meeting. This man communicated with Mr. Schulte, who was evidently greatly surprised by the news. He went to the Jockey Club office, room 17 Courier-Journal office building, and told Mr. Price that he had been elected to serve in the judges' stand. Mr. Price stated that he was glad of it. Mr. Lew P. Tarlton, of Frankfort, had served as associate judge with Mr. Price last year, and Mr. Price naturally thought that Mr. Schulte had been appointed to fill the position held the year before by Mr. Tarlton... [Note: When M. Lewis Clark died, W.E. Applegate named Price presiding judge.[31]]

Mr. Price has served as Secretary of the Jockey Club for the past eight years. After the death of Maj. B. G. Bruce, Col. M. Lewis Clark offered him the post of Secretary and he accepted. At that time he was a well-known Louisville newspaper man.

As Secretary of the Jockey Club he immediately became a highly efficient and very popular officer. Col. Clark was his warm friend, and they served together as judges at many tracks. Besides being an associate judge in Louisville, Mr. Price has acted as presiding judge at Latonia, Oakley, Ideal Park and other tracks. He was presiding steward of the California Jockey Club at San Francisco, last winter, and gave complete satisfaction.

The spring meeting of 1901 got off to an early start. The Kentucky Derby as usual was on opening day, but not as usual, the race was in April, on the 29th. His Eminence, another colt by Falsetto, with Leamington in his pedigree, won. It was the first of consecutive victories by African-American jockey Jimmy Winkfield.[32] In the field of five, his start was relatively easy — just one false break — but later in the meet, a send off by veteran starter Curly Brown had the crowd up in arms. Evidently the barrier machine (perhaps his invention) could not ensure a fair start.

William F. Schulte at home in St. James Court, *ca.* 1902.

FROM "HISSED STARTER CURLY BROWN," *THE COURIER-JOURNAL*, 5 MAY 1901

A remarkable demonstration occurred at Churchill Downs yesterday afternoon just after the horses had been sent away in the fifth race. Starter Curly Brown, the most capable man who has handled the starter's flag at Churchill Downs in ten years, was hissed, yelled at, cursed and insulted by a large crowd of people for a bad start he had just made.

The people who made the demonstration may be ashamed of their action; for what they did was done when they were excited. The scene reminded one of a mob exhibition on one of the worst sort of outlaw tracks racing in the winter.

And the worst feature about the exhibition was, that Starter Brown was not to blame to the extent that he was given credit for. He made an unsatisfactory start. There is no doubt of the fact, but it was clearly unintentional, and it was the first bad start he had made. St. Marcos, a quick breaker, got off running just as the flag fell, and in a few jumps opened up a gap of several lengths on the field behind him. This is where the crowd roared it disapproval, and Starter Brown, goaded by the jeers and insults of the multitude, tipped his hat and bowed. Then a mob of several hundred men made a rush for the judges' stand, but the police were there, and prevented any violence. After the excitement was over Starter Brown tendered his resignation, but it was not accepted, and he will continue to act in that capacity.[33] ...

President and Judge Schulte came in for a share of the disapproval. Men made megaphones of their hands and called him names, but, of course, the presiding judge kept his temper and refused to answer the insulting epithets. It was half an hour before the police finally restored order. No blows were struck, but it needed only a spark to kindle the wrath of the angry bettors into a conflagration which would have hurt a number of men.

FROM "LAST WEEK OF THE MEETING," *THE COURIER-JOURNAL*, 19 MAY 1902

Considerable comment was caused yesterday because of a rumor which stated that Mr. W. F. Schulte was to retire as president of the Jockey Club and that ex-Sheriff Henry Bell was to succeed him. Mr. Schulte was asked about this rumor yesterday afternoon and he stated that he had no intention of retiring and that if he was to be removed he had not heard of it. "Please say for me that there is no truth in the rumor so far as I know," said Mr. Schulte.

The spring meet of 1902 was marginally successful due "not because the attendance was larger than in previous years, but because more books remained throughout the meeting than for many years." *The Courier-Journal* went on to reveal on 26 May 1902 that W. E. Applegate was considering significant alterations in the physical plant and, indeed, in its management. The changes were so substantial they must have been on Applegate's mind for some time. The reason for such sweeping plans was, as *The Courier-Journal* headline pointed out, an "effort to get society people interested in the sport." Applegate was fundamentally altering the appeal of horse racing away from the bettors and bookies and trying to make it once more appealing to those who enjoyed it as a sport. M. Lewis Clark's vision was being revisited. William Edward Applegate has remained obscured in the history of Churchill Downs. And yet without the dramatic changes he effected in 1902 and 1903, Churchill Downs would be just another footnote in Louisville horse racing like Oakland, Woodlawn, Greenland, and Douglas Park.

FROM "MANY IMPROVEMENTS AT CHURCHILL DOWNS," *THE COURIER-JOURNAL*, 26 MAY 1902

When the spectators go to Churchill Downs next spring to witness the running of the twenty-ninth Kentucky Derby they will be surprised at the changes which will have been wrought between now and the date on which this classic race is decided. Mr. W. E. Applegate, who, it is said, owns 85 percent of the stock of the Jockey Club, and who, at any rate, owns a controlling interest in the association, is determined to make a number of elaborate improvements. One of the finest and best appointed clubhouses at any race track in the South or West will be built during the summer and fall to the south of the present grand stand. It will be large and commodious, with a wide veranda extending around the entire building. His idea is also to have the betting shed underneath the stand where the paddock is now located. The paddock will be removed north of the stand at the present location of the betting shed. Within the inclosure, that is, in the infield, golf links will be laid out; tennis courts will be marked off, and other landscape features added.

It is possible that between now and fall there will be a reorganization of the New Louisville Jockey Club. For some unknown reason the sport has not advanced as rapidly as it should have proceeded, and it is quite likely that a number of very prominent men, who are well known in local business and social circles, will be identified with the club before the snow flies again. The present owners of the track realize that this step is necessary. In years gone by the most important men in Louisville and Jefferson county were numbered among the stockholders of the Louisville Jockey Club. And in years to come it is expected that the spring meetings will be great social features, both as regards Kentucky and the entire South. Just who the men are who will be connected with the club has not yet been announced, nor will it be until all the details have been completed. As a matter of fact, none of the details has been discussed as yet, and the plans so far are in a crude state. But the general idea has been outlined, and the result will be awaited with interest.

William E. Applegate, principal owner of Churchill Downs, *ca.* 1925.

FROM "LAST WEEK OF THE MEETING," *THE COURIER-JOURNAL*, 19 MAY 1902

Mr. W. E. Applegate, who owns a controlling interest in the Jockey Club, spent yesterday in Indianapolis on business. He sent the following denial of the rumor yesterday afternoon:

Indianapolis, Ind., May 18 — W. W. Douglas, Sporting Editor Courier-Journal: Please deny story that there is to be a change in presidency of Jockey Club. There is not one word of truth in it. Depend on that. The rumor originated in some imaginative brain. The matter has never been discussed by the Jockey Club directors.[34]

—W. E. Applegate.

No such crowd was ever gathered in one spot in the State of Kentucky as was gathered at Churchill Downs, now transformed into the State Fair Grounds, yesterday....They all wanted to see the fair, of course, but with the fair they wanted to see the collision between the two great locomotives, which had been held temptingly before the people of the State for two months as one of the prime attractions. They all saw the collision, they were all thrilled by it, and they all came away pleased and satisfied....

From 35,000 to 40,000 human hearts beat rapidly as monster freight locomotives crashed into each other at the State fair grounds yesterday afternoon. It was a head-on collision and there were no fatalities. The engineers of the doomed locomotives knew of the danger ahead, and jumped in ample time.

Charles F. Price, general manager of the California race tracks, has resigned his position, which pays $10,000 a year, and hereafter he will confine his efforts in the racing game to the Middle West.

It was rumored yesterday that Mr. Price would accept the presidency or the secretaryship of the New Louisville Jockey Club, in a short time, but this is certainly premature and indefinite. It can be stated authoritatively that Mr. Price has not been approached by the management or owners of the New Louisville Jockey Club with an offer to take either place mentioned, and it is no certainty that he will be offered either place. As a matter of fact he did not resign his place to take the Louisville office, and was surprised, in fact, to learn that the place was available.

Late in the Autumn of 1902, Charlie Price, former newspaper editor, and the Secretary at the Churchill Downs race track, dropped into my office, sat down, and, without preliminary, bluntly asked me to buy the Churchill Downs property. "Why should I do that?" I encountered.

"Because," replied Price, "if you don't buy it, the track will have to close and there won't be any more Kentucky Derbies." I was dumbfounded. I had heard that the operators of the Downs were having some financial difficulties, but it never occurred to me that they were of such magnitude that they could not carry on....

I called some of my most intimate friends into an informal meeting; Mayor Charles Grainger, of Louisville; Col. Andrew Vennie;[35] W. E. Applegate, who was Vice President of the Downs group; Sam S. Brown, J. C. Boardman, and others and told them what Price had told me. I asked them if they wanted to chip in and buy the Downs, if the price was reasonable. Nobody was very enthusiastic, but it was suggested that I get the rock-bottom figures from Charlie Price. He named $40,000 for the physical property, the real estate being under lease from the Churchill family....

Racing judge Charles F. Price at Churchill Downs, *ca.* 1925.

"I am not at liberty to state who will be the new owners of the Jockey Club. In fact, this is a matter that I have not asked about in detail. I know the New Louisville Jockey Club has cost me a lot of money; that I own the controlling interest of the stock, and that I believe other people can make more out of it than I did. With a new deal all around I believe the New Louisville Jockey Club will prove a big success, and I will be glad to see it. I will also be glad to get out of the club."

So I went back to Charlie Grainger and my other friends who were interested in saving the Derby, among them Saunders P. Jones, Louis Seelbach, the hotel owner, and Frank Fehr.[36] I had discussions with W. E. Applegate who was with the operating group that wanted to sell. Applegate sketched out the financial picture for me and it wasn't too cheerful....

I called up Charlie Price. "Find a buyer?"

"No."

"All right. We'll take it. Get your lawyer to come over and we'll draw up a contract." This he did promptly and in a few days we owned the long-established "white elephant." The thing to do was to learn what had made it such, and to try to remedy the situation.

Sports reporter and biographer Frank G. Menke was named director of press relations when he came to work at Churchill Downs in 1938.[37] According to Matt Winn, he asked a lot of questions — dates and details — which were for newspaper articles and radio programs. Sometime in 1944, Menke proposed a book. This was forty-two years after the management at Churchill Downs had changed, and the details had become hazy. Col. Winn had been in charge for so long, it seemed like he always had. But the changeover did not take place as Menke's book described. W.E. Applegate took the initiative and devised a way to save the track and preserve his investment.

FROM "BIG CHANGE IN THE JOCKEY CLUB," *THE COURIER-JOURNAL*,
1 OCTOBER 1902

A meeting of the stockholders and directors of the New Louisville Jockey Club will be held at noon to-day in the office of the Jockey Club, room 17 Courier-Journal building. This will probably be the most important meeting the Jockey Club has ever held, for to-day the stock will change hands, a new board of directors will be elected, new officers will be selected for at least a year and probably for the next five years, and there will be a new deal all around....

The old officers, who will retire to-day, are: William F. Schulte, president; W. E. Applegate, vice president; Charles Bollinger, treasurer; and D. F. Dressen, secretary. The old board of directors which will retire is composed of Messrs. W. E. Applegate, William F. Schulte and Charles Bollinger.

Exactly who will acquire a controlling interest of the stock has not been made clear, nor will this be stated until after the meeting to-day. It has been stated that Louis V. Bell, the wealthy New York horseman, has purchased a controlling interest in the club, but this is denied by those most directly interested. However, those who deny it refuse to make public the names of the new owners or the prospective owners. It is stated, however, that Messrs. Grainger and Price will control the destinies of the track and club no matter who the new purchasers are. Both are well known and popular and they should be able to put the club on a paying basis.

FROM "RECORDS WERE SMASHED BY CROWDS AT KENTUCKY STATE FAIR," *THE COURIER-JOURNAL*, 24 SEPTEMBER 1902

The card for to-day and to-night will be equally interesting. An automobile race will be had at 3:30 o'clock in the afternoon between six amateur drivers of Kentucky. J. Kemp Goodloe, Dr. W. T. Durrett and Worth Otter, of Louisville, have entered, and there is an entry from Bardstown and one from Maysville. All the machines are gasoline motors and weigh less than 1,000 pounds.

Doc Wohlgamuth, superintendent of the grounds, has promised to have the track in first-class condition. He put a force of workmen to cleaning and rolling the track immediately after the horse rings were through with last night. By this afternoon, when the race is called, the track will be as smooth as on Derby day, and it is expected that the best that is in them will be got out of the machines.

FROM "IMPROVEMENTS ARE TO BE MADE," *THE COURIER-JOURNAL*, 2 OCTOBER 1902

The first object in the change of management of this great factor in the racehorse world is to attempt to place Churchill Downs on a par with the great tracks of this country. The new management will give better stakes and purses, erect a new club-house — but, above all, will exert their utmost to attract the great thoroughbred magnates of the country, secure their entries, and thereby, with tremendous influence, make Churchill Downs what it should be, the equal of Saratoga as the best speeding ground of the nation's tracks. The attraction of these high-class turfmen of the horse world is thoroughly recognized as an all essential. The new management wants to get the Whitneys, Belmonts, Keenes and all that ilk of typical horsemen to come to the Downs and by their aid assist in retrieving the old renown of the great course.

Col. W. E. Applegate, who at present owns a controlling interest in the Louisville track, arrived in the city yesterday after a lengthy business trip in the East and at Chicago. He left here shortly after the close of the meeting at Churchill Downs and returned only yesterday to rearrange matters regarding the local racing situation.

"Yes, a meeting of all who are financially concerned in the New Louisville Jockey Club will be held to-morrow at the office of the club, in the Courier-Journal building," said Col. Applegate yesterday afternoon. "I can't outline what will be done, but I am of the opinion that there will be a complete change in the directory of the club, a complete change in the ownership and also a very considerable change among the officers."

"I believe that after the new directors have been elected they will elect Mayor Charles F. Grainger president, Charles F. Price secretary and Matt Winn vice president. I don't know who will be the new treasurer, but it may be some one whose name has not yet been mentioned."...

FROM "IMPROVEMENTS ARE TO BE MADE," *THE COURIER-JOURNAL*, 2 OCTOBER 1902

The complete change in the directory, ownership and management of the New Louisville Jockey Club, which was exclusively announced in yesterday's Courier-Journal, took place as predicted, and to all intents and purposes Col. W. E. Applegate, Charles Bollinger, Hamilton Applegate, William F. Schulte, Des F. Dressen, etc., have no further connection with the local racing body.

According to the announcement made after yesterday's meeting the new officers of the Jockey Club and the new Board of Directors are as follows:

President — Charles F. Grainger. Vice President — M. J. Winn. Secretary and Treasurer — Charles F. Price. Treasurer — J. C. Boardman. Board of Directors — Saunders P. Jones, Charles F. Price, Walter E. Glover, Louis Seelbach, M. J. Winn, J. C. Boardman, Charles F. Grainger....

The meeting was held in the Jockey Club office, room 17 Courier-Journal building, and after it was over it was announced that there had been a complete reorganization of the club, etc. It was given out that 83 per cent of the stock, which had been held by Messrs. W. E. Applegate, H. C. Applegate and Charles Bollinger, had been transferred to Charles F. Price, Matt Winn and J. C. (Billy) Boardman, who will have an option on the purchase of the stock for seven years, which is the remaining number of years the club has a lease on Churchill Downs. These new stockholders, it seems, simply hold the stock in trust, or as trustees, holding an option on the stock for that length of time if they desire to buy it during that period.

This means that the story regarding the purchase of the stock by Louis V. Bell, of New York, is untrue, and that he will have no more voice in the operation of the club than any other stranger. From what was announced it is evident that the Jockey Club has been placed entirely in the hands of Charles F. Price and Mayor Grainger, and, as both are experienced and popular, they should be able to put the club back on the same plane it was placed on by the late Col. M. Lewis Clark.

Mayor Grainger, it is stated also, will be at the head of the club, and will take care of the social feature, while Mr. Price will have charge of the racing end of the business. He will be the presiding judge at the Louisville meetings. Mayor Grainger will also be in the stand, as will another man of racing experience.

According to a well-informed man it will be Mayor Grainger's ambition to get local society intensely interested in the move, and to that end additional stock will be issued to persons of well-known social standing, and the money thus acquired will be spent in various improvements, chief among which are a clubhouse, a cafe and summer garden.[38] The present paddock will be removed and a new paddock built on one end of the betting shed. Many of the old stables will be torn down and new ones erected....

As to the new club-house, it will be exclusive to club members, their friends and the guests of the Jockey Club. It will be so located as to command the best of views of the races. The exterior will have two circling balconies, with cafe, buffet and public and private dining-rooms.

New paddocks will be erected and the betting shed will be reconstructed. The old stables will be supplanted by new ones. In fact, there will be a complete renaissance.

With the end of next season's spring meeting, the Downs will be put to a different purpose. It will be transformed into a summer garden, with every necessary night illumination attendant. The best of attractions will be given. Mr. Winn, vice president, and Mr. Boardman, the treasurer, will have charge of the amusement and catering features.[39]

William E. Applegate had effected the change in direction he had floated in the press many months before. He had turned the operation over to an invigorated management team. No money had changed hands; no deeds were signed. He still retained controlling interest and his son, Hamilton C. Applegate, would become secretary of the board of directors and, in time, treasurer of the track.[40]

Col. Applegate could now turn his attention to straightening out Latonia which he also headed, and which was unable to meet its payments.[41] Churchill Downs was in the capable hands of Charles Grainger and Charles Price.

Charles F. Grainger (1854-1923) was the sitting mayor of Louisville, having served as an alderman and chairman of the Board of Public Works. During his term from 1901 to 1905, the Louisville Free Public Library, the jail, and the armory were built. He then became president of the Louisville Water Company. Through it all, he was president of Grainger & Co., his father's old Phoenix Foundry (est. 1833) which he took over in 1888. His wife was Jeannie Miller, the daughter of Silas F. Miller, whose mansion housed the University of Louisville before the Belknap Campus was established. If not stretched too thin, Mayor Grainger was the right

Above: Caricature of Mayor Charles F. Grainger, president of the New Louisville Jockey Club. From *Kentuckians As We See Them* (1905). Below: Clubhouse porch, 1904. Opposite: From *The Courier-Journal*, 3 May 1904.

man to change the image and fortunes of Churchill Downs.

The idea of a clubhouse with a wide veranda to be located south of the grandstand had been announced in *The Courier-Journal* on 26 May 1902, so the architectural firm that had conceived the grandstand had probably been at work preparing conceptual drawings and obtaining cost estimates early in 1902 and even before then. The structure would have the same location relative to the grandstand that the earlier clubhouse had had, but this one would be connected to the grandstand as was a popular and accepted arrangement at other tracks.[42]

D. X. Murphy & Bro. was the logical firm to tie the existing and proposed structures together. They accomplished this structurally, but stylistically, the clubhouse and grandstand were distinctly different. In the intervening eight years, architectural preferences had changed. The previously favored Victorian Romanesque style of the brick grandstand had given way to yet another version of Classical Revival displayed in the clubhouse. The public would associate the Classical Revival with the mansions of the old South, and this style would prevail in all the changes and improvements at Churchill Downs until the massive rooftop boxes

AS SEEN FROM THE NEW CLUB HOUSE

were added in the 1960s. However, to the Murphy firm's credit, the massing of the clubhouse balanced the betting shed to the north of the grandstand, and the designers were able to taper the grandstand's abrupt termination on the south side by providing the new clubhouse with an interesting triangular shape. (Although the clubhouse has been removed, the curve of the tip end is still evident in the brick foundation in the basement.) This was a rather modest addition. Clubhouses were generally massive oversized houses, separate, but connected by a walkway to the left side of the grandstand as viewed from the track. Washington Park in Chicago of 1896 was the epitome. Its connector at the second floor level veranda was quite long and covered by an awning.[43]

At the same time, the D. X. Murphy & Bro. firm was working on drawings for improving the betting shed north of the grandstand and for building a new paddock. The decision had been made not to locate the betting operation under the grandstand where the paddock had been. The paddock structure would be positioned along the track beyond (north of) the betting shed (for a photograph, see *The Courier Journal*, 1 May 1903).

FROM "JOCKEY CLUBHOUSE READY FOR MEMBERS,"
THE LOUISVILLE HERALD, 30 APRIL 1903[44]

The clubhouse of the Louisville Jockey Club is ready for the reception of members and their guests. It is the coziest clubhouse to be found at any race track. A broad veranda encircles the building, and the portion fronting the track is filled with easy benches and chairs. Every inch affords an unobstructed view of the track. On the roof there is a magnificent promenade. From its broad walks every jump of the horses can be seen from start to finish. The furnishing of the clubhouse was completed yesterday afternoon. The main cafe, which opens on the front veranda with colonial doors and windows, is furnished with oak. The draperies are green and orange, the colors of the club. A massive red brick fireplace is screened with palms and ferns, and all over the spacious hall are clusters of palms and ferns.

Opening into the cafe on the north are women's reception and toilet rooms. The reception room floor is covered with green matting, and the draperies are the same as those of the cafe. The furniture is mahogany, and consists of a dressing table, a six-foot mirror, a large center-table and a chiffonier. Easy chairs are scattered about the room.

Back of the main cafe is the gentlemen's cafe. The sideboard is finished in white and the counter of the bar is mahogany. The large windows are screened in green silk, relieved by delicate figures.

The kitchen is in the basement and takes up the entire space under the clubhouse. It is fitted with the most modern hotel ranges, ice boxes, linen closets and laundry. The china and glassware arrived yesterday. Each piece of china bears the monogram of the club.

The club now has a membership of nearly 200, and it is expected this number will be reached by Saturday. There is a bridge from the grand

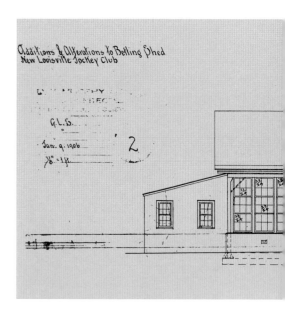

FROM *THE EVENING POST*, 18 APRIL 1903

If any fault was to be found with the Derby in late years it lay in the fact that the race seemed in a measure surrendered to the sporting element and lacked something of the social pre-eminence of former days. The grandstand used to focus the aristocracy of the Bluegrass State, and people who cared little for horse racing as a regular sport still flocked to the Derby, impelled by a State patriotism and general enthusiasm. This year will see a revival of the old regime, in that the new management of the Louisville Jockey Club has bent its best efforts toward the uplifting of the racing game, and has, by the erection of a spacious and commodious club house, made it possible for the society element to come and find the accommodations it likes...

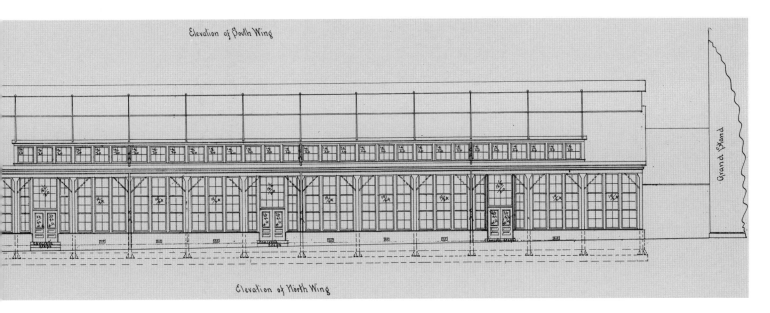

Elevation of South Wing

Grand Stand

Elevation of North Wing

Above: Rear (Central Avenue) elevation of betting shed by D.X. Murphy & Bro. For a size reference, note height of the three doorways. Right: Front of betting shed, showing corner of 1903 paddock. Seating on platform was skirted by a balustrade with elaborate grillwork.

FROM "READY FOR RUNNING OF DERBY AT CHURCHILL DOWNS NEXT SATURDAY," *THE LOUISVILLE HERALD*, 26 APRIL 1903[45]

Under the efficient management of Secretary Charles Price and Assistant Secretary D. F. Dressen numerous improvements have been made at the track, and the racing plant at the corner of Fourth and P [now Central Avenue] streets is one of the most complete in the West. During this past winter several new barns have been built and unsightly old ones removed; the new club house has been erected and a new paddock has been built at the end of the betting shed.

stand to the promenade of the clubhouse, and a broad brick walk leads from the entrance to the veranda...

The comfort of non-members has not been overlooked. The old paddock under the grand stand has been converted into a cafe — cool red bricks pave the floor, and the furnishings are the same as those of the clubhouse. Next is the public bar, so long familiar to the public. Then come the betting ring and the new paddock, all ready for Saturday's crowd.

Mr. J. C. Boardman will have charge of the clubhouse and cafes.

Dinner parties will be the rule after the races are over — nearly every table has been engaged for Derby evening. Mr. Clausman, the chef from the Union League Club, of New York, who has charge of the kitchen, will remain with the club during the summer. He was engaged on the recommendation of the celebrated Oscar, chef of the Waldorf-Astoria, who wrote that Mr. Clausman was the equal of any man in his profession in New York.

Jockey Club Park Entrance, Louisville, Ky.

Entrance to Jockey Club Park off Central Avenue, *ca.* 1907.

FROM *THE EVENING POST*, 18 APRIL 1903

Another new feature will be the resumption of jumping races.[46] In past years these races were run at Churchill Downs every year, but lately they were abandoned, and only a few neglected hedges stood out in the infield as reminders of the obsolete sport. This season will again see the timber-toppers racing on the steeple course....There are six jumps to the mile, including the water jump, which is the most trying leap of the course, and lies directly in front of the grandstand.

FROM "THE DERBY," *THE LOUISVILLE HERALD*, 2 MAY 1903

The main intent of it, to try out the three-year-olds of the year, is still the one purpose. But the weights have increased until the fillies are no longer in it, and the distance has been cut down...and the result is that the increased impost has year by year cut down the number of starters until now the field averages half-a-dozen.

The impost, or the total of the various entry fees, was $160 in 1903.[47] When the winner's purse was increased in 1896, so too were the number of horses nominated — 171. It would not be until 1928 that that number was exceeded. The number of horses running in the Kentucky Derby did not exceed ten until 1915. Jimmy Winkfield was aboard the favorite in the 1903 Derby, but he did not go on to win — a victory that would have tied him with Isaac Murphy as the winningest Derby jockey to that time.[48]

It should also be noted that the 1903 Derby was the first run on a Saturday afternoon. Also 1903 was made different by the extended use of the plant and grounds when the meeting was over.

FROM "FIRST CONCERT AT JOCKEY CLUB PARK," *THE COURIER-JOURNAL*, 1 JUNE 1903

Weber's Military Band, of Cincinnati, began an engagement at the Jockey Club Park yesterday afternoon. The opening was not as gay as was expected, owing to the inclemency of the weather. However, a fair-sized crowd was present in the afternoon and an enjoyable concert was given.

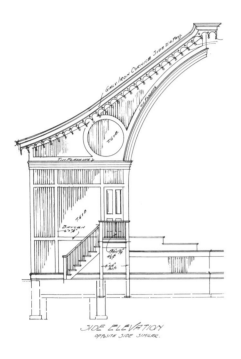

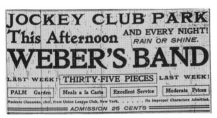

Above right: *ca.* 1905 post card of bandstand in front of grandstand. Above: South elevation of bandstand by D.X. Murphy & Bro. Bottom: From *The Courier-Journal,* 7 June 1903.

Since the close of the races at the noted course, two weeks ago, active preparations have been made to make the opening a grand success. Members of the New Louisville Jockey Club have made the park one of the most attractive places in the country for summer amusements. In place of the betting shed is a cafe. A bandstand has been erected on the grass, and on the beautiful lawn, benches and chairs have been placed.[49] The members of the Jockey Club can now point to the park as one of the most attractive places and a marked success. Then there are tanbark walks, growing flowers, Japanese lanterns and other embellishments to make the place attractive by day, gay by night and popular the summer through.

The selections of the band were received yesterday with great applause. While the programme embraced music of serious worth, the lovers of rag time came in for their full share. All the encores were responded to in that kind of music. Mr. John C. Weber, the director of the band, has dedicated a piece to the New Louisville Jockey Club, and it had the first place on the programme. It is a spirited march, and was well received.

FROM "CHARLES F. PRICE RESIGNS AS SECRETARY," *THE COURIER-JOURNAL,*
29 SEPTEMBER 1904

Charles F. Price, secretary and general manager of the New Louisville Jockey Club, and one of the most widely known racing officials in the country, yesterday afternoon resigned his position with the local racing organization. The resignation went into effect at once and was accepted by the directors of the club.

Mr. Price's successor was elected immediately after his resignation had been accepted. The new secretary is Lyman Davis, who during the past year has been the assistant secretary as well as the track superintendent of the New Louisville Jockey Club....

While the new secretary is known to comparatively few Louisville people he is a man experienced in thoroughbred racing and is well known to horsemen in the West. With the advice of Mr. Price at his command there is no reason why he should not prove an efficient and popular official. He acted as Mr. Price's assistant during the last spring meeting and has since then filled the position as track superintendent made vacant by the resignation of former Supt. Wohlgamuth.[50]

Lyman H. Davis had been a stable clerk at Latonia beginning in 1893, and after serving as secretary and handicapper there, he went to the Worth track near Chicago. Davis came to Churchill Downs in 1903 as assistant secretary and handicapper. He also worked at Empire City, Juarez, and other tracks, but never severed his association with Churchill Downs. He was superintendent of the greenhouses when he died in 1941 at the age of 71.[51]

Sometime in 1905 or shortly thereafter, Davis's duties as secretary and general manager were divided, and Matt Winn took on the added responsibilities of general manager.[52] Winn already had his hands full with his new duties as president of the American Turf Association.[53] This group had broken away from the Western Jockey Club which succeeded the American Turf Congress that Schulte had headed before tendering his resignation over the undesirable racing dates Churchill Downs continued to receive. In *Down the Stretch*, Winn says that when he requested more and better racing dates and was ignored, Churchill Downs departed the controlling organization. Winn helped formulate a competing racing body, of which he was elected president.[54] Capt. S. S. Brown, who owned the Kentucky Association track at Lexington, supported Winn's initiative, and when Ed Corrigan brought his Washington Park into the fold, another turf fray was underway.[55]

In the meantime, Winn had also become part of Mayor Grainger's administration as a member of the Louisville Board of Public Safety. During this 1904-1905 stint, he was made a Kentucky Colonel by Governor J. C. W. Beckham.[56]

FROM "FAMOUS BAND TO BE HEARD AT THE NEW JOCKEY CLUB PARK,"
THE COURIER-JOURNAL, 9 APRIL 1905

Lovers of music are looking forward with a good deal of pleasant anticipation to the coming series of concerts which will be given at New Jockey Club Park during the summer. Last year this was almost all the stay-at-homes in the southern part of the city had as a matter of recreation or pleasure in the warm months.

Manager Matt J. Winn, who will be at the head of the concerts during the coming season, was asked yesterday what arrangements had been made to gratify the local musical appetite. His reply was surprising, when the attractions during the past seasons are considered. The full list of attractions has not been made up to date, but what has been secured is certain to please the most critical.

The Duss band, J. S. Duss, conductor, will open the season June 11 and will play for two weeks. This famous orchestra will be followed by Morin's French military band. The conductor is Henry Morin, and the organization is one of the most noted bands in Paris. It contains fifty

FROM "APPOINTS," *THE COURIER-JOURNAL*,
26 MARCH 1904

Mayor Charles F. Grainger yesterday appointed the new Boards of Public Safety and Public Works, Matt J. Winn filling the place formerly held on the Board of Public Safety by Edward T. Tierney. No other change was made in the personnel of the two boards, but under the new boards every person holding position by appointment by either board will have to be reappointed.

Mr. Winn, the new member of the Board of Public Safety, is one of the best-known business men in the city, and although he has never taken any part in politics has always been a Democrat and for years has been a close personal friend of Mayor Grainger's. He was offered the position several days ago, and yesterday morning notified the Mayor that he would accept. The Mayor then called in the old members of the two boards and announced their reappointment. Mr. Winn was a caller at the office and was notified of his appointment.

In Mr. Winn the universal expression of opinion was that the Mayor has made a wise selection and that the new member will make an excellent official. He will not give up his business, but will devote all the time necessary to the position at the City Hall. Mr. Winn is a member of the Elks Lodge, is a leader in the Louisville Council, Knights of Columbus, and is vice president of the New Louisville Jockey Club.

pieces and two singers, and will play here for two weeks. Following Morin comes Creatore, the peculiar. All Louisville remembers Creatore. Last year on one night at the Jockey Club Park more than 5,000 people paid to see his eccentric gyrations—more people than ever before attended a musical production in this city. Creatore will be here for two weeks, and will be followed by Weber's band of fifty pieces. Next to Creatore, Weber is said to be the most popular musician who ever conducted a band in Louisville.

This ends the list up to date; but Manager Winn is negotiating with half a dozen of the most attractive bands of Europe to fill out the summer season. He said yesterday that he was after novelties because the local appetite seems to be for musical productions from abroad rather than for American bands.

FROM *THE THOROUGHBRED RECORD*, 21 OCTOBER 1905
Charles F. Grainger, President of the Louisville Jockey Club and Mayor of Louisville, closed a deal Wednesday for the purchase of Churchill Downs. The price is said to be $135,000 cash. Mayor Grainger is acting as trustee for a syndicate...The Jockey Club has been paying $4,500 a year to the Churchill heirs for the lease of the land, which comprises 81 acres. This lease has continued since 1874, and the club has paid $130,000 in rentals. Mr. Grainger and his associates thought it good policy to own the land instead of paying rent. It is evident that the owners of the Jockey Club have confidence in the future success of the racing game in that city or they would not invest so much ready cash.

The deed was recorded in Jefferson County Deed Book 631, p. 341, on 1 November 1905. Why Grainger and others purchased the property and not the New Louisville Jockey Club itself, is not known. But later, asserting that the property should fall under the control of the club, an agreement, dated 10 May 1907, was prepared and signed to effect that arrangement for a term of five years. At the end of the term, the amalgamation of the club's assets and the land was to be worth $300,000. The club's assets were to represent $138,000 and the land $162,000. No rent would be paid during the period, but Grainger and the other owners would "look to their appropriate part of the profits of the joint enterprise as compensation for the use thereof." After five years, a new corporation would be organized and capitalized at $300,000 and the two parties would receive the same proportional amounts of stock. The agreement was extended on 1 May 1912 for an additional four years.[58]

FROM *THE COURIER-JOURNAL*, 13 DECEMBER 1905
A man who ought to know stated yesterday afternoon that Lum Simons received a check for $25,000 as his part in the transaction which transferred Douglas Park from J. J. Douglas to Louis A. Cella and others prominent in the Western Jockey Club, the rival of the American Turf Association.[57] The same man declared that Mr. Douglas received $150,000 in New York [in] exchange for Douglas Park and other pieces of real estate, and that this amount was deposited by Mr. Douglas in a local bank on Monday. The Courier-Journal's informant also stated that Mr. Douglas's property, including three houses and lots on Douglas avenue and Bailey avenue, went in with the sale, the entire property embracing 126 7/8 acres and three dwelling houses, each of which rents for $25 per month. Mr. Douglas, it was stated, sold all the property possible in one lump in order to be rid of the worry connected with the ownership.

FROM "MR. VENNIE SAYS THERE IS NO WAR," *THE COURIER-JOURNAL*,
13 DECEMBER 1905

Andrew Vennie, of New York, arrived in the city yesterday from New Orleans and declared that there is no turf war at the Crescent City. Mr. Vennie is a stock-holder in the New Louisville Jockey Club and came here to visit Matt J. Winn, president of the American Turf Association. He will go to Pittsburgh with Messrs. Winn, Price, W. W. Hite and others, who will attend the funeral of the late Capt. S. S. Brown.

Samuel Smith Brown died on 11 December 1905 at the age of 63, at his home in Pittsburgh. A millionaire many times over, he became prominent in racing circles when Milton H. Young of Lexington sold him Troubadour with which Brown won the Suburban Handicap in 1886. Capt. Brown and Col. Young remained intimate friends, and Brown was proprietor of Senorita stock farm in Fayette County, named for his favorite horse. He had a half interest in the 1884 Derby winner Buchanan and owned the 1905 winner, Agile. In 1904, Brown purchased Lexington's old Kentucky Association race track from Charles Green of St. Louis. He made extensive improvements and put racing back on its feet in the Bluegrass. The plant was sold in 1935 and dismantled for a federal low-cost housing project. The old iron gates with the Kentucky Association letters cast in them now fittingly mark the entrance to the Keeneland Association grounds. Brown was also a stockholder and director of the New Louisville Jockey Club when he died.[59]

FROM "FIGHTS ANNEXATION," *THE COURIER-JOURNAL*, 10 MARCH 1906

The New Louisville Jockey Club and a number of residents in the vicinity of Churchill Downs yesterday filed suit to prevent annexation to the town of Oakdale of the territory occupied by them....

The plaintiffs say that their property is too sparsely settled to be converted into a town and that the cost of making alleys and streets would be intolerable to the property owners.[60]

FROM "PLUNGERS GET BUSY AT CHURCHILL DOWNS," *THE COURIER-JOURNAL*,
3 MAY 1906

The largest number of books to cut in for the regular three-day draw, some twenty-six in number, since the establishment of racing at the historic course in 1875, did business at the Downs yesterday. Many Knights of the Chalk, who occupy stools in the great betting enclosures of the metropolitan plants, were in line, among whom were to be seen the familiar faces of such top pricers as Steve L'Hommedieu, "Hops" Laudeman, Fred Cook, Herman Elrod, Freddie Peich, Joe Yeager, William Shannon, Paul Hoffman, J. Davis, and many others of equal note.

For Derby Day and considering the unknown quantity of many of the starters, the books laid prices that were exceptionally liberal, and the percentage was on a par with any first-class plant in the country.

FROM BARRY BINGHAM, SR., "THE KENTUCKY DERBY: A VERY SPECIAL RITE OF SPRING," *THE COURIER-JOURNAL & TIMES*, 28 APRIL 1974[61]

The First Kentucky Derby winner I ever saw was Sir Huon. I was asleep in my cradle when he took the purse in the Churchill Downs classic in 1906, but a few years later I was introduced to him at Bashford Manor. (The farm belonged to my great-uncle George Long, who owned two Derby winners and bred a third.) A stable boy, holding me tightly, put me up on Sir Huon's back for a moment. Another kept a grip on the handsome bay's halter.

Since then I have seen many Derby winners in their hour of triumph...I have watched the English Derby, with its hordes of humanity spilled across the greensward of Epsom Downs, its gypsies, its "pearlies" calling the odds in raucous Cockney accents. I have gone to the races in Singapore, in the company of an entrepreneur with the wonderful name of Run-Run Shaw; in Nairobi; at ramshackle tracks on Caribbean islands; and amid the elegance of the Longchamps course in Paris. But nothing has for me touched the drama of our own Kentucky Derby...

Tell a person anywhere in the world that you are from Kentucky and watch his face light up. "Oh yes," he will respond, "that's where they run the Derby." All the services of all the public-relations experts on Madison Avenue couldn't have bought us that spark of recognition, that touch of instant interest.

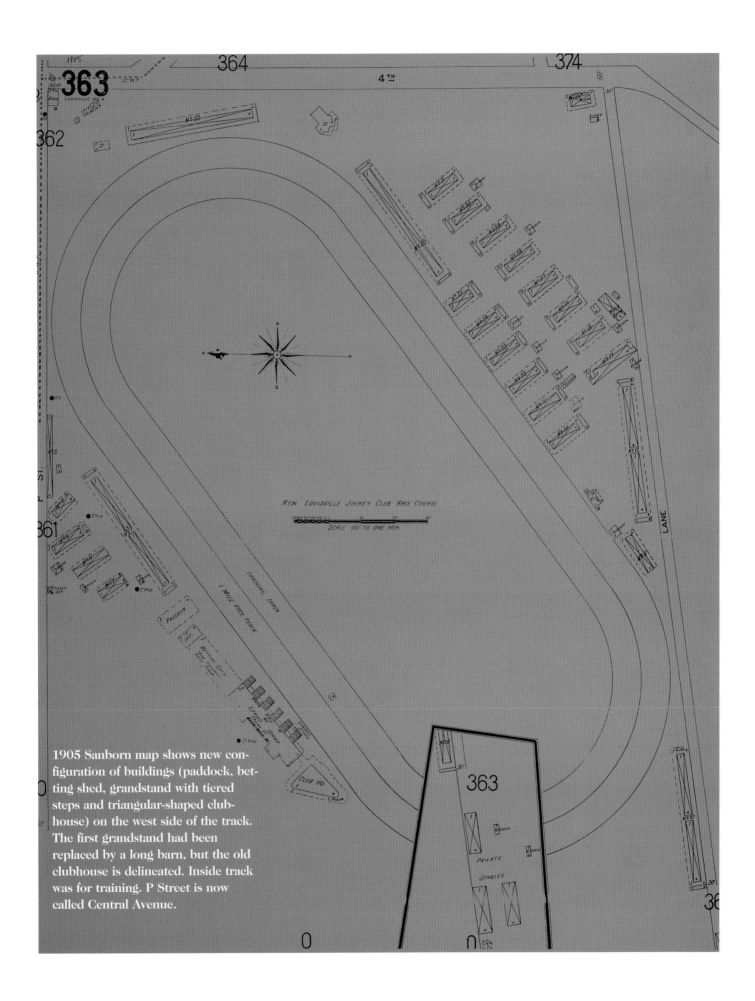

NEW LOUISVILLE JOCKEY CLUB RACE COURSE

SCALE 100' TO ONE INCH

1905 Sanborn map shows new configuration of buildings (paddock, betting shed, grandstand with tiered steps and triangular-shaped clubhouse) on the west side of the track. The first grandstand had been replaced by a long barn, but the old clubhouse is delineated. Inside track was for training. P Street is now called Central Avenue.

Sir Huon won the 32nd Kentucky Derby on 2 May 1906. The third Falsetto colt to win the Derby was also the third winner bred by George Long. He owned two of them at the time they raced.

George James Long (1853-1930) followed in his father's footsteps at the Dennis Long Company, manufacturing cast-iron pipe. In the late 1880s, he became interested in race horses and purchased Bashford Manor, the old J. B. Wilder place on the Bardstown Road. He traveled to Erdenheim Farm to acquire the dam of his first (1892) Kentucky Derby winner, Azra. Long served on the committee on appeals of the American Turf Congress, was appointed to Kentucky's first racing commission. He was a director of the Kentucky Jockey Club and its successor, the American Turf Association, at his death. By that time he had dispersed his stock and Bashford Manor's colors would not be seen on the track again.[62]

FROM "BROWN DICK DYING AT THE DOWNS," *THE COURIER-JOURNAL*, 3 MARCH 1906

"Brown Dick," the most widely known colored horseman in the world, a man who has trained some of the most noted horses both East and West for the last forty years, is dying of pneumonia in the living part of stable No. 11 at Churchill Downs.

This news will come as a shock to all men who own thoroughbreds throughout America, because "Brown Dick" is as popular and as well liked on the metropolitan tracks of the East as he is here, at Memphis, New Orleans or in California.

"Brown Dick" owned Ben Brush, one of the greatest race horses of his day, and sold him for $20,000. He owned and trained Plaudit, which he sold to John E. Madden as a two-year-old for $12,000, and with which Madden won the Kentucky Derby in 1898. He has owned and trained hundreds of crack thoroughbreds, but these two were his latest successes.

Years ago Brown Dick was a familiar figure at Monmouth Park, Long Branch, Saratoga and at other great racing centers in the East, but of late years he has confined his efforts mostly to training horses for the Western races, and has been uniformly successful.

"Brown Dick's" real name is Ed Brown. At present he is in charge of the horses belonging to Dr. J. D. Neet. He had been feeling bad for several months and concluded that his ailment was stomach trouble. He went to West Baden Springs and remained ten days, returning here about two weeks ago, when he contracted pneumonia. The attending physicians stated last night he was dangerously ill and that they had little hope for his recovery.

Edward Dudley Brown's body was returned to Midway for burial. "Six colored trainers will act as pallbearers." But the days were dwindling when blacks would play a prominent part in horse racing. Isaac Murphy had been dead for a decade. Jimmy Winkfield, after losing the 1903 Kentucky Derby on the favored horse and forgoing his third straight win, had gone to ride in Russia. Only William Walker was around to carry on

FROM "BROWN DICK PASSES AWAY," *THE COURIER-JOURNAL*, 12 MAY 1906

"Brown Dick" was a Negro gentleman, and it was fitting that this man, who had handled and owned some of the most noted horses this country has ever produced, from Lexington to Ben Brush, should die in the home of another noted colored trainer, Bob Campbell, who handled the horses of the famous "Lucky" Baldwin. He sold horses for many thousands of dollars, but he died practically penniless and yesterday afternoon when word of his death reached Churchill Downs a subscription was at once started among the horsemen to defray the funeral expenses, and Ed Corrigan started off the list with $50.

the tradition. Racing was altogether different. The old horse farm operations, tied to the land for generations by sporting tradition and a network of loyal black trainers and jockeys, were being undermined by the likes of George J. Long, who made their fortunes far from the land, and who could start in racing from scratch and become competitive in just a few years.

Fine horses were no longer a necessity; the breed need not be improved. Transportation was being mechanized over night. Henry Ford and others were seeing to that. The emphasis was shifting from the farm to the track, and racing was becoming increasingly urbanized. Edward Brown had been born on the eve of the Civil War. He had done on the track what no African-American man had ever done before, or would do to this day. His only son, Lee L. Brown, after attending Eckstein Norton Institute, taught school, was a deputy sheriff, secretary of the board of the Louisville Urban League, a Republican, and a member of the Boy Scout Court of Honor.[63]

From sketches in "Western Jockey Club Magnates Confer In Louisville, But Do Nothing Important," *The Courier-Journal*, 2 May 1906.

FROM "LOCAL RACING MEN WELL PLEASED," *THE COURIER-JOURNAL*, 7 MARCH 1906

Both officials [Matt Winn and Charles F. Grainger] are well satisfied with what they learned in the State Capital regarding the Jack Chinn Race Track Bill, and Mr. Winn, who is president of the American Turf Association, will leave for New Orleans to-night to attend a meeting of the association which he has called for Thursday afternoon at the Crescent City.

Most of the details concerning the bill have been printed in the Courier-Journal, but it was not known until last night, when Messrs. Winn and Grainger arrived, that the measure which is sure to become a law this week, was calculated to benefit the New Louisville Jockey Club or the American Turf Association, the controlling body, and would make the opposition, the Western Jockey Club, which owns Douglas Park, "be good."[64]

The bill was framed by the breeders of the Bluegrass, who claim to have the interests of the turf in Kentucky at heart, and at least three of them, or a majority, will be members of the commission. The other two members will be appointed from the race track interests of the State.[65]

FROM "PRESIDENT CHOSEN," *THE THOROUGHBRED RECORD*, 12 MAY 1906

Breckinridge Castleman, a son of Gen. John B. Castleman and a young man well-known in Louisville society circles, has accepted the presidency of the newly named Castleton Jockey Club, which, up to Wednesday, was known as the Douglas Park Jockey Club.[66]

Thursday morning Gen. Castleman declined the presidency in a letter to Presiding Judge A. W. Hamilton. Gen. Castleman, in this letter, stated that he found it impossible to accept the presidency on account of his connection with and the development of Louisville's park system.

FROM "PEACE ON TURF A CERTAINTY," *THE COURIER-JOURNAL*, 1 JUNE 1906

The turf war is now over. Both the Western Jockey Club and the American Turf Association factions are satisfied, and the peace pact between Joseph Rhinock, representing Latonia, and Louis Cella, representing the various tracks of the Western Jockey Club, has been ratified by the American Turf Association...

It is quite probable that a new turf body will be formed within the next few months, or prior to the fall meetings in Louisville. It is said that the name of the new body will be the United Turf Association. Realizing the great executive ability and the honesty of Col. Matt J. Winn, who served as president of the American Turf Association, members of both factions will endeavor to persuade him to head the new body.

Col. Winn is anxious to retire from the game, and it is known that he will refuse to accept the honor. However, such a strong fight will be made that it does not seem as though he can refuse to accept. Louis Cella is one of those who fought Col. Winn in the past, but who will now urge that he be elected as president of the United Turf Association.

The conflict was avoided principally because the improvements at Douglas Park were not ready in time for the announced summer meet. The merger of the Western Jockey Club and the American Turf Association into the United Turf Association did not take place, and Matt Winn certainly did not retire from racing as *The Courier-Journal* had indicated he was wont to do. He was poised, actually, to expand his base of influence. Douglas Park opened its new plant in September and it was well received — even by Matt Winn.[67]

FROM "SPLENDID OPENING OF FALL MEETING AT DOUGLAS PARK,"
THE COURIER-JOURNAL, 4 SEPTEMBER 1906

A beautiful race track, bright and new in all the glory of fresh paint and flying pennants; with a splendid card of six races composed of the highest class thoroughbreds now performing in the West; a crowd of more than 20,000 people on holiday-pleasure bent — these were the conditions under which the initial meeting at Douglas Park was begun yesterday afternoon. A more auspicious opening could not have been wished for by the most ardent supporters of the Western Jockey Club, under the auspices of which the meeting is being held....

In all the vast crowd it was easy to pick out men, who, until a few short weeks ago, constituted the backbone of the American Turf Association, the rival of the organization which has invaded Kentucky. Matt J. Winn, president of the American Turf Association, was there and had only words of praise for the plant, for the size of the crowd and the class of the sport; Congressman Joe Rhinock, a heavy stockholder in Latonia and City Park tracks, had come all the way from Washington to be present at the opening; Pat Dunne, Edward Corrigan's nephew, was not only present, but started horses in the various races....

James J. Douglas driving at Churchill Downs, *ca.* 1905. Balconies with ornate railings cantilevered over space between steps. Opposite: Grandstand scene while the 1906 Derby was being run.

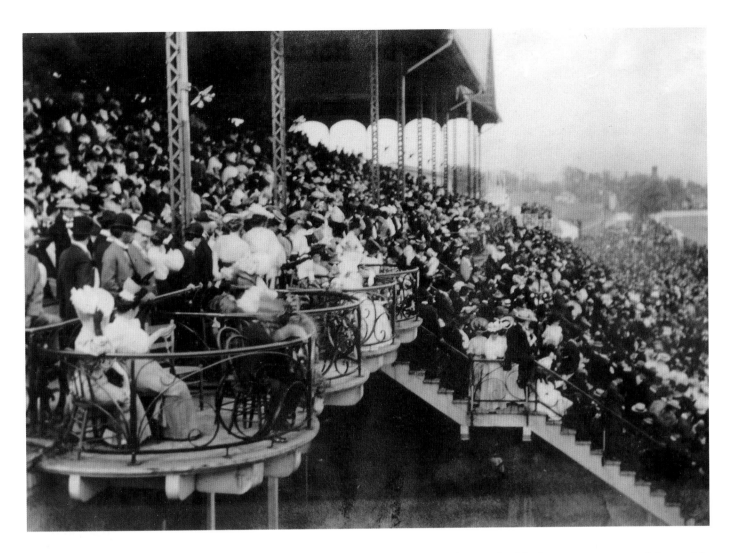

FROM "NEW JOCKEY CLUB IS INCORPORATED," *THE COURIER-JOURNAL*, 10 MARCH 1907

The Louisville Racing Association filed articles of incorporation yesterday....The incorporators and their respective holdings are: M. J. Winn, fifty shares; C. F. Grainger, fifty shares; H. C. Applegate, fifty shares; Louis Cella, 147 shares; John Hachmeister, three shares. It is provided that there shall be no limit to the maximum debt.

The women were perfectly charmed with the arrangement of the architecture of the grand stand that allows them to have a good look down into the betting shed.[68] Being barred from the betting shed, the next best thing is to hang over the banisters and feast their eyes on the seething tumult below. They left the boxes, and between races draped themselves over the railing at the back of the grand stand and felt themselves right in the midst of things, as it were.

FROM "BIG TURF DEAL GOES THROUGH," *THE COURIER-JOURNAL*, 26 FEBRUARY 1907
The interests financial and otherwise of Louisville's two big race tracks, Churchill Downs and Douglas Park, will be pooled within a few days and formed into a holding company which will conduct both organizations. This company will be controlled by the following officers and directors: President — Charles F. Grainger. Vice President and General Manager — Matt J. Winn. Secretary — Hamilton Applegate. Treasurer — John Hachmeister. Directors — Charles F. Grainger, Matt J. Winn, Hamilton Applegate, John Hachmeister and Louis A. Cella.

These officials will conduct the race meetings at both the local tracks, the plan being to give a thirty-day meeting at Churchill Downs in the spring and a meeting of the same duration at Douglas Park in the fall. The same officials who will officiate at Churchill Downs in the spring will act at Douglas Park next fall and the profits of the two meetings will be divided among those interested.

This is the biggest deal that has taken place in turf circles hereabouts in a number of years. It has been on for some time, but became known yesterday only because one of the directors who had promised not to talk of the affair until the deal was actually consummated saw fit to give out the story.

When the lease agreements between the Louisville Racing Association and its two tracks expired in 1912, the New Louisville Jockey Club paid the Douglas Park Jockey Club $7,500 in settlement and satisfaction of all claims, and the tracks parted company — at least for a while.[69] Even though additional improvements would be made at Douglas Park, it would flounder until 1918 when the Kentucky Jockey Club, a new holding company controlling (in part) Churchill Downs, purchased the nearby track for a training site.[70]

FROM "READY TO HELP STATE FAIR," *THE LOUISVILLE TIMES,*
3 SEPTEMBER 1907

Col. Matt J. Winn, upon whom the turf spot light is centered, by reason of his most recent achievement in making the Empire City race meeting, at Yonkers, such a great success, is back home to lend his assistance, in making the State Fair, to be held at Churchill Downs, the biggest event of its kind ever held in Kentucky.

The Empire City track was owned by James Butler, a fifty-year-old native of Ireland who had already made a fortune establishing the first chain of grocery stores in this country when he met Matt Winn in Chicago in 1905.[71] They had a mutual friend in Ed Corrigan, who introduced them, and Butler was anxious to get Winn's help in re-opening the track he had acquired in Yonkers. Winn may have turned forty-four but he was a mere novice in racing, yet they became fast friends and forged several major track projects during the next two decades. As Winn recalled for Frank Menke in *Down the Stretch* (p. 65), after the success of the initial meeting at Empire City, Butler told him: "You team up with me here, and as soon as we get this place established, we'll buy or build some other race tracks, and have a lot of sport, and make ourselves a lot of money." This appealed to Winn, who had nothing to show for his days in the grocery business and who had a large family to support. He would lead Churchill Downs in a new and dynamic direction. Whereas Meriwether Lewis Clark had spread the race track's influence through his service as a track official, Matt J. Winn used his skill as an owner and operator to bring Churchill Downs to the forefront of racing. While he probably never once started a race, Winn certainly put a great many in motion.

FROM "FINE START FOR RACE MEETING," *THE COURIER-JOURNAL,* 11 AUGUST 1907

New York, August 10 — For the first time in eight years thoroughbred race horses were seen in action to-day at the Empire City track, near Yonkers. Since 1900 nothing but trotting events have been held on this course, but the Empire City Trotting Club succeeded in getting dates from the Jockey Club and inaugurated a midsummer meeting which will last eighteen days. Everything gives promise of a successful meeting. Only two favorites won this afternoon, but the card was a splendid one and the racing gave general satisfaction. It was conceded on all sides that the sport was of a much better class than was expected.

For those who journeyed to the track to-day Secretary Lyman Davis had prepared a bumper card of six races, which consisted of a handicap at one mile as a feature, three selling events and two allowance affairs. In all, the fields were well balanced and made up of horses of good class,

with the result that a large attendance was on hand to do battle with the "bookies."

More than 10,000 people journeyed from New York to see the sport. The scene both in the betting ring and paddock was typically Western. It looked as if the regulars at Churchill Downs and Latonia had been transplanted here....

Many noted Kentuckians were seen in the big crowd. Congressman Ollie James and Joe Rhinock led the division. Arthur Board, George Coder, Verney Sanders, Victor Henderson and others were here from Louisville. Matt J. Winn entertained all his friends in splendid fashion.

Above: Covered walkway from P Street (Central Avenue) into grandstand. Back of clubhouse is pictured at right, *ca.*1907. From Charles F. Price, *Churchill Downs....(ca.* 1909). Right: From Illustrated Sunday Magazine of *The Courier-Journal*, 5 May 1907.

OFFICERS OF THE NEW LOUISVILLE JOCKEY CLUB

CHAS. F. GRAINGER PRESIDENT AND ASSOCIATE JUDGE.

MATT J. WINN VICE PRESIDENT & GENERAL MANAGER

CHAS F. PRICE PRESIDING JUDGE.

WILLIAM SHELLEY ASSOCIATE JUDGE.

LYMAN H. DAVIS, SECRETARY AND HANDICAPPER

HAMILTON APPLEGATE TREASURER

FROM "AUTOMOBILE AND HORSE RACES," *THE LOUISVILLE TIMES*,
19 SEPTEMBER 1907

A running race and three automobile races composed the card at the State Fairgrounds [at Churchill Downs] yesterday. With the exception of the first automobile race, made in unusually slow time, the sport was excellent....Some 200 machines paraded around the track before the automobile races.

FROM *THE COURIER-JOURNAL*, 27 MARCH 1908

Steeplechase races will be one of the big features at Churchill Downs this spring....Harry Carr, superintendent of Churchill Downs, has the steeplechase course on a par with the best Eastern courses, the turf of the course being as level almost as a billiard table. Big green mounds mark the route for the jumpers.

Carr has been engaged for weeks in grading the track. Every low spot has been filled, and the silt, which has washed down in the ditches, is now being thrown back onto the track proper. It will liven up considerably in the next few days.

FROM "DERBY COLTS GET GALLOPS," *THE COURIER-JOURNAL*,
26 MARCH 1908

Messrs. Winn and Grainger selected the places for locating the eleven pari-mutuel machines which will be used at the Downs henceforth....the system of wagering which comes into vogue again after nearly thirty years of disuse and which promises to prove the salvation of racing insofar as betting is concerned.[72]

FROM "MAYOR DECLARES AGAINST BETTING," *THE COURIER-JOURNAL*,
4 MAY 1908

Mayor James F. Grinstead, in a letter which was received yesterday by Charles F. Grainger, president of the New Louisville Jockey Club, has declared that no betting on the races will be tolerated at Churchill Downs during the race meeting which is scheduled to begin there tomorrow.[73]

Start of a five-mile handicap at Churchill Downs. From *The Courier-Journal*, 9 July 1910.

FROM "CHURCHILL DOWNS THE FASTEST AUTO COURSE," *THE COURIER-JOURNAL*, 9 SEPTEMBER 1908

The track is considered one of the fastest for automobile racing in the United States.[74]

This fact was not known until racing experts learned of the time made on it at the meeting of the Kentucky State Fair last year.

The Mayor, in his letter to Mr. Grainger, states that he has directed the Board of Public Safety to detail for duty at Churchill Downs during the race meeting a sufficient number of policemen to protect the public against rogues and pickpockets, and also to prevent betting by what is known as the pari-mutuels system, pool selling, or any other system, in use at race tracks....

In a lengthy statement given out by W. Marshall Bullitt, chairman of the Board of Public Safety, last night, he compares the pari-mutuels system of betting with the old-fashioned gambling game of keno...He further argues that racetrack betting is tolerated in but four States of the union, namely—Kentucky, New York, California and Louisiana, and that in two of these States an earnest effort is being made to abolish the practice of betting at race tracks.

FROM "CHAT OF THE COURSE, "*THE COURIER-JOURNAL*, 8 MAY 1908

The machines are unquestionably the fairest way that has ever been devised to wager on a horse race....While you do not know what odds you are going to get before the race...you are bound to get an equal break with the others who bet on the race.

FROM "PARI-MUTUEL WAGERS UPHELD," *THE COURIER-JOURNAL*, 7 MAY 1908

The right of the New Louisville Jockey Club to sell combination pools or accept wagers with the pari-mutuel machines was fully sustained to-day by the Court of Appeals....It was decided that the Legislature had intended, by exempting from the provisions of the gambling act of 1893 combinations or French pools, to allow betting by such methods.[75]

FROM REPORT OF CHARLES F. GRAINGER TO THE
STATE RACING COMMISSION, 1908

I have known of no meeting that has been so free from criticism. This I attribute not so much to the vigilance of the officials as to the protection offered in the revival of the Pari-Mutual system of betting. Under the former mode of bookmaking, whether justly or unjustly there was much complaint of fraud.

Bookmakers owned and raced large stables of horses, engaged by contract skilled jockeys, employed clockers, and paid for and secured stable information, gaining to them advantages not possessed or attainable by the public. Adverse comment followed and in some cases scandal.[76]

This objectionable feature, one which will pertain to bookmaking as long as it continues, has been entirely eliminated by the Pari-Mutual system. Under the latter there is practically no incentive for fraud. There is no remuneration for dishonesty as is possible with bookmaking. No jockey, owner, bookmaker or other can become a beneficiary of fraud or connivance thereof, for the reason that no direct or assured benefits can accrue.

FROM "OLLER TALKS OF PARI-MUTUELS," *THE COURIER-JOURNAL*,
27 SEPTEMBER 1908

H. C. Applegate, treasurer of the Louisville Racing Association, has returned here from a trip to Paris, his mission abroad being to personally interview M. Joseph Oller,[77] the inventor of the pari-mutuel method of wagering on races, which was revived in America by the New Louisville Jockey Club at its meeting last spring at Churchill Downs. A return to the

French system after a lapse of many years aroused keen interest, and it has since been the subject of wide comment, ranging from praise to condemnation. So confident are Charles F. Grainger, president of the new Louisville Racing Association, and M. J. Winn, the general manager and vice president of that organization, that the method will prove the salvation of the speculative end of the turf that they never have wavered in their opinion. Because of this firm attitude they assigned Mr. Applegate to pay a visit to Oller, in order that he might thoroughly acquaint himself with every detail of the system.[78]

Applegate experienced no difficulty in locating Oller in Paris. It is related of the inventor of the pari-mutuels that he is one of the most popular, clever and enterprising citizens of the great capital of France. In addition to operating a mammoth establishment for printing pari-mutuel supplies, he owns and operates racecourses and is the promoter and manager of several theatrical enterprises. At 83 Oller is alert and active in the manipulation of his extensive business interests....

Mr. Applegate made an investigation relating to the totalisator, which shows the various amounts staked on horses as the betting progresses. He ascertained that in 1867 Oller had, with M. Leon Sari, the late manager of the Folies Bergère, assisted by Garnier, the famous clockmaker, invented the totalisator. This machine not only totalized the sums, but it also did all the calculations, and, after deducting the percentage, showed on a special dial the return on the winning and placed horses.

FROM MATT J. WINN IN *DOWN THE STRETCH*, PAGE 76

The original machines, built 40 or 45 years before in France, no longer were suited to our purpose. And six weren't enough. So we called in a man named Schuman, who was both a patent attorney and a draftsman.[79] We gave him our ideas for an improved machine. He made blueprints, which went to Grainger, who manufactured the first American machines in his iron foundry, in Louisville.

FROM "ENTRY LIST IS GROWING FAST," *THE COURIER-JOURNAL*,
6 SEPTEMBER 1908

The Churchill Downs racetrack is now being put in readiness for the races. A force of men are working daily in rolling the track in order that it will be as hard as is possible to make it....so compact that there will be little or no dust raised by the racing cars. The grounds....will look like they do on Derby day.

By 1909, horse racing had been curtailed or abolished in all but three states – Kentucky, New York, and Maryland. Winter racing, therefore, was precluded, and as Matt Winn made clear in *Down the Stretch*, racing could hardly survive without it. The gravity of the situation brought on by the reform movement was not lost on the eastern racing establishment — John G. Follansbee in particular. The native Californian, educated at Harvard, had been in racing in the East for some years and he had cattle

Jockey Club Juarez had the same configuration of structures as Churchill Downs and was also designed by D.X. Murphy & Bro.

and mining interests in the West and in Mexico. His uncle was the Wall Street financier and racing mogul, James R. Keene, who along with his brother-in-law, Foxhall Daingerfield, had made Castleton Farm, Lexington, into "the most prominent Thoroughbred breeding nursery in the world."[80] Follansbee interested others in racing just across the Rio Grande River from El Paso, Texas, where reformers could be expected to stay clear of the likes of Pancho Villa. Matt Winn was brought on to put the operation into working order as he had done at Empire City. Jim Butler provided additional financial insurance; the management team and crew from Churchill Downs came along too. D. X. Murphy & Bro. drew up the plans for the track buildings.

John Follansbee, the president of the Jockey Club Juarez, died in late 1914. Winter racing survived in Mexico until 1917, despite the civil unrest, but by then the track had fulfilled its mission to help racing survive during the doldrums of the progressive movement before the first World War.[81] Matt Winn had definitely established a niche for himself in racing.

FROM "DEATH KNELL TO BOOKMAKING," THE COURIER-JOURNAL, 11 DECEMBER 1909

By a decision of the Court of Appeals this morning upholding the constitutionality of the act creating the State Racing Commission, the death knell of bookmaking at racetracks in this State was sounded. The decision of the court fully and completely sustains the Racing Commission and the powers which are given it under the act of the Legislature. The court holds that the commission has complete control of racing in Kentucky, except where expressly excepted, and can regulate the manner of betting at those racetracks.

Left: Flight by Glenn H. Curtiss, 18 June 1910. Above: From *The Courier-Journal*, 12 June 1910.

After months of delay the famous Latonia case was decided to-day. The Latonia racetrack defied the Racing Commission and refused to do away with bookmakers, when granted dates for a meeting. The commission wanted betting conducted with the pari-mutuels as at Louisville, but the officials of the Latonia Agricultural Association, as the Latonia track corporation is called, wanted bookmaking, so the orders of the Racing Commission were disobeyed.[82]

FROM "AEROPLANE RACE FEATURE OF DAY," *THE COURIER-JOURNAL*,
20 JUNE 1910

For the first time in his experience, Glenn H. Curtiss had a real neck and neck race with a competitor who used the Curtiss machine. He and James C. Mars flew at 5:45 o'clock yesterday afternoon, and tore off lap after lap around and above the race track at a speed of sixty miles an hour. The crowd which braved the threatened rain cheered wildly at the spectacular sight, for at times the two aeroplanes were but fifty feet apart....

Several motorcycle races took place and some exceptionally fast time was made by Freddy Huyck, the world's champion cyclist.

A month before Meridian won the 1911 Kentucky Derby, a landscaper from Bolton Abbey, Yorkshire, England, was hired by Matt Winn. Within a year, he was made superintendent of Churchill Downs — a position he would hold until he died in 1963. His influence and contributions to Churchill Downs, and the various other tracks that came under its purview, were enormous. The appearance of the grounds, and the structures as well, bore Tom Young's imprint. Flowers became his trademark, necessitating the construction of greenhouses. Even the track was manicured. He also became the person who dealt with the architects, taking advantage of his background in blueprint reading.

Thomas Young (1887-1963) had come from England to visit an uncle in Buffalo. He studied botany and landscaping in Canada before starting to work for the Buffalo firm of landscapers and architects, Townsend and Fleming.[84] Bryant Fleming had received commissions in Louisville to landscape William E. Chess's property called Winkworth (now Boxhill) and to design George W. Babcock's nearby residence (Rockledge), and to landscape Samuel C. Henning's place. Tom Young was sent to Louisville to supervise the work. Fleming would also later design Arden Valley (soon called the River Valley Club).[85]

FROM THE COURIER-JOURNAL, 4 MAY 1911

General Manager M. J. Winn opened a school of instruction for the clerks who will operate the new pari-mutuel machines this spring. The machines, twenty-one in number, are a big improvement over the old-style machines heretofore in use. Instead of taking two men to operate a machine one man is sufficient.

The betting ring with its long line of machines has the appearance of a large banking house and accommodation for the largest crowds is afforded without the inconvenience of past years.

FROM THE COURIER-JOURNAL, 9 MAY 1911

The New Louisville Jockey Club track was rolled for the first time this spring, and every night now Superintendent Keegan has it thoroughly drenched. He will roll it several more times this week, and he says unless there is a deluge of rain it will be fast for the Derby Saturday next....

Capt. W. H. Fenchler, steward of the Jockey Club Juarez track, arrived here last night to see the Kentucky Derby run next Saturday and will remain in attendance at Churchill Downs during most of the coming meeting here. He reports that on leaving El Paso, Tex., he met Price McKinney,[86] the Pittsburgh [Cleveland] steel magnate, and J. G. Follansbee, of New York, and both informed him they would be in Louisville to see the 1911 Kentucky Derby run. McKinney is a heavy stockholder in the Juarez racing plant and Follansbee is a steward at the Mexico track and a son-in-law of the famous turfman J. R. Keene....

FROM "FIELD AT RACE COURSE," THE COURIER-JOURNAL, 14 MAY 1911

Thousands of persons witnessed the running of the Derby from the field yesterday. It was free, and the spectators who occupied it arrived early, many having their lunches with them. They were scattered about over the spacious green, some taking shelter from the blazing sun under hedge rows, while others hoisted umbrellas in their efforts to avoid the burning rays until time for the historic race to be run. In the center of the track-inclosed green was what was termed by some the "German village." It was covered by a huge tent, and chairs were drawn up to tables for the

---

FROM "CURTISS MAKES A TRIAL FLIGHT," *THE COURIER-JOURNAL*, 18 JUNE 1910

Rising in the air as gracefully as a bird, the roar of the propellor blade startled the group of onlookers who had been hanging around all day watching the machine assembled. Glenn H. Curtiss last evening shortly before dusk made two short practice flights around the Churchill Downs track.[83]

Curtiss was on nettles all day, anxious to feel the throb of his engine behind him and when his mechanicians had put on the last touch he could not resist the temptation to try it out.

The machine was pulled from its tent and pushed to the middle of the infield. The propellor was revolved once and the mighty sixty-horsepower engine responded at once. Curtiss manipulated a few valves and in less than three minutes he was ready to fly.

accommodation of those who had the price of liquid refreshments. A score or more of coatless men, perspiring from every pore, were kept busy dispensing beer and sandwiches. They worked like Trojans, and popping sounds that accompanied the uncorking of bottles resembled a fusillade of shots.

Vehicles of every description, from the coal cart to the highly-polished automobile with brass trimmings, occupied the field. For the most part they were drawn up near the finish line, and each was filled to capacity. Pretty girls, wearing white dresses, picture hats and dainty, high-heeled slippers, smiled patronizingly from a big touring car upon a bunch of dusky damsels who occupied a two-horse coal wagon. Despite the contrast the two vehicles occupied points of vantage side by side, and it was hard to tell which party enjoyed the running of the Derby most.

It was a gala day for the colored lovers of racing. Negroes made up two-thirds of those in the field. Half-grown colored boys scampered over the grass-covered inclosure, their teeth shining like ivory and their eyes round with excitement. Bent old men leaned heavily upon their canes, waiting for the race of the day to be run. Newsboys, most of whom had taken an entire day off, bet pennies on the result of the Derby. Nearly everybody in the big inclosure was desirous of making a wager, no matter how small. As there were no betting machines in the field most of the wagers were made between friends.

FROM *THE COURIER-JOURNAL*, 9 MAY 1911

While racing hereabouts has lost some of the spectacular features which [it] obtained in the day of the bookmaker, it has, as a consequence, come to be recognized as a sport and not solely a medium of speculation. This is a condition that is expected to elevate it materially in the eyes of the better classes and make for it thousands of staunch supporters.

FROM "McCURDY STAR OF ELKS' MEET," *THE COURIER-JOURNAL*, 3 SEPTEMBER 1911

With the possible exception of a few sprained collar buttons, due to the numberless varieties of plain and fancy sky-gazing indulged in by a crowd of about 6,500 people, and one bad spill, in which Will Shymanski, entrant in the international mule race, vaulted lightly over the head of his mount, there were no casualties at the opening of the Elks' aviation meet at Churchill Downs yesterday afternoon.

In a Gnome-driven biplane J. A. D. McCurdy made six flights, racing an automobile, attempting to reach an altitude record of 3,000 feet, and giving an exhibition of bomb throwing from aerial heights at a supposed battleship, blocked out in the infield.[87]

FROM "POOR MAN'S HORSE WINS AMERICA'S RICHEST RACE," *THE COURIER-JOURNAL*, 8 OCTOBER 1911

A poor man's horse won the Kentucky Endurance Stakes, the richest race run in America this year. The name of the horse is Messenger Boy, and while he was entered in a woman's name, he belongs to Eugene Lutz, of Cincinnati. After this splendid 3-year-old had galloped down to the wire, in front of Nadzu, a rich man's horse, a short, stockily-built man made his way toward the judges' stand. He wore a black sweater, a golf cap, and in appearance was anything but an ideal owner of the winner of the richest stake run in America this year....

Infield, Derby day, 10 May 1910. Tote board and judges' stand took up part of the training track. Old clubhouse was still standing in background (over the judges' stand).

Mr. Lutz tried to make a speech. He stammered and stalled and messed about and practically said nothing. What he actually did say was that he wished that he had time to fill the gold cup with wine and treat the assembled company. Of course, nobody wanted to be treated, and after Mr. Lutz had made his talk he went down the steps with the gold cup in his hand. In front of the stand waiting for him were half a dozen men who are worth many millions of dollars, and who own horses that are racing at the present meeting. He paid no attention to this brilliant company although each turfman tried to intercept his progress and say something of a congratulatory nature. He hurried across the track and sped through the emerald green of the infield, carrying the Tiffany cup in his hand. Far across the course his wife and two little girls were waiting for him....

Gene Lutz bought Messenger Boy from R. F. Carman, the Eastern millionaire, two years ago for $135. To-day the New Louisville Jockey Club has a check for Mr. Lutz for $4,950, and somewhere out in the southern part of the city there is a rather happy family and on the sideboard in the dining-room is a solid gold cup made by Tiffany & Co., of New York, which cost the Kentucky Racing Commission $1,000. This is the first valuable cup of any description that the Lutz family ever owned, and the check which awaits the winner in the office of the New Louisville Jockey Club is more money than they had ever dreamed of.

The Courier-Journal had carried on 18 May 1911 the announcement the State Racing Commission would sponsor a four-mile race at Churchill Downs in the fall, called the Kentucky Endurance Stakes. On the day of the race, 7 October 1911, the newspaper recalled: "Thirty-one years ago

Four mile Kentucky Endurance
Stakes, 7 October 1912, won by
Sotemia in world record time, 7:10
4/5. Trophy was presented by
Governor James B. McCreary to
trainer M. Feakes. Cars were parked
on south side of P Street
east of Seventh (Rodman) Street
(present site of Kentucky Derby
Museum).

Oct. 7. 1912
Time 7:10⅘ (World's Record)
Jockey E. Martin

Jim Malone won the last four-mile race ever run in Kentucky. This was in 1880. Previous to this or thirty-three years ago, on July 4, 1878, Molly McCarthy and Ten Broeck fought out their memorable battle." The mighty Ten Broeck's standing record for four miles of 7:15 3/4 had been eclipsed by Messenger Boy's 7:14 1/5. But, of course, when Ten Broeck set his record at Churchill Downs on 27 September 1876, it was his fourth win in two weeks and followed within three days his record three-mile Post Stakes victory.[88]

There was no going back, however, to the endurance tests of yesteryear as the State Racing Commission had envisioned. The Kentucky Endurance Stakes was run twice again — in the fall of 1912 and 1913 — and then abandoned.

FROM "DERBY TEEMS WITH SENTIMENT," *THE COURIER-JOURNAL*, 5 MAY 1912
This fascinating picture will loom in all of its radiance and splendor on the clubhouse lawn of the Jockey Club, back and forth on the lower promenade, up the broad stairway and bloom again in the newly-built boxes, twenty-six in number, on the roof of the building set apart for the exclusive use of the club members of the Jockey Club.[89] This is an innovation provided by Mr. Winn out of compliment to society, not alone in Louisville, but Kentucky and the union, for year after year the elite journey to Churchill Downs to bestow their approval and patronage upon a sport characteristic of Kentucky and dear to the heart of every man and woman appreciative of a contest between blooded racers both fleet and courageous.

Mr. Winn's ideas concerning the comfort of the patrons of the Jockey Club, the beautification of the plant, remodeling it in keeping with up-to-date methods, the elimination of everything unsightly, the substitution of something better and pleasing, always elicit from his business associates,

Clubhouse with boxes just added to second level, 7 October 1912. From a panoramic photograph which distorted the curve of the track.

FROM "DERBY TEEMS WITH SENTIMENT," *THE COURIER-JOURNAL*, 5 MAY 1912
But at the clubhouse it will be found that the most extensive transformation has been wrought. On the roof over the promenade where the beauty and the chivalry of the whole country have on so many occasions formed such gay scenes there will be colonial style boxes, extending the entire length of the clubhouse. Each box will seat as many as ten persons. The boxes will be snow white and on Derby day will be decorated. Behind the boxes will be a promenade. Between races "Beauty Row" will be packed by women and their escorts visiting the occupants of the various boxes. Here, on Derby day, will be representatives of highest society extending from the four corners of the Republic. From this elevated position the clubhouse members and their guests may view the races without any obstruction whatever, never losing sight of the horses from start to finish at any part of the course.

Top: Donerail winning the 1913 Derby. Bottom: Caricature of Matt Winn and his wife and seven daughters. From *Kentuckians As We See Them* (1905).

Mr. Grainger and Col. Andrew Vennie, hearty approval, so when he decides to make alterations and improvements no discussion ensues as to the advisability of doing this or that simply because it represents a heavy expenditure of money. Liberality and progressiveness are the keynotes with the Jockey Club, judging by what has been done heretofore, by what is being done now and what Mr. Winn has in contemplation for the future.

This system is what has made Mr. Winn the foremost and most successful manager of race courses in both America and Mexico. It brought to him in New York, before adverse legislation there closed the race tracks, unreserved admiration from the metropolitan turfites. It has enabled him to securely establish in Mexico one of the greatest racing plants to be found anywhere....

In order to relieve the congestion of previous Derby days Mr. Winn will have thirty-two pari-mutuel machines in operation. Three will be available for clubhouse members, which will be located just outside the entrance to the clubhouse, almost opposite the judges' stand. In the betting ring proper will be twenty-nine machines. Where the boards heretofore displayed the entries in the six daily races along with the names of the jockeys will hereafter be occupied by five cashiers' stands for the cashing of $25 and $10 tickets. In all there will be twenty-three cashiers. Every arrangement has been made to facilitate everything in connection with the pari-mutuel system.

This will be the last spring for the big stable which stands alongside the paddock.[90] This summer it will be removed. All of the ground adjacent to the paddock will be graded and sodded. Trees will be planted, just as they have been in the infield, which has been graded and planted with grass seed....Mr. Winn will close the inside track to trainers and beautify it. Here flowers will bloom from the far stretch turn to a point far beyond the clubhouse turn.

Mary Doyle "Mollie" Winn, 45, died on 15 August 1912, leaving seven daughters without a mother and Matt J. Winn a widower. Three children had died in infancy. She was the daughter of John and Mary Doyle and was educated at Nazareth Academy. The Winns were married on 20 November 1888. At the time of her death, they resided at 606 West Broadway.[91]

Before departing for Juarez, Mexico, for the 100-day meeting beginning there on Thanksgiving Day, 1912, Matt Winn went to Colorado for a rest. Preparations for the Juarez meet were taking place at the New Louisville Jockey Club, despite reports of revolutionary activity in Mexico.[92]

Also at Churchill Downs, 290-horsepower race cars and motorcycles were tearing up the course.[93]

FROM *THE COURIER-JOURNAL*, 10 MAY 1913

There will be a greater sprinkling of Eastern turfmen on hand to see the Derby run off to-day than ever gathered on a race track in Kentucky.

CHURCHILL DOWNS
DERBY DAY
MAY 9th 1914

Among those of national reputation, and a majority of whom are leading lights as members of the Jockey Club, are A. Belmont, chairman of that organization....This is Mr. Belmont's first appearance on Derby day at Churchill Downs, and he will be accompanied by his wife, formerly Miss Eleanor Robson.[94]

The 1913 Derby was a bittersweet day for Matt Winn, who had witnessed the 1889 race with his bride, and probably many more after that with her. But for Churchill Downs the future was finally promising. Donerail, ridden by Roscoe Goose, won in a then-record time, paying a whopping

Infield section from a slightly deteriorated panoramic photograph.

FROM *THE COURIER-JOURNAL*, 4 MAY 1914

A big improvement has been made in the carriage entrance to the Downs and this is now one of the most pleasing aspects of this portion of the grounds.

FROM *THE COURIER-JOURNAL*,
10 MAY 1914

While no filly has ever won the Kentucky Derby, in the last three sessions, members of this sex have finished in the show hole every time. In 1912 Flamma was third; last season it was Gowell and yesterday Bronzewing ran in that position.

$184.90 for a $2 ticket (first available at Churchill Downs in 1911). Thomas P. Hayes, of Louisville, owned, trained, and bred Donerail.[95]

FROM *THE COURIER-JOURNAL*, 9 MAY 1914

Rain, which fell intermittently throughout the day and far into the night, forbade any hopes for a fast track this afternoon, and as a result the Derby field will not be as large as anticipated, but the class of the 3-year-old division of thoroughbreds, trained to the minute, will be ready to sport silks before the concourse which will gather at historic Churchill Downs this afternoon.

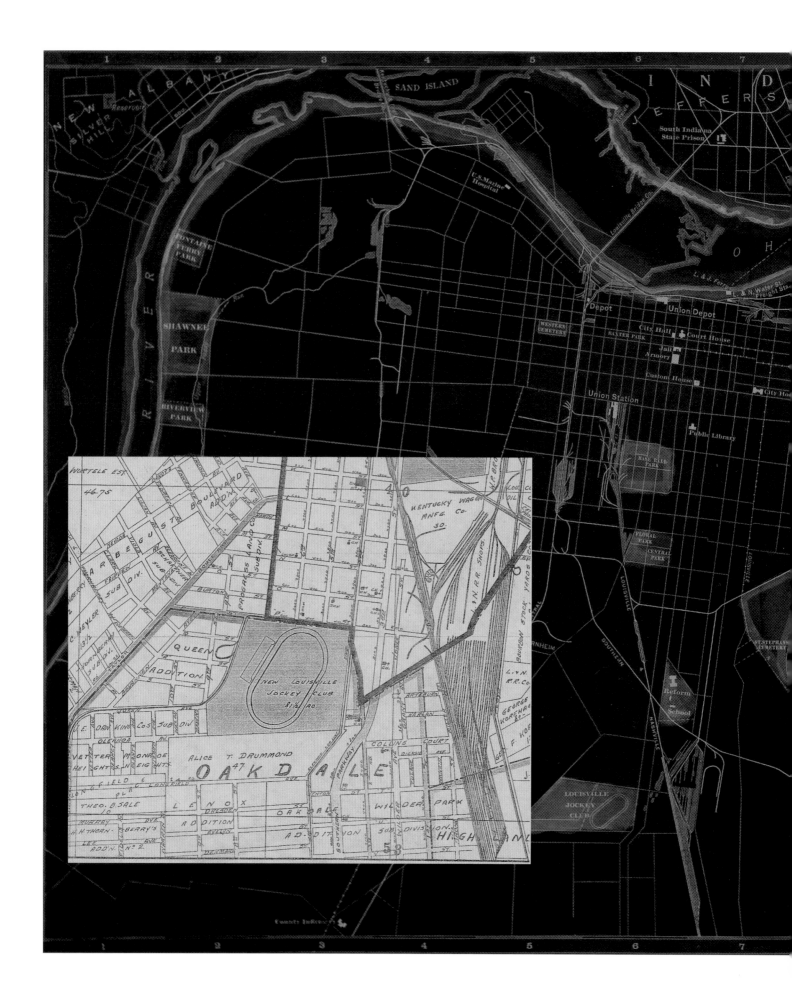

The 40th renewal was won by Old Rosebud, whose owner, Hamilton Clarke Applegate, produced a well-known whiskey by that name. Ham Applegate was also treasurer of the New Louisville Jockey Club, and his father was its principal stockholder. This may have been added incentive for Superintendent Tom Young, who found his track potholed with rain water on Saturday morning. Undaunted, he ordered a 25-man crew with buckets to sponge the hoofprints dry. It was a Derby-day story he would never forget, nor would Applegate. Old Rosebud set a track record that would stand until 1931. Young's dehydrated track was listed as fast.[96]

FROM "MR. DERBY HIMSELF TELLS HOW HE DID IT," *THE COURIER-JOURNAL,*
4 MAY 1941

Colonel Winn recalls that wide national publicity started pouring in 1913 when Donerail won the Derby and paid $91.45 [$184.90] for a $2 ticket, and the following year it continued when Old Rosebud set the track record of 2:03-2/5, which existed until 1931 when Twenty Grand won the Derby in 2:01-4/5.

At that same time that these stories were making the country's papers, Colonel Winn was making friends in the racehorse business all over the country, at tracks in New Orleans, Mexico, Maryland and New York. [Note: James Butler, Price McKinney, and Matt Winn purchased the Laurel Race Course near Baltimore from its builder, H. D. "Curly" Brown, in 1913. Winn was made general manager.[97]]

The constant encouraging of Eastern owners to ship their horses here, coupled with the publicity in '13 and '14 had its effect, and in 1915 Harry Payne Whitney shipped his filly, Regret, here and won the Derby.

Colonel Winn believes the Regret Derby was the year that Churchill Downs came into its own, for after it the Eastern horses began being shipped here in droves, resulting in increased news and larger crowds.

FROM "CHURCHILL DOWNS RADIANT FOR RECEPTION OF VAST DERBY CROWD,"
THE COURIER-JOURNAL, 8 MAY 1915

Apart from the grooming of the grounds, the planting of thousands of shrubs, evergreens, and blooming plants, the clipping of the lawns and park until a practically perfect emerald-green turf has been achieved, the outstanding features of the new additions to the plant include the terracing of the lawn in front of the grandstand and clubhouse, so that it is possible to see the entire track from any part of the lawn, the erection of a new building [note: see page 5 for illustrations to house the forty-one pari-mutuel machines, a new cashier's apartment, new banking department and stockroom, the refurnishing and equipping of the restaurant, a new sanitary kitchen and the connecting of the clubhouse with the grandstand. A charmingly furnished dressing room and lavatory for ladies has also been added to the grandstand....

While the "rostbeef" sandwich stand which is in the nature of a Derby day institution, retains its old position, new environment has been provided for the restaurant, together with the addition of a big, new, sanitary

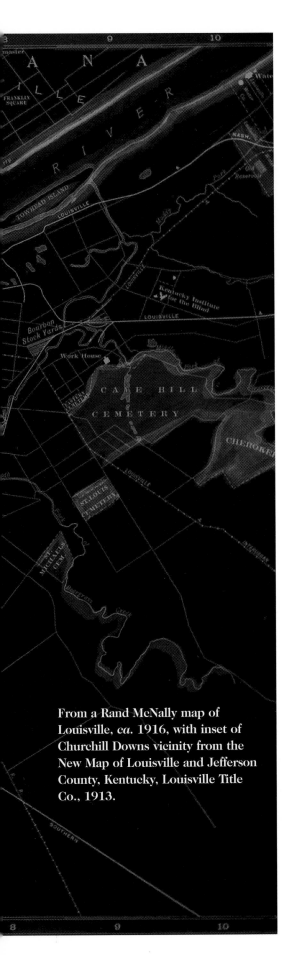

From a Rand McNally map of Louisville, *ca.* 1916, with inset of Churchill Downs vicinity from the New Map of Louisville and Jefferson County, Kentucky, Louisville Title Co., 1913.

Derby day, 1916, showing terraced area in front of grandstand and a steeplechase jump in the infield.

kitchen, the equal of that possessed by any Louisville club. Tables and chairs of the best design have been provided. Both the restaurant and the new dressing room for ladies are located to the right as one enters the grandstand.

The room of the secretary and the jockeys' room have been removed to the extreme end of the paddock, and the cashier's department has been taken out of the main betting shed. It is the belief of those who planned the new building, which includes the roster of the forty-one pari-mutuel machines, the cashier's department, banking department and stockroom to care for the paraphernalia of the machines, that the arrangement and equipment represent the last word in providing for the comfort of the public. Seven of the new machines are of the type which had been brought to such perfection through the efforts of President Grainger, who designed them....

Supt. Young, who has this year doubled the capacity of the greenhouses of the Downs, has provided a wealth of rare [and] beautiful flowers to decorate the clubhouse, as well as supervising the setting out of thousands of plants in paddock, park and lawn. A beautiful bit of landscape gardening has also been provided by the superintendent, who has utilized to the fullest extent the possibilities presented by the stretch of land lying between the track and the centerfield, facing grandstand and clubhouse. As usual, the name "Churchill Downs," will appear in the vivid colors of growing plants in front of the timer's stand.

FROM "CHURCHILL DOWNS RADIANT FOR RECEPTION OF VAST DERBY CROWD," *THE COURIER-JOURNAL*, 8 MAY 1915

The lawn in front of the clubhouse and grandstand has been raised nearly three-feet and terraced toward the track, thus giving sufficient elevation to enable spectators in the rear to see over the heads of those in the foreground, doing away with the heartbreaking suspense of the moments when the horses are out of view because nature unkindly made some folk taller than others. In addition to raising the grade, the lawn has been widened eight feet for a distance of 300 feet, this gain having been made by stripping this amount of space from the track while the track was not looking.

FROM PETER CHEW, *THE KENTUCKY DERBY* (1974), PAGE 3

The center of American racing gravity, then as now, lay in New York. Winn courted the big eastern stables that raced there. A number of New York notables, including August Belmont II, were on hand for the 1914 race won by Old Rosebud, a first-class local horse. Winn's big break came the next year when Harry Payne Whitney agreed to run his superb filly, Regret, in the Derby.[98] She led from wire to wire, the only thoroughbred of her sex ever to win the race.[99] "I do not care if she never wins another race, or if she never starts in another race," said an exultant Whitney. "She has won the greatest race in America, and I am satisfied."

The Derby was made.

From Matt Winn in *Down the Stretch*, page 128

In the summer of 1918, while I was directing racing at Empire City, Pat Hanlon came on from Louisville, and asked if I cared to sell Churchill Downs. Hanlon, who had been an official in the American Tobacco Company, had retired, and then decided to get into horse racing, [revealed]: "A syndicate has been formed in Louisville, and the idea is to get control of all the Kentucky tracks. Douglas Park, Latonia and the Lexington track will go in. But we need Churchill Downs to complete the circuit. What price do you place on it?"

I told Hanlon that I never had given a thought to selling the property; that no deal concerning it ever would be made without full sanction of my associates; that never having thought about selling it, I could not fix a price. [Note: Winn owned 21% of the New Louisville Jockey Club stock. By then W. E. Applegate and his son controlled 29%, Andrew Vennie had 21%, and Charles Grainger 20%; the remaining 9% was in sixteen different hands.[100]]

From Bill Levy, *The Derby* (1967), page 27

It was in 1918, too, that Matt Winn and his associates sold Churchill Downs to a Louisville syndicate for $650,000, more than sixteen times the amount Winn and company had paid in 1903. Winn had planned to leave Kentucky and operate exclusively in the East, but when Jim Brown, who headed the syndicate, told him there was no deal unless the dynamic former tailor remained at Churchill Downs, Winn agreed to stay as vice-president and general manager.[101]

Caricature of James Brown by Robert M. Hooe, *Kentuckians As We See Them* (1905).

The placing of Kentucky's race tracks under the ownership and management of a holding company would have had great appeal to James Buckner Brown (1872-1940), but whether he was the head of the syndicate trying to effect such a merger is doubtful. He certainly had enough working knowledge of finance, but at that point he lacked the personal wealth or political clout to galvanize the high powered group that wanted to turn the operation of Kentucky race tracks into a profitable business. But his meteoric rise in the worlds of banking and journalism would make him an influential part of the takeover group.[102]

When the corporation papers for the new racing entity were recorded in February 1919, it was speculated that Patrick J. Hanlon would be the association's president. The former vice president of the American Tobacco Company from St. Louis had retired briefly, but instead of taking over the Kentucky Jockey Club, he moved to New York to work for the P. Lorillard Tobacco Company.[103]

CHURCHILL DOWNS
LOUISVILLE, KY.

SIR BARTON
Winner Kentucky Derby 1919

November 2=13
11 Days

FROM "THE STALLION STAKES," *LOUISVILLE COMMERCIAL*, 18 SEPTEMBER 1886

Murphy showed his superior ability as a jockey in his finish on Silver Cloud. It looked to most every one that he got second place, but, of course, the judges were in the best position to decide the matter. It was a finish that the photographer should have taken. The instantaneous camera is now used frequently at race courses. There has been one at this meeting, but it was not present yesterday.

Opposite: Poster for fall meet, 1919, showing Derby winner Sir Barton.

The finish of the 1886 Stallion Stakes at Churchill Downs was captured by the noted New York horse painter and illustrator Gean Smith, who died on 7 December 1928 at the age of 77 (see *The New York Times*, 9 December 1928). The huge oil painting is on display at the Kentucky Derby Museum. While the first and fourth horses are obvious from their positions, the second and third are virtually tied. From Frederick M. Burlew's seminal work on racing silks, "American Racing Colors, 1865-1915," in two volumns at the Keeneland Library, it is possible to determine that D. T. Pulsifer's Sir Joseph is ridden by West in the striped silks, while E. J. "Lucky" Baldwin's Silver Cloud is ridden by Isaac Murphy in the black silks.

Chromolithograph, copyrighted 1890, displays products marketed by John G. Roach & Co., liquor wholesalers, with Churchill Downs' grandstand in background. Infield shows no evidence of steeplechase course, and other liberties have been taken with structures to the left of the grandstand as well as the location of the clubhouse where the gentlemen are sitting, which would now be the site of the present grandstand.

Incredibly, active politicians were pictured drinking with Roach (at right) in this early piece of advertising art. At left was John Griffin Carlisle (1835-1920), former editor of the old *Louisville Daily Ledger*, U.S. Congressman, and in 1890 U.S. Senator. To his left was James Proctor Knott (1830-1911), former U.S. Congressman, governor of Kentucky, and in 1890 a member of the state's constitutional convention.

To his left (and to Roach's right) was Joseph Clay Stiles Blackburn (1838-1918), former U.S. Congressman, and in 1890 U.S. Senator. Blackburn was Luke P. Blackburn's brother who was married to Julia Churchill. John Gaines Roach (1845-1907) had been president of the Bel-Air Distillery, and in the early 1900s owned Glenview, the old J.C. McFerran farm east of Louisville noted for its trotting stock.

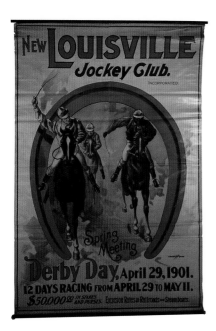

Above: African-American jockeys were still very much in evidence (if in caricature). Jimmy Winkfield won the 1901 Derby on His Eminence and repeated on Alan-a-Dale the following year. Only twice (1901 and 1945) has the Kentucky Derby not been held in May. Right: This 1897 poster obviously has misrepresented Churchill Downs. The clubhouse depicted in the background is Washington Park's in Chicago.

Color photography was still novel when this Derby day sequence was made in 1941. In the confusion on the presentation stand, Matt Winn is attempting to give the Derby trophy to Whirlaway's owner, Warren Wright, who is hidden behind jockey Eddie Arcaro in red.

Contemporary scenes on the backside.

When I first came here to work in 1967, there was a sign on the gate back here that said no females were allowed after six o'clock. Since females have been allowed back here, we have doubled our room spaces. We reopened the upstairs of all the tack rooms. When they were closed, everything was left in them like the old coal stove boxes. We found a newspaper article dated, I think, 1896.

—FROM AN INTERVIEW WITH BUTCH LEHR, 24 MAY 1993

Top: The roof of the Kentucky Derby Museum mirrors the twin spires of Churchill Downs. Louisville's skyline to the north can be seen in the distance. Above left: Interior of old Churchill Downs museum in 1978. Above right:

The centerpiece of the Kentucky Derby Museum, opened in 1985, is its three hundred and sixty degree, multi-image presentation which gives visitors a sense of the exhilaration that pervades the yearly "Run for the Roses."

KENTUCKY JOCKEY CLUB
(A holding company owning or controlling Churchill Downs, Latonia, Douglas Park, the Kentucky Association, Fairmount Park, Lincoln Fields and Washington Park, 1919-1928)[1]

PRESIDENT
Johnson Newlon Camden

VICE PRESIDENT AND
GENERAL MANAGER
Matt J. Winn

SECRETARY AND TREASURER
Sherman Goodpaster

RESIDENT MANAGER,
CHURCHILL DOWNS
Charles F. Grainger; Andrew Vennie; Daniel E. O'Sullivan

DIRECTORS
Robert Worth Bingham, William F. Bradshaw, James B. Brown, J. Graham Brown, Johnson N. Camden, Henning Chambers, James T. Clark, Jr., Samuel A. Culbertson, Fred Forcht, Jr., Maurice L. Galvin, Charles F. Grainger, Arthur B. Hancock, Patrick J. Hanlon, Alvin Tobias Hert, R. Baylor Hickman, Lawrence Jones, George J. Long, Stuyvesant Peabody, Andrew Vennie, Matt J. Winn

Battery F, 81st Field Artillery, Kentucky Army Horse Show, 18 October 1919.

Sir Barton, foaled at John E. Madden's Hamburg Place and owned by J. K. L. Ross, won the Kentucky Derby on 10 May 1919. Four days later, he won the Preakness and four weeks later the Belmont Stakes — the first Triple Crown winner, although the combination of wins was not so termed until Gallant Fox's victories in 1930.

FROM "KY. RACETRACKS ARE ORGANIZED," *THE COURIER-JOURNAL*, 22 FEBRUARY 1919

Articles of incorporation were filed yesterday afternoon by the newly-organized Kentucky Jockey Club, which is to take over Latonia, Douglas Park, the Kentucky Association and Churchill Downs — the four race-tracks in this State.

The papers were signed by Lawrence Jones, P. J. Hanlon and A. J. Carroll. The latter is the attorney for the association, while Mr. Hanlon will likely be its first president. Mr. Jones is a prominent member of the syndicate....

According to the papers, the purpose of the new owners is to conduct race meetings and improve the breed of thoroughbred horses. While the greater portion of the stock has been underwritten by the syndicate, over $1,000,000 was placed in the hands of brokers last week, and it is said that most of this has been purchased by owners and breeders. J. E. Madden, of Lexington, probably the best known breeder and owner in this country, is said to have been a large purchaser of the stock.

The final papers for the transfer of the tracks have been drawn up and it is said that the purchase price will be paid to the present owners early next week, although the options do not expire until March 1.[2]

FROM "NEW GRANDSTAND AT CHURCHILL DOWNS," *THE COURIER-JOURNAL*, 6 APRIL 1920

When the new 300-foot addition to the grandstand and other vast improvements which represent a cost of more than $200,000 are completed at Churchill Downs, the local racing plant will rank second to none in America in respect to housing large crowds. In excess of 50,000 persons may be cared for comfortably under the new arrangements, and this figure has been arrived at by measurements, allowing so much space per person. The total length of the grandstand and clubhouse combined is

Betting shed has been dismantled and steel framing for grandstand extension is shown being erected, 6 March 1920. Tiers of steps leading to grandstand seats have also been removed.

now seven hundred and fifty feet.

In the grandstand alone will be accommodations for 10,000 persons, while the lawn in front of it will provide standing room with an excellent view of the races for 18,000 more. This lawn runs an eighth of a mile. The clubhouse and its surrounding grounds and the stretch of lawn beyond the paddock will afford points of vantage for close to 25,000 persons.

There will be two hundred and eighty-nine boxes in the grandstand, the old portion of it being devoted exclusively to seats of this kind. In the new section there will be no reserved seats except in the row of boxes in front.

All stairways leading into the grandstand will be on the inside of the structure, instead of in front of it as before. This arrangement was made so as to avoid the crowding and blocking on the steps so prevalent in past years, especially when the horses were preparing to start in a race at a mile or further and had to pass the grandstand twice. The Downs stand will be the only one of its kind in this respect in this country.

The new administration buildings will be modern in every detail, and much larger than before. In them will be located every office but that of the racing secretary.

From a standpoint of beauty, Churchill Downs will surpass any other racetrack of the present day when completed. The huge columns supporting the grandstand will be artistically decorated and on the name of each will be engraved the name of previous Derby winners, and the year in which they won the classic. Flower beds will be laid out in all directions, and the infield in front of the grandstand will be a profusion of plants and shrubbery. All of the flowers to be used were grown in the green house at the racetrack, and there will be more than enough to go around.

Matt J. Winn, general manager of the Kentucky Jockey Club, built the beautiful Jockey Club Juarez course and also superintended the reconstruction of the Laurel racetrack, one of the prettiest in America, but the rebuilding of the historic old Downs plant is his master effort.

FROM *THE LOUISVILLE HERALD*, 8 MAY 1920

Since the last meeting, the club has spent a fortune in constructing a large addition to the grandstand, which will afford a seating capacity equal to that of any race track in the country. Other improvements including the sloping and paving of the grandstand lawn, the construction of additional entrances, enlarged pari-mutuel quarters, and additional parking space for automobiles will serve to make Churchill Downs the most commodious and up-to-date racing plant in the country. The creation of a new mile chute is another noteworthy undertaking. Efficiency and preparedness are things that the Kentucky Jockey Club is noted for. Derby Day finds beautiful Churchill Downs clothed in its spring garb, all ready to receive the club's guests. The decorative scheme has always been one of Churchill Downs' unique claims to distinction, and this year with the deep green of the centerfield, the glory of the geraniums here and there and everywhere the spick and spanness of every detail, the attention to every comfort, past records are going to fall by the wayside and a new notch be set.

FROM SAM H. McMEEKIN, *THE COURIER-JOURNAL*, 8 MAY 1921[3]

Stephen Collins Foster wrote the accompaniment for the joy-paean wafted upward from Churchill Downs yesterday afternoon. To the strains of "My Old Kentucky Home" Kentuckians gave vent to their delight. For Kentucky triumphed in the Derby!

After several years of planning and renovation, My Old Kentucky Home in Bardstown was dedicated on 4 July 1923 as a state shrine. Interest in Stephen Collins Foster and the song that he had composed, "My Old Kentucky Home," in Judge John Rowan's residence, had recently been rekindled, so its singing at the 1921 Derby may have been the start of a treasured tradition and the most poignant moment in all of sports.[6]

Alvin Tobias "Tobe" Hert, 56, an influential director of the Kentucky Jockey Club, died on 7 June 1921, while attending a Republican National Committee meeting in Washington.[5] Hert had been mayor of Brazil, Indiana, and superintendent of the state reformatory at Jeffersonville before starting up in 1904 a small plant in Shirley to make a new coal tar product called creosote. The wood preservative, used principally for railroad ties, made Hert extremely rich and powerful. Mrs. Hert, who took up her husband's political mantle, continued to reside at Hurstbourne which they had purchased in 1915.[5]

Top: Charles F. Price presenting 1921 Louisville Cup to Col. E. R. Bradley, owner of Bit of White. Bottom: "Souvenir" service presented to owner of 1922 Kentucky Derby winner, Morvich.

FROM *THE COURIER-JOURNAL*, 13 MAY 1922
"Durby" or "Darby?" That is the question...the vexing problem of its pronunciation is on everybody's mind...The "smart" and "chic" thing to do is to pronounce the word as it sounds. If you want to continue calling it "darby," you should also pronounce clerk "clark."

FROM *THE COURIER-JOURNAL*, 9 MAY 1922

This solid fourteen-karat gold buffet service will supplement the winner's portion of the $50,000 added Kentucky Derby stakes. The service, which is one of the finest gold services made in recent years for a competitive event, consists of a combination loving cup and centerpiece seventeen inches high, with richly hand-pierced mesh for flowers, a plateau for the cup eleven inches in diameter, two nine and a half-inch candlesticks and two compotes.

The service, which is of a Renaissance pattern, is embellished with fine hand-engraving with Acanthus leaves and scrolls as the motive. It is also enriched by heavy honeysuckle and lamb's tongue mounts characteristic of the period. It is valued at $7,000.

This service is now on display in the window of James K. Lemon & Son. Benjamin Block, owner of Morvich, was an interested gazer at the window yesterday. He laughingly remarked that it would look well on his sideboard.

The highly-favored Morvich triumphed in the forty-eighth Derby, but never won again. New York stockbroker Benjamin Block took the first Kentucky Derby trophy ever awarded back to New York.

The prototype of the present cup was awarded in 1923, and then modified with a finial of a horse and jockey designed by the famous New York sculptor, George Louis Graff, for the fiftieth Kentucky Derby in 1924. Made by Lemon & Son, the 22-inch high, 14-karat gold cup contained 55 ounces of gold.[7]

FROM "RACETRACK CROWDS RUSH UP FOR POSITIONS AS MOVIE CAMERA CLICKS," *THE COURIER-JOURNAL*, 16 MAY 1922

A young woman swathed in flame-colored draperies and accompanied by a man rushed stealthily from the clubhouse at Churchill Downs during the second race yesterday afternoon.

The couple cast nervous glances to the right, darting hither and thither with a hunted air, finally disappearing into the startled crowd. Two minutes later they strolled up to the camera fanning calmly. The "movie" folks were having an afternoon of it.

Ten yards away Jack Pickford [(1896-1933), brother of Mary Pickford] leaned across the wire fence with a lazy eye on the "ponies." Behind him the crank of his own camera wound and wound, collecting atmosphere by the half-reel. But Jack Pickford was not working. His pictures here finished, he cast a leisurely gray-green eye about the field, killing time until he could leave to make more race track reels at the Metropolitan races in New York. Even the events being beaten out on the field did not move him to throw his hat in the air or wave his head as the multitude who pointed him out in breathy whispers hoped he would. He stood with a calm, even sophisticated grace with hat jammed firmly on his ears....

"To be sure, I've got more sympathy for jockeys since I jockeyed myself yesterday, but no—no thrill in it." Mr. Pickford ran in a race of his own staging Sunday with a handicap and the understanding that for the sake of the picture, the jockeys were to stay behind and let him win. The jockeys, apparently, did not gather the purport of their directions, however, and Mr. Pickford was obliged to race in earnest. He won.[8]

LETTER FROM ROBERT W. BINGHAM TO JAMES B. BROWN, 12 MARCH 1923[9]

I inclose copy of a letter that I have today sent to Mr. Goodpaster resigning as Director of the Jockey Club.

At the time you asked me to accept a directorship, I did so without familiarizing myself with the work of the Jockey Club. I understood it in a general way, and in fact knew very little about it. As I stated at that time, I thought racing, as an incident of the breeding industry, should be supported. But I cannot approve of the methods that I have since found are employed by the Club in the matter of participating in State politics, and I, therefore, think that in justice to yourself and your associates on the Board, as well as to my own ideas in that respect, I should not sit upon the Board.

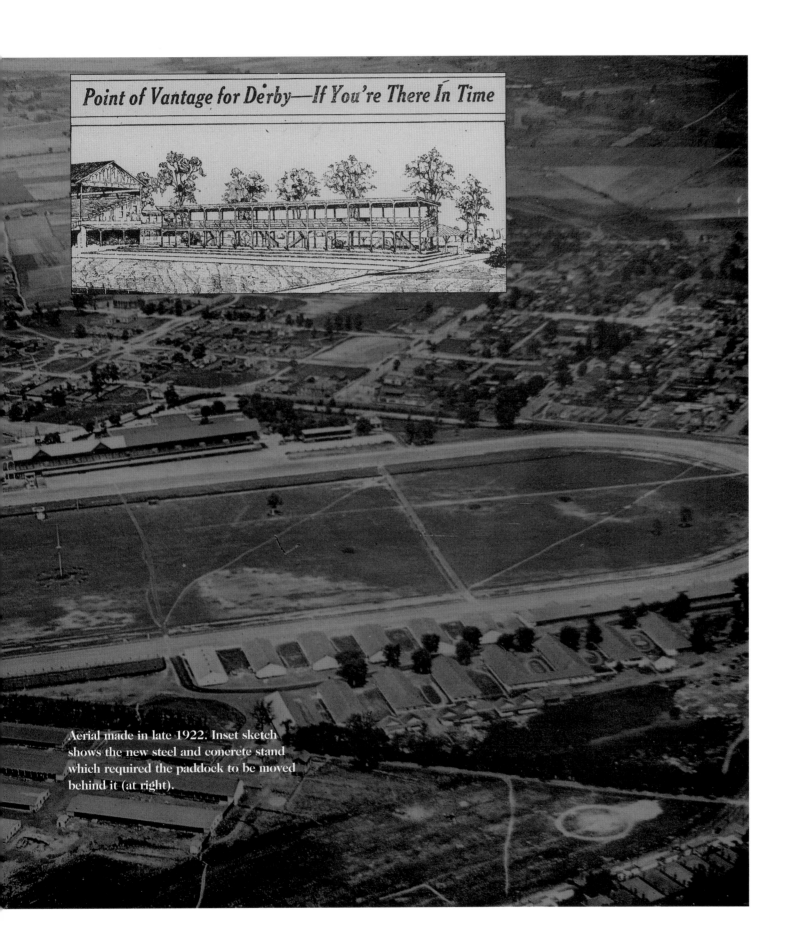

Point of Vantage for Derby—If You're There In Time

Aerial made in late 1922. Inset sketch shows the new steel and concrete stand which required the paddock to be moved behind it (at right).

An adversarial relationship was developing between the two former Democratic party insiders. Robert Worth Bingham had served as county attorney and interim mayor of Louisville before running on the Republican ticket for the Kentucky Court of Appeals. Subsequently, he was appointed chancellor of the Jefferson Circuit Court by Republican Governor Augustus Willson. Judge Bingham purchased controlling interest in *The Courier-Journal* and *The Louisville Times* in 1918. James Buckner Brown, who had been appointed president of the Board of Sinking Fund Commissioners by Mayor Bingham, was president of the state's largest banking institution, the National Bank of Kentucky, and a director of the Louisville Gas & Electric Company as well as the Standard Oil Company of Kentucky. In January 1924, Brown purchased *The Louisville Herald*, the daily established by Augustus Willson and other prominent Republicans. It was later owned by the Louisville Jockey Club director, General Eli H. Murray. Representing Jim Brown in the *Herald*'s purchase was the Republican attorney from Covington, Maurice L. Galvin.[10]

So, while Matt J. Winn was making certain that the state's race tracks were turning a profit for the Kentucky Jockey Club, fellow members of his board of directors were beginning to exert their influence in state politics as part of the somewhat nebulous but very real power known as the bipartisan combine. This was a loose but well-oiled coalition of race track, liquor, coal, textbook, and railroad interests that operated irrespective of party affiliation. One of the principal players in the combine was Maurice L. Galvin, a director of the Kentucky Jockey Club with direct ties to the Latonia race track.[11]

Left: Scene around the racing secretary's office and jockeys' quarters, viewed from the stadium probably on Derby day 1923. The structure was later used as a hospital. The old paddock appears at left. Above: Looking toward old paddock area and secretary's office (left) in 1923. Lawn is now site of the Kentucky Derby Museum.

FROM VERNEY SANDERS, "PASSING OF 'CHARLIE' GRAINGER, SPORTSMAN, MOURNED BY MANY," *THE LOUISVILLE TIMES*, 14 APRIL 1923[12]

It was through his management that the Kentucky Derby has become the greatest sporting event in America... No expense has been spared to make the historic Downs the best advertisement Louisville can boast of. That was due to Charlie Grainger.

Charles F. Grainger from *Club Men In Caricature and Verse* (1912).

From "C. F. Grainger, Ex-Mayor Of City, Is Dead," *The Courier-Journal*, 14 April 1923

The first Kentucky State Racing Commission had Mr. Grainger as a member. In 1906 [1902] he became president of the Louisville Jockey Club, holding the position until the formation of the Kentucky Jockey Club in 1918. He then became resident manager of Churchill Downs, and remained as such, until his death.

Evidence of Mr. Grainger's services to racing in Kentucky is shown in the fact that the value of the Kentucky Derby was raised from $5,000 to $50,000 during the time he held office in the Jockey Club. But the conditions surrounding racing enlisted his interest as much as the sport itself. He was the first to introduce the pari-mutuel betting system in the United States, in this way doing away with bet-making at the tracks and providing the only betting medium that has been sanctioned by the Legislature. He never placed a bet himself at Churchill Downs in consideration of the fact that he was interested in the running of the track.

The school for jockeys and boys who exercise the horses at Churchill Downs was financed out of Mr. Grainger's own pocket. The teachers were hired by him, and the McKinney cottage furnished as a school in order that the boys might obtain an education during their time at the track.[13]

FROM CHARLES A. BERGIN, "RACING SEASON BEGINS AT LEXINGTON COURSE
WITH BRIGHT OUTLOOK," *THE LOUISVILLE HERALD*, 22 APRIL 1923

Lexington, which from time immemorial has had the distinction of opening the spring season again, will lead off this year....

The running of the Kentucky Derby on the second Saturday of the
meeting at Churchill Downs will be quite a departure from the precedent
of having the big race an opening day feature, but it avoids a conflict with
the running of the Preakness Stakes at Pimlico, and insures the best horses contesting in the latter race as starters in the Derby.[14] The conflict of
last year was greatly deplored, and there would have been the same conflict in 1923, but for the graceful action of the Kentucky Jockey Club.

The Derby has been run as early as May 3. This was in 1909. In 1907,
it was run on May 6, and in 1908, on May 5. It has been the custom for
the past twelve years to open the Downs meeting the second Saturday in

Opposite: Clubhouse fashion, track-side, 1922. Below: Parking in front of clubhouse, 1923. Right: Crowd anticipating Derby. The start had been moved into the straightaway, requiring the finish line to be placed in front of the clubhouse, 1923.

May, but the Derby always has been the opening day feature. In the opinion of many horsemen, it is well that the Derby should be run later than the Preakness Stakes which is set at one mile and an eighth, while the Derby is one mile and a quarter. It is best that the shorter distance should come before the longer, but what is of great importance is that the new arrangement assures every chance for a horse to try for both rich prizes. Sir Barton has both to his credit, and this year there is a possibility that another colt may duplicate that enviable achievement.

This season will mark the first year that the Derby will be started on a straightaway, and it was the contention of General Manager Matt J. Winn, of the Kentucky Jockey Club, that a removal of the finishing line, which automatically placed the quarter post in the home stretch, off the bend, was necessary because of the probable large field. Under the old conditions, more than one-half the horses would have been forced to take the worst of it, because of the start being effected on a turn.

Seventeen horses were entered in 1920, and with the start then placed up in the grandstand turn, it was a real disadvantage for the horses posted inside. In 1923, an even larger field was expected, and for the first time more than twenty horses were entered. Anticipating the bottleneck at the start in the curve, the starting line was moved into the straightaway. This, of course, necessitated moving the finish line, as well as the judges' stand. To balance the recent additions at the north end of the grandstand, the 1902 clubhouse was remodeled, tying it into the south end of the grandstand. Its classical revival features fronting the track were removed, but the verandas on the parking lot side were retained. A covered area, called

New paddock, pictured during 1924 Derby, was accessible from the track through the grandstand and along a walkway cordoned off by a balustraded wooden fence, later made of stone.

the pergola, was erected south of the new clubhouse seats, and in between was positioned an elevated press box with an open area on its roof for cameramen. The finish line was moved from the south end of the grandstand to the end of the old clubhouse.

In 1941 the finish line was moved again (see *The American Racing Manual*, page 146). The length of the stretch from last turn to judges' stand was increased from 1,100 feet to 1,234.5 feet, and the distance from the judges' stand to the first turn was decreased from 300 feet to 113.5 feet. This change may actually have been made in 1938 when the old tote board at the finish line (on the infield side) was replaced by the current presentation stand, and a simple, thin pole was erected at the finish line.

As the golden anniversary of Churchill Downs approached, other improvements were underway, but always with an eye to cost containment. The 1903 paddock behind the north end of the extended grandstand was now inaccessible to most patrons. When a larger paddock was constructed at the center of activity behind the old part of the grandstand, it was made from metal reused from the paddock erected in 1912 at Douglas Park where racing had subsequently ceased.[15] The 1903 wood-beamed paddock would be used for other purposes, and remains as a pavilion today.

Obviously, when the paddock was relocated, there was no way to get horses from the barns on the backside to it to be saddled, nor was there a way once saddled to get them onto the track. So an 18-foot-wide passageway was created through the new connection between the old grandstand and the improved clubhouse stand.[16]

To handle the anticipated crowds for the fiftieth Kentucky Derby, the pergola erected just the year before was removed and the clubhouse stand was extended southward an additional 400 feet. The D. X. Murphy & Bro. architectural firm was also kept busy planning construction of a large dining room with a porch that was placed perpendicular to the clubhouse stand and overlooked the clubhouse garden. Another pergola was positioned south of this dining room to create a southern entrance to the clubhouse area.[17]

Zev (left) with Earl Sande up, after winning the 1923 Derby.

FROM *THE COURIER-JOURNAL*, 11 MAY 1924

Mrs. Kathleen Wheeler, who made a model in bronze of the winner of last year's Derby, has been commissioned by Johnson N. Camden, president of the Kentucky Jockey Club, to model the winner of the Derby for this year. Mrs. Wheeler will have an exhibition in the window of the W. K. Stewart Book Company during the first week of the races of thoroughbreds which she has done. The models will include: Zev, In Memoriam, Chacolet, Lady Madcap, Morvich, Man o' War and several others. The entire exhibition will be shown on Derby Day at Churchill Downs.

FROM "THE DERBY," *THE COURIER-JOURNAL*, 17 MAY 1924

The fiftieth anniversary of the Kentucky Derby! How many who saw the first Derby in 1875 will see the fiftieth Derby in 1924? Not one of the true sportsmen who inaugurated racing then at Churchill Downs and hung up the first Derby stakes of $1,000 will see the winner of today's Derby take down the stakes of $50,000. They are all gone....

Bonaventure was the name of the horse that won the first race ever run on the Churchill Downs course and the superstitious—what lover of horse races isn't a bit superstitious?—might regard that as an omen of good luck amply realized in the history of the track. For Churchill Downs, now one of the most prosperous race courses in the world, is the oldest one in this country in point of continuous operation. There are two or three racing associations in the United States which were established before that of the Louisville Jockey Club, but they have all had lapses in their operation while the Louisville Club has never missed a season....

It was a different sort of racing we had in those days, in more respects than in the scanter money prizes to be won. Then a race horse had to cover ground....Steeplechases were common, exciting and murderous to rider and horse.

But even the old-timers must admit that there is something to be said for the new fashions of racing. Shortening the Derby distance greatly increased the popularity of the race among horsemen.... And they must admit also that the new fashions in racing have their merits. They bring more races and larger fields. They bring more money to horsemen, breeders as well as racers. They have enabled the local Jockey Club to make the Kentucky Derby the best known race in America and the most effective advertisement Louisville has ever had.

If the Jockey Club will confine itself to its legitimate business, horse-racing, and cut loose from politics, it and the Kentucky Derby may continue to enjoy prosperity. Kentuckians will never lose their love for the thoroughbred horse, nor for horse-racing as the finest sport known to man. It is the abuse of racing, the abuse of the power which money gives a racing association, that can seriously hurt racing in Kentucky.

FROM *THE COURIER-JOURNAL*, 17 MAY 1924

Running of the Golden Jubilee Kentucky Derby, together with "close-ups" of celebrities, "shots" of the winning horse, its jockey, the owner and other intimate views will be shown at noon tomorrow and all next week at the Alamo Theater in *The Courier-Journal Pictorial News*.

The showing will be the first time in the history of the Derby that Louisvillians, unable to attend the event, will have an opportunity on the following day to see the classic reproduced on the screen. The pictures will be taken by the Louisville Film Company.[18]

The Golden Jubilee Kentucky Derby was won by Black Gold, a great-grandson of Ben Brush and the odds-on favorite, owned by Mrs. Rosa M. Hoots. Matt Winn would long recall her gracious acceptance speech upon receiving the first gold cup, prepared to commemorate the anniversary. Mrs. Hoots was the first woman to own a Derby winner.

Just behind Black Gold, but out of the money, was Altawood, owned by C. Bruce Head. The native of Harrodsburg, whose grandfather had discovered a mineral springs there about 1807, had been in the railroad construction business in New York until 1917, when he returned to Kentucky and purchased Waldeck Farm at Crestwood where Altawood was bred.[19] About the time that Altawood won the Latonia Cup later in 1924, Head was involved in the construction of a new track, Fairmount Park, at Collinsville, Illinois, near East St. Louis.

According to Matt Winn in *Down the Stretch*, after Fairmount Park opened on 26 September 1925, he was sought out by Head who told him, "I want you to buy the track." According to Winn, Head "wanted to get out of operating a race track." Actually Matt Winn and others from

Presentation stand, 1924. Mrs. Rosa M. Hoots at right; Matt Winn at left; Charles Price and Johnson Camden are between trainer Hedley Webb and jockey John Mooney. Opposite: Design option for the Kentucky Derby Trophy by George Louis Graff, an employee of the Elgin Silver Co., of New York.

I remember vividly that cousin Brainard Lemon brought three 8 x 10 glossy photographs of mockups of the Derby trophy for my mother to see. My mother was Ethel Whitney and she married Clarence F. Price. He was the son of Judge Charles F. Price and he also worked at Churchill Downs. Mother was related to cousin Brainard and he called her Lady Bug. He asked her, which one do you like? She picked the one.
—FROM AN INTERVIEW WITH ETHEL PRICE LANG, 24 OCTOBER 1994

Churchill Downs had been deeply involved in the preparation of Fairmount Park for its opening. Robert E. Dundon wrote in *The Louisville Herald* on the day Fairmount opened that "the Kentucky Jockey Club has loaned to Collinsville, for the reorganization of the turf in that locality, the services of Col. Matt J. Winn, managing director of Churchill Downs and Latonia." *The Thoroughbred Record* on 3 October 1925 reported: "General Manager Bruce Head and Managing Director Matt J. Winn and many of their associates in the enterprise, including Joseph Rhinock and J. B. Respess, expressed themselves highly appreciative of the generous patronage." Eventually, the Kentucky Jockey Club took over Fairmount Park, and Bruce Head remained as its manager. Later he would also be general manager of Lincoln Fields and Hialeah.[20] The Fairmount Park clubhouse, designed by the Louisville architectural firm of D. X. Murphy & Bro., has been completely remodeled; the original grandstand burned in 1974.[21]

When evaluating the situation in East St. Louis, Winn became interested in racing in the Chicago area, outside the confines of Cook County. Land near the town of Crete was purchased for a track and Stuyvesant "Jack" Peabody was brought in as Lincoln Fields' first president. Matt Winn always pointed to Lincoln Fields with great pride "because it was built under my supervision, and was the dream come true of a race track perfect in all its appointments." The layout was the same as at Fairmount Park and Churchill Downs with the clubhouse and betting shed located on either end of the grandstand. The brick clubhouse was a copy of the

Top: Rendering of clubhouse for the Fairmount Jockey Club, 1926. Bottom: Grandstand at Lincoln Fields, 1926. Both race tracks' buildings were designed by D.X. Murphy & Bro., Louisville.

FROM "FLAMES DESTROY CHURCHILL DOWNS BARN AND DAMAGE THREE ADJOINING BUILDINGS,"*THE COURIER-JOURNAL*, 15 OCTOBER 1924

Fire, spreading with great rapidity, Tuesday morning destroyed Stable A at Churchill Downs, damaged a substation of *The Courier-Journal* and The Louisville Times, a grocery and two residences and scorched several other buildings on Fourth Street, causing a total loss estimated at $21,000....

Thomas Young, superintendent of the track, said the stable would be replaced. The only horse quartered there, Green Gold, was being exercised when the fire broke out.

D. X. Murphy & Bro. firm's facility at Fairmount Park; only the two compartments on the third level were combined into a full enclosure. Their framing plans, in fact, were interchangeable. The plant included a polo field and golf course. Recently, the plans for the golf course were discovered, but no record can be found of the track's early days. The grandstand burned in 1952, and when Benjamin F. Lenheimer, who had operated Washington Park since 1935 and Arlington Park since 1940, purchased the track in 1955, he changed its name from Lincoln Fields to Balmoral Park.[22]

As Winn was conceiving Lincoln Fields in Crete, Thomas E. Bourke, who had reopened Ed Corrigan's old Hawthorne track, built a new track in Cook County in Homewood, naming it Washington Park for the once premier racing establishment in Chicago. Bourke and his partners soon sold their Washington Park to none other than Curly Brown, who immediately contacted Winn about a possible purchase. This was effected in early 1927. The Kentucky Jockey Club then also controlled racing at Churchill Downs, Latonia, Fairmount Park, Lincoln Fields, as well as indirectly at Hawthorne in the Stickney suburb of Chicago. The latter was opened in 1891 and taken over in 1909 by Ed Corrigan's partner

Thomas F. Carey. The track was leased to the Chicago Business Men's Racing Association and evidently the Kentucky Jockey Club assisted the group financially and gained control of a bare majority of its stock holding. Charles W. Bidwill, Sr., became Hawthorne's managing director. He also owned the old Chicago Cardinals professional football team (now the Arizona Cardinals) and in 1946, he acquired nearby Sportman's Park. He operated Hawthorne for the Carey family until he died in 1947, whereupon Robert F. Carey assumed management. Presently, his son, Thomas F. Carey II, is head. Charles W. Bidwill, Jr., is president of Sportman's Park and is on the board of directors of Churchill Downs.[23]

Entrance to "Churchill Downs, Kentucky Jockey Club," 1926.

ROBERT E. DUNDON, "NEW MAJOR LEAGUE OF RACE TRACKS IS COL. WINN'S PROJECT," *THE LOUISVILLE HERALD*, 30 OCTOBER 1925

Col. Matt J. Winn, general manager of the Kentucky Jockey Club, and managing director of the Fairmount and new Chicago enterprises, is certain to put new life and vigor into racing in Illinois. It is probable that under his supervision, a "major league" circuit of racing, embracing Chicago, Greater St. Louis, Louisville and Latonia (Cincinnati), will be effected. There will be as much difference between this organization and the smaller tracks as between the big leagues in baseball, and the minors. Of course, all four cities have a large population. Louisville, being the smallest, naturally will have the briefest season, but it will continue to be best, for it will have the blue ribbon of the turf, the Kentucky Derby, the greatest race on the American continent.

Those who have watched Colonel Winn's remarkable career have not the slightest doubt that he will be able to achieve for Chicago and St. Louis what he has already done for Louisville and Cincinnati.

With these four major tracks under his direction, the colonel will be able to draw divisions of the greatest Eastern stables to Kentucky and Illinois, for the entire spring, summer and fall. In fact, Chicago actually threatens the supremacy of New York, in a turf way, and every business and hotel interest of the Western metropolis will feel the impetus of its becoming the sport capital of the United States....

With Chicago and St. Louis racing successful, due to the hard work of Colonel Winn and his associates, hundreds of Kentucky farmers, in Southern and Western, as well as Central and Eastern sections of the State, will receive enhanced prices for their yearling horses. That is plenty of gain for one year....

In conclusion, if additional proof were needed that Kentucky benefits by having this improved type of racing, just make a few inquiries as to the number of wealthy men who are buying Bluegrass farms, not only to raise their own blooded stock, but on which to spend at least a portion of their time. Florida is having a tremendous boom, but that of Kentucky, we really think, is the more substantial, if less spectacular.

The idea of a "major league" was perhaps a trial balloon floated by Robert E. Dundon. As sports editor for *The Louisville Herald*, owned by Kentucky Jockey Club director, James Buckner Brown, Dundon would have been privy to such planning. The concept would become a reality as a holding company known as the American Turf Association.

FROM "WIDENER SPENDS DAY IN LOUISVILLE INSPECTING HORSES AT DOWNS,"
THE COURIER JOURNAL, 11 JANUARY 1925

The great fault that I find with the Kentucky race courses, especially Latonia, is their hard footing, he said.[24]

FROM THE TEXT OF CREDO HARRIS'S "RADIOCAST," PUBLISHED IN
THE COURIER-JOURNAL, 17 MAY 1925

We are radiocasting to you, for the first time in history, the running of a Kentucky Derby. For this purpose the engineers of WHAS, *The Courier-Journal* and *The Louisville Times*, have, through the courtesy of the Kentucky Jockey Club, installed wires, microphones, amplifying panels and other equipment high up in one of the cupolas rising from the top of the famous Churchill Downs grandstand; and from this dizzy place we get a picture, not only of the track, and of the big race that is to come, but of the country for many miles in every direction. All of these things we shall try to tell you about as briefly as possible, just as they appear to our eyes. In other words, we are going to see if, for a little while, we can let our eyes be your eyes, and translate the pictures from here into your own imaginations. If we succeed we shall be glad.

We are, as I have said, high up in a cupola, as if looking down from a basket of a captive balloon, taking a bird's-eye view of the most classic assemblage of horse-lovers that American racing has ever known. For this is the fifty-first consecutive meeting of the great Kentucky Derby—the most coveted race on the Western Hemisphere—a trial of stamina and gameness for 3-year-olds, in whose veins course the most royal blood that centuries of breeding has been able to produce. [Note: The newspaper reported the radiocast had "probably the biggest audience any station ever had. Probably 5,000,000 or 6,000,000 heard the race results."]

Andrew Vennie (1859-1926), Matt Winn's long-time and most intimate friend, died on 20 May 1926. He was a member of the syndicate that took over in 1902, and he owned 21% of the track's stock when the New Louisville Jockey Club was taken over by the Kentucky Jockey Club, of which he was also a director. He had assumed the position of resident manager of Churchill Downs when Charles Grainger died in 1923. Vennie was succeeded by Daniel E. O'Sullivan, a Bowling Green, Kentucky, native, who had been managing editor of *The Courier-Journal* and *The Evening Post*, editor of the *Louisville Commercial*, as well as founder of *The Critic*. He was the city of Louisville's first director of safety and served as assistant city attorney.[25]

**View of infield from grandstand,
Derby day, 1926.**

FROM "SACKETT SCORES STATE COMBINE," *THE COURIER-JOURNAL*,
12 JULY 1927

The Kentucky Jockey Club, supported by the American Book Company, maintains a sinister but effective control of legislation in Kentucky, United States Senator Fred M. Sackett declared in an address before Republican leaders here at noon today in which he strongly indorsed the candidacy of Robert Lucas for Governor.

The coal industry in the State also was scored for its "unholy alliance with the Jockey Club," and the Senator predicted that the coal men would feel the people's resentment of that alliance following the downfall of the Jockey Club, which he said was inevitable. Working through a bi-partisan group, these interests have been able to control legislation and keep themselves in power, Senator Sackett said.[26]

FROM "JOCKEY CLUB IS HIT BY BECKHAM," *THE COURIER-JOURNAL*,
3 AUGUST 1927

The Kentucky Jockey Club is guilty of trying to buy the Democratic nomination for Governor for its Oldham County candidate, J. C. W. Beckham charged here tonight in an address before hundreds of Western Kentucky voters....

At Dixon this afternoon and here tonight, Mr. Beckham scourged and lashed the Jockey Club "for its attempt to make a Pennsylvania, an Illinois or an Indiana out of Kentucky—for its attempt to buy, bribe and intimidate."[27]

FROM LETTER BY "KENTUCKY FOGEY," *THE COURIER-JOURNAL*, 6 AUGUST 1927

M. Lewis Clark, a beloved Kentuckian, founded the Louisville Jockey Club more than fifty years ago, and up to the time of his death he continued its responsible head as president. Its announced policy was the development of that great Kentucky farming industry, the thoroughbred horse.

With no practice nor franchise for legalized gambling, it did exercise control over its betting privilege for protection of its patrons. The honest methods of M. Lewis Clark made the Jockey Club an institution of a holiday with a free field on Derby Day for all Kentucky. One dollar was the grandstand price every day so that the poor as well as the rich, from far and wide, could enjoy the races.

Then what happened? Along comes one Johnson Camden, with his millions from West Virginia, to organize Jockey Club control, and perform the magic trick of legalizing gambling, within its gates, as a virtue, while outside its gates a bet on a race is a felony under the law.

Johnson Newlon Camden, Jr., (1865-1942) was the son of a Parkersburg, West Virginia, railroad and coal operator who served twice as U. S. Senator. The younger Camden was trained at Virginia Military Institute, then in law at Columbia and the University of Virginia, but when he married Susanna Preston Hart in 1888, he took over her family homestead, Spring Hill Farm near Versailles. Camden also accumulated great wealth

Steel stadium and standing room only for 1926. The stadium, erected in 1922, had been enlarged. Sometimes called the "baby grand," its north end was demolished in 1962 when it was tied into the grandstand.

in coal, rail, and banks, and he was briefly the U. S. Senator from Kentucky (1914-1915). He also served on the State Racing Commission, three times as chairman.

His wife died in 1929, and two years later he married the widow of Brutus Clay. Spring Hill Farm, where the 1896 Kentucky Derby winner Ben Brush was buried, was sold to Silas Mason, and the Camdens moved to the Clay farm in Bourbon County called Runnymede. Built with Greek Revival features by Charles Todd Garrard, and called Locust Grove by the grandson of Kentucky's second governor, the cattle farm on Stoner Creek had been purchased by Col. Ezekiel Field Clay, who entered the Thoroughbred business with his brother-in-law Catesby Woodford. Ironically, there they bred Ben Brush. Col. Clay was a member of the first State Racing Commission. His son Brutus inherited the farm. When Camden died on 16 August 1942, he was survived by two daughters and six Clay stepchildren. He had been president of the Kentucky Association, the Kentucky Jockey Club, and chairman of its successor, the American Turf Association.[28]

FROM "CHURCHILL DOWNS GOES REPUBLICAN," *THE COURIER-JOURNAL*,
28 SEPTEMBER 1927

No matter how long a man had worked for the Kentucky Jockey Club, no matter what his ability was or what his character was, so the story goes, he was completely out of luck in applying for a job if his party affiliation was Democratic.

Four hundred jobs were available at the track Friday, the day preceding the opening of the fall race meeting, and there were a large number of Democrats present who thought they would surely be employed because they had had experience and their applications had been endorsed by Democratic legislators who had supported the Jockey Club at the General Assembly.

In November 1927, the Commonwealth of Kentucky followed Churchill Downs and went Republican. Senator John Crepps Wickliffe Beckham was defeated by Judge Flem D. Sampson of Barbourville, who had been chief justice of the Kentucky court of appeals. Referred to as "Flim Flam," Sampson's poor showing as governor only served to emphasize the magnitude of Beckham's defeat. As Robert F. Sexton has pointed out, "The 1927 election marked the end of the anti-gambling movement and the end of the progressive movement in Kentucky."[29]

Senator Beckham had promised to make pari-mutuel betting illegal, but the bipartisan combine had again been able to thwart such a campaign. Supporting Beckham, who had already twice served as governor, was a coalition of church and civic leaders in Louisville, some of whom had been active in the progressive movement since the overturn of the 1905 municipal elections.[30] The group, forged mainly from the Louisville Churchmen's Federation (later the Louisville Area Council of Churches), had supported Alben Barkley in his unsuccessful 1923 primary effort. But "despite Barkley's loss," as Sexton has commented, "the 1923 primary proved the anti-gambling crusade had become a viable political issue." However, in the face of racing interests, the Democrats were not able to remain united in 1927 and suffered a humiliating defeat. And the influence of the Kentucky Jockey Club was reaching well beyond the commonwealth's borders.

Matt J. Winn was no stranger to politics, but as the 1920s came to an end his focus did not seem to be on Kentucky. He was quite prominent in *Collyer's Year Book* for 1928, published in Chicago. He was listed as executive director of the Lincoln Fields Jockey Club (Stuyvesant Peabody was president, Marshall Field III vice president). He was noted as chairman of the board of directors of the Fairmount Jockey Club and pictured as executive director of the Illinois Turf Association which governed racing in Illinois. Charles W. Bidwill, Sr., was secretary-treasurer of the association, and H. D. "Curly" Brown, who had built and was operating Arlington Park, was among its board members.

Opposite:1928 Sanborn map, showing considerable development since its 1905 edition. The structure on the southwest corner of Fourth Street and Central Avenue was first listed in the 1904 city directory as the South Louisville Savings and Deposit Bank.

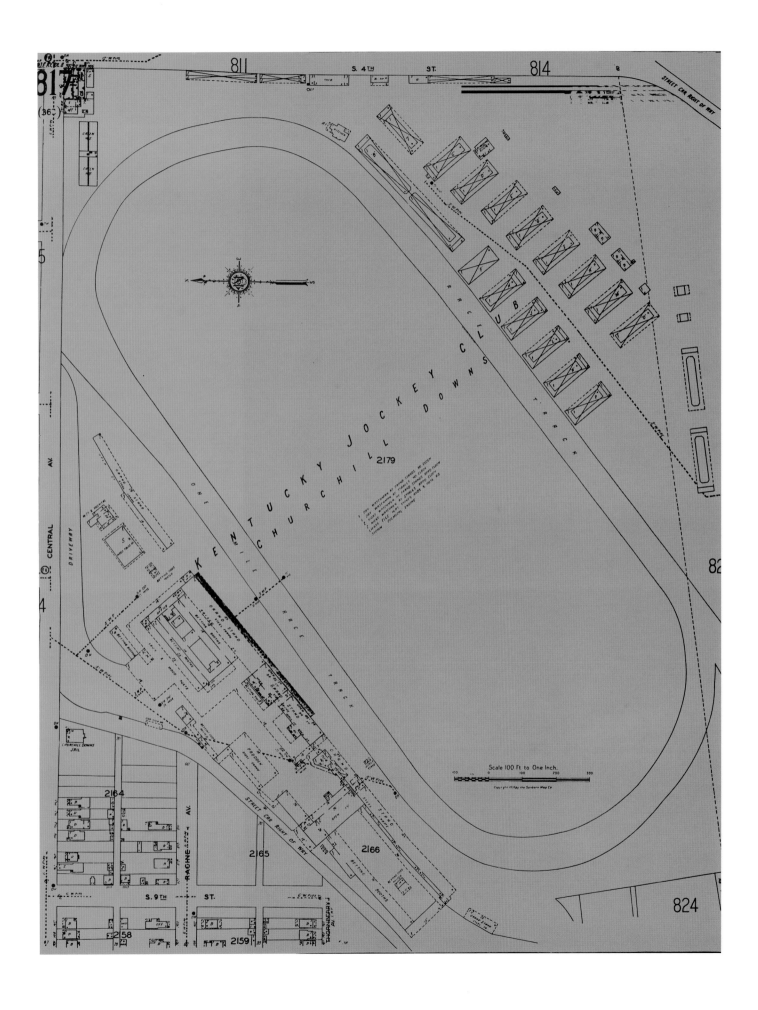

PART FOUR

American Turf Association

1928-1942

CHURCHILL DOWNS-LATONIA, INC.
(1937-1942)[3]
CHAIRMAN, BOARD OF DIRECTORS
Samuel A. Culbertson

PRESIDENT
Matt J. Winn

VICE PRESIDENT
A. J. Carroll, Polk Laffoon

SECRETARY AND TREASURER
Maurice L. Galvin; Henning
Chambers; Sam H. McMeekin

SECRETARY
Sam H. McMeekin

TREASURER
Stanley F. Hugenberg, Sr.

RESIDENT MANAGER
Daniel E. O'Sullivan;
Russell Sweeney

DIRECTORS
J. Graham Brown, A. J. Carroll,
Henning Chambers, James T.
Clark, Samuel A. Culbertson,
Charles I. Dawson, Maurice L.
Galvin, Henry O. Gray, Stanley F.
Hugenberg, Sr., Lawrence Jones,
Warner L. Jones, Jr., Polk Laffoon,
Sam H. McMeekin, Samuel H.
Stone, Roger Sullivan, Matt J. Winn

First turn during 1933 Kentucky
Derby. Winner's enclosure was
between the pagodas visible behind
the horses. Judges' stand in the
infield at right would be replaced
in 1938.

Looking north at clubhouse garden and 1929 Derby day crowd around the paddock area beyond.

102062

FROM "PLAN STOCK RAISE FOR JOCKEY CLUB," *THE LOUISVILLE TIMES*, 29 DECEMBER 1927

The plan of the directors of the Kentucky Jockey Club to dissolve the club and place its assets under a holding corporation, incorporated under the laws of Delaware, provides for a capitalization of $6,000,000, an increase of $2,600,000 over the present capitalization, it was learned Thursday....Tracks the holding company would control were Lincoln Fields, Washington Park and Hawthorne at Chicago, and Fairmount, East St. Louis, Ill.; Churchill Downs, Louisville, and Latonia, Covington.[4]

FROM "JOCKEY CLUB IS DISSOLVED HERE," *THE COURIER-JOURNAL*, 17 JANUARY 1928

Plans for dissolution of the Kentucky Jockey Club...were legally consummated Monday... Col. M. J. Winn will be manager of all tracks under the jurisdiction of the American Turf Association, a holding corporation marked to take over the stock of the Kentucky Jockey Club and several others....

Directors in the American Turf Association are Mr. [Johnson N.] Camden, Colonel Winn, Henning Chambers, Lawrence Jones, George J. Long, Baylor Hickman, C. Bruce Head, Stuyvesant Peabody, James T. Clark and others who formerly made up the directorate of the Kentucky Jockey Club.

FROM "$3,000,000 TURF STOCK PLANNED," *THE COURIER-JOURNAL*, 25 MARCH 1928

Announcement also was made that Samuel A. Culbertson has been elected president of Churchill Downs, Incorporated.[5]

Churchill Downs is a separate corporation from the American Turf Association, and was organized as a company in January. Articles of incorporation were filed by James B. Brown, Henning Chambers and Lawrence Jones.[6] The corporation was capitalized at $250,000 and 25,000 shares of common stock were to be issued....

The association is reported to be planning full ownership of an Eastern track with the funds derived from the shuffle, thus completing the association's chain of racing properties. The only Eastern track officials of the association are known to have an interest in is at Laurel, Md., where Matt J. Winn and associates are said to have investments aggregating 51 percent.[7]

FROM LETTER OF ROBERT WORTH BINGHAM TO JUDGE OSSO W. STANLEY, DATED 19 JANUARY 1929[8]

I think it is undoubtedly true that the great majority of our fellow-Kentuckians are decent, law-abiding and patriotic, but they have not been able to express in government the principles and ideals for which this majority of our people stand. I believe the root of the whole trouble for a long time has been the manipulation of the organizations of both parties through the medium of the enormous amount of money spent for this purpose by the controlling influences in the Kentucky Jockey Club. The people in the state, in their effort to secure better conditions, have

Kv. Derby, 1930

Left: The Earl of Derby witnessed
the 1930 race from the presentation
enclosure. Flags of Great Britain
and United States flew that day.
Racing secretary Charles F. Price
watched the race more intently with
binoculars. Above: Churchill
Downs Chairman Samuel A.
Culbertson was ever resplendent in
his younger days.

shifted from one party to the other without accomplishing anything
because they found the same influences in control, regardless of the party
nominally in power....

My view upon this subject has no connection with racing, to which I
have no objection, and not even to betting, which is, to say the least, a
minor matter compared with the major principle involved. This Jockey
Club control, in my judgment, is as bad, or worse, than the old machine
of liquor control, to which it succeeded. In the end it will go the way of
the other control, but, meanwhile, it has set our state back a generation.

FROM "JOCKEY CLUBS NAMED IN SUIT," *THE COURIER-JOURNAL*, 21 MARCH 1929
Renewed charges of conducting a lottery contrary to law and other sinis-
ter and illegal activities were contained in a petition in equity filed
Wednesday against the Kentucky Jockey Club, Latonia Jockey Club and
Churchill Downs by the Commonwealth of Kentucky through Attorney
General J. W. Cammack in the Jefferson Circuit Court.

The petition asked for $1,000,000 damages....and all three of the cor-
porations be dissolved....

The motion was opposed by attorneys for the Jockey Club, consisting
of Maurice Galvin, A. J. Carroll and H. E. McElwain. [Note: The suit was
first initiated by Attorney General Frank E. Daugherty in November
1927. His sucessor, James W. Cammack, dismissed the suit and filed a
new petition naming in part the old corporate entity, the Kentucky Jockey
Club. Jefferson Circuit Court dismissed the suit and the Court of Appeals
upheld the validity of the pari-mutuel laws in February 1931. See "Jockey
Club Case Decision Made Final," *The Courier-Journal*, 17 June 1931.]

Looking south at the odds board at the end of the clubhouse garden in 1930.

FROM "RACE TRACKS IN KENTUCKY UP FOR SALE," *THE COURIER-JOURNAL*, 19 MARCH 1931

Property of the American Turf Association formerly owned by the Kentucky Jockey Club was offered for sale sixty days ago, it was learned Wednesday. Joseph E. Widener, noted turfman, said in a telephone conversation from the Savoy Plaza Hotel, New York, that an official of the American Turf Association approached him two months ago and offered the property for sale. "I explained that I was not interested, did not have time to devote to it," Mr. Widener said he replied. Mr. Widener said his answer was final on the subject. He added, "I would like to see racing properly conducted in the State, and it would mean a great deal to get it out of politics."....

It had been reported that Mr. Widener might have been interested if the organization could have been operated more as a business enterprise than as a gambling venture under State laws. He was asked concerning this and the report that he would be willing to take over the Kentucky organization provided it could be reorganized and operated so as to return interest of 6 per cent on the investment, the arrangement to provide also that all receipts above the 6 per cent return would go to the State Treasury.

FROM "CAMDEN TO QUIT AS HORSE BREEDER," *THE LOUISVILLE TIMES*,
24 MARCH 1931

Johnson N. Camden, chairman of the board of directors of the American Turf Association, master of Hartland Stud, a magnificent estate of 1,900 acres near Versailles, Tuesday made known his decision to retire from the breeding of blooded stock....If he resigns his post as chairman of the association, it would mark the end of a long connection with the track. He was formerly president of the Kentucky Jockey Club and has been a breeder of notable animals for thirty-seven years.[9]

Last Thursday Mr. Camden scouted at the possibility of genuineness of the tender of Kentucky property of the association reported by Joseph E. Widener, New York sportsman, as having been made to him by an unnamed negotiator. Mr. Camden said that the subject had never been discussed at a meeting of the board, and that he felt certain that he would know of any move to sell the Kentucky tracks.

It is known, however, that the subject of the sale of a large block of American Turf stock has been broached to brokers. This move may have led to the rumor that the tracks were for sale. This stock is thought to be that pledged on several large notes in the National Bank of Kentucky.

In 1930, the assistant starters used small boxes to help position the horses. A grid system on wheels had been devised by the next year, but as can be seen, the horses were still not restrained in back or in front.

FROM *THE COURIER-JOURNAL*, 17 MAY 1931
"Derby broadcast very clear and interesting," said a cablegram from London to Credo Harris, manager of WHAS, radiophone of The Courier-Journal and The Louisville Times, at 7:45 o'clock Saturday night. The message was from Miss Henrietta Bingham, daughter of Judge Robert W. Bingham, publisher of the newspapers.

The Derby radiocast was given over short wavelength through WHAS to Lawrenceville, N.J., and was picked up in England by the British Broadcasting Company.

FROM "EXPERTS RIDE RADIO 'HOBBY,'" *THE COURIER-JOURNAL*, 17 MAY 1931

A hobby-horse that ran like a thoroughbred was radio at the fifty-seventh running of the Kentucky Derby. And as half America saw the Derby better with its ears than it possibly could have seen it with its eyes, the greatest radio jockeys of the Nation gave a thrilling ride in a record-breaking event....

Lightning switching made a smooth race for the hobby-horse, a three-year-old with the National Broadcasting Company's stables of features this year. Since 1929 NBC has been putting the race on the air, but never before as Saturday afternoon. Never before was there such a day since the hobby-horse ran his first race in 1925, when WHAS and WGN put the turf classic through the ether for the first time. Up on top of the clubhouse, near the press box, William Burke "Skeets" Miller, formerly of The Courier-Journal, waved his hand out of the radiocast booth window, and Graham McNamee greeted the listeners from coast to coast. When the horses started onto the track, McNamee atop the clubhouse was ready to tell about the parade before the stands while [Clem] McCarthy climbed the stairs to the roof to be on hand for the start.[10]

Inside the little NBC radiocast booth, McCarthy glued his eyes to a pair of telescopic binoculars and squinted down to the starting gate. Not a move of the nervous horses escaped him, and from the moment he cried, "They're off!" he had the situation wholly in hand. McCarthy never misses a detail when he rides a race for the radio. No faltering, no explanation that he thought he was right but wasn't, only facts, about as fast as human minds can grasp them....

But the National Broadcasting Company was not the only concern to have entries in the hobby-horse Derby. The Columbia Broadcasting System entered its star microphone jockey, Ted Husing,[11] and the editor of the National Turf Digest, Ed Horn, helped him. The CBS pickup was managed by Herbert B. Glover. And then Station WGN of Chicago had its own sports ace, Quin Ryan, mounting a mike in one of the grandstand cupolas which was a pigeon roost before WGN reclaimed it and pressed it into radiocast service in 1925, the same year that WHAS first turned the trick of letting all America into the Derby without anyone's having to climb the fence. The WGN string of jockeys for the air ride was augmented by L. Sabath, Chicago racehorse owner, and Westbrook Pegler. French Lane and Harvey Woodruff spoke from the press box after the race.

FROM "FIGHT STARTS FOR RACE TRACK CONTROL," *THE HERALD-POST*, 22 MARCH 1933

Factions within the American Turf Association which controls four of the nation's leading thoroughbred racing establishments, including Churchill Downs and Latonia, were soliciting stockholders' proxies Wednesday in preparation for a fight for control and management of the corporation at the annual meeting in Chicago April 3.

On one side are Walter H. Girdler, James G. Kirwan, Donald McDonald, Jr., Sam H. Stone and Milton H. Trost, all of Louisville, representing a "Stockholders Protective Committee" which charges mismanagement and inefficiency in the operation of the corporation....

In a letter sent to stockholders Tuesday the Protective Committee declared that there was urgent necessity for displacing the officers now in control and charged that during the last five years "greatly excessive" sums have been paid to present officers in the way of salaries.

FROM "DIRECTORS DENY CHARGES," *THE COURIER-JOURNAL*, 24 MARCH 1933

Directors of the American Turf Association today denied the charges of a committee of Louisville stockholders, that administration of the organization's affairs has been wasteful and extravagant.

Against the plea of the Louisville group that the present officers be voted out of office at the coming annual meeting in Chicago April 3, nine directors said in a circular letter to stockholders that those now in office seem "better fitted to successfully conduct the business than would be those who are entirely without experience."

The dissenting stockholders had suggested that James C. Stone of Louisville, former chairman of the Federal Farm Board, be chosen president to direct the association and its control of racetracks at Washington Park and Lincoln Fields in Illinois, and Churchill Downs and Latonia in Kentucky.

FROM "TURF STOCK RULE UP TO CONTROLLER," *THE LOUISVILLE TIMES*, 24 MARCH 1933

The decision of S. G. Awalt, Acting Controller of Currency at Washington, as to the disposition of a block of American Turf Association stock in possession of the receiver of the National Bank of Kentucky, was expected Friday to play an important part in the fight of a group of stockholders to oust the present management.

This fight and the stake of the bank's depositors in it were brought to his doorstep this week by Johnson N. Camden, president, and Maurice Galvin, attorney for the association, and Seldon R. Glenn, State Tax Commissioner. They called on Mr. Awalt Wednesday and Thursday and held conferences attended by A. M. Anderson, receiver, who holds about one-fourth of the capital issue of 482,000 shares. These shares were acquired as assets of the bank largely through defaulted loans.

Depending on Mr. Awalt's decision, the receiver can take one of three courses. He can sell the stock to the present management, which would assure their retention of control at the annual meeting in Chicago on April 3. He could hold it and vote it with the stockholders' committee rebelling against the management, a course that this committee has been hopeful he would take. The third alternative would be not to vote it at all, which is what his predecessor, Paul C. Keyes, did.

GEO. HERMAN (BABE) RUTH OF N.Y. YANKEE BASEBALL FAME & JOHN (BUD) HILLERICH OF HILLERICH & BRADSBY BAT MFGRS. SHOWN AT CHURCHILL DOWNS MAY 5 1934 WHEN "CAVALCADE" WON THE KY. DERBY.

It would appear that George Herman "Babe" Ruth came to the Derby three times. Churchill Downs' centennial book pictures him in connection with the 1931 race. The caption under the R.G. Potter photograph above asserts that the Bambino was about to watch Cavalcade win in 1934. The Kentucky Derby Museum has a 1935 Derby program signed by Ruth. In fact, he was the guest of Louisvlle Slugger maker John "Bud" Hillerich (right) at the 1936 Derby when he feigned a hand injury (note bandaged finger) to avoid signing autographs. (See Tommy Fitzgerald, "More People Fooled At 1936 Derby By Ruth Than By Bold Venture," *The Courier Journal*, 19 August 1948.)

Above: Political dignitaries and Churchill Downs executives posed at the 1934 Derby (l to r): Matt J. Winn, Maurice L. Galvin, Governor Ruby Laffoon, Dan E. O'Sullivan, Postmaster General James Farley, unidentified, and Samuel A. Culbertson. Right: "The Fighting Finish," was an apt caption for the best known racing picture of all time, made in the 1933 Derby by *Courier-Journal* photographer Wallace Lowry. Down the stretch Herb Fisher on Head Play battled with Don Meade on Brokers Tip (right), the eventual winner.

From "Plan Drawn To End Turf Fight," *The Louisville Times*,
1 April 1933

Aerial view dated 11 September 1933. Area to the left of the chute is now used for parking. Longfield Avenue runs diagonally at right.

The major points of the settlement have been accepted by the management. Under the compromise, three members of the committee, Sam H. Stone, Walter H. Girdler and James G. Kirwan, are to be elected to the board of directors. Two of the three, probably Messrs. Stone and Girdler, are to go on the association's executive committee of four.

Another point agreed upon was that the association retire from politics. This change of policy was insisted upon by the minority....

With the liberalization of racing laws in a number of States, members of the stockholders' committee believe that the breeding industry in Kentucky is due for a boom. California and Ohio have passed new racing laws, and New York is about to approve the pari-mutuel form of betting. They expect this activity to be reflected in a demand for Kentucky thoroughbreds and in the racing industry generally.

The compromise was worked out in conjunction with the sale of 87,000 shares of capital stock at $8 a share to the management by A. M. Anderson, receiver of the National Bank of Kentucky, acquired through default on notes given the bank for its purchase. The management cannot vote the newly-bought stock Monday, but its acquisition prevents its being voted by the receiver on the side of the dissenting stockholders.

Matt Winn made the cover of *Time* on 10 May 1937. The accompanying article heaped praise on the "fat, white-haired Louisville Irishman ... whose habit [once] was to invest all his spare funds in bets at the track," and who is "more than any other individual responsible not only for the popularity of the Kentucky Derby but for the popularity of U.S. horse racing as a whole."

FROM "TURF BODY ADDS 7 NEW DIRECTORS," *THE LOUISVILLE TIMES*, 3 APRIL 1933

Seven new directors were added to the old directorate of nine in compromise of the stockholders' fight at the annual meeting of the American Turf Association Monday in Chicago. Matt J. Winn, as had been anticipated, was re-elected president.

In the settlement of the stockholders' grievances none of the old directors was removed. The seven added were Walter H. Girdler, Donald McDonald, Jr., members of the stockholders' protective committee, Henry O. Gray, all of Louisville; Edward J. Hughes, Secretary of State of Illinois; Charles W. Bidwill[12] and C. E. Ellis, all of Chicago, and Bruce A. Campbell, of East St. Louis....

The protesting stockholders were not averse to the retention of Mr. Winn, but as their objective was the corporation's elimination from politics, they centered fire on Mr. Galvin. The compromise, however, brought with it a promise of a change in future policy and cessation of all political activities.[13]

FROM "WINN KEEPS CONTROL OF RACING GROUP," *THE NEW YORK TIMES*, 4 APRIL 1933

Chicago, April 3 (AP). Colonel Matt J. Winn, the man behind the Kentucky Derby, still is the head of the American Turf Association, more firmly entrenched than ever. Today, the 71-year-old guiding genius of racing was re-elected president of the association, sweeping aside all opposition that had threatened to oust him from administrative control of the Washington Park, and Lincoln Fields race courses in Chicago, and Churchill Downs and Latonia tracks in Kentucky. These four major race courses, with other interests, are owned by the American Turf Association.

FROM A NEWSPAPER CLIPPING, 4 MAY 1934[14]

A man, who played an important part in the history of the Kentucky Derby, will be missing from the crowd that visits Churchill Downs tomorrow. Tom P. Hayes, who furnished Donerail, 1913 winner, Layson, which finished third to Agile and Rams Horn in 1905, and who saddled Head Play for the 1933 race, has gone to the great beyond. No more popular or efficient trainer was to be found anywhere in his day. Mr. Hayes never missed a running of the classic if it was possible for him to be here. He died at his home at Lexington last August. Still another to be missing will be William "Billy" Walker. Walker, a negro, was astride Baden-Baden in 1877 and last year his memory of that battle with Leonard and King William was still fresh. Walker, during his last years, made Louisville his home and never missed a running of the Derby.[15]

FROM *BOARD OF TRADE JOURNAL*, APRIL 1935

Louisville's first Derby Festival Week is being celebrated as this issue of the Board of Trade Journal comes to press. It marks the fruition of an idea which was conceived a year ago when Mayor Miller and the Board of Trade made a beginning by arranging some special entertainment for guests to the Kentucky Derby.[16]

FROM POWELL LEE, "CHURCHILL DOWNS DIRECTOR GIVES ARCHITECTS LESSONS," *THE LOUISVILLE TIMES*, 23 DECEMBER 1935

Although the clubhouse and grandstand enclosures contain more than 2,000 boxes, said [resident manager Daniel] O'Sullivan, "the number this spring will be greatly increased. Last Derby Day every box and seat in both enclosures was sold before the gates opened. Thousands of requests have already been received for the 1936 Derby and interest in the famous race is more evident, it seems, than ever before."

Changes in no way affect the fountains and gardens which have lent charm and originality to the entire picture of the course.... The columns on the rear porches of the old clubhouse are being torn down and the plan is to extend the building to the line dividing the grandstand and the clubhouse by moving the runway, where horses are taken from the paddock to the track, northward and have them brought from the paddock thence under the stands to the track.

Colonel Winn's office, now on the roof, will be moved to the second floor over the space where the present paddock runway goes between the buildings. Facing the track from his office will be a "presentation" balcony to be used in bad weather when the stand on the track is exposed.

FROM "DOWNS, STEP BY STEP, FOR THREE-QUARTERS OF A CENTURY," *HERALD-POST*, 30 APRIL 1936

For years those who visited the clubhouse section and dined in the restaurant, wondered why, when additions were made to seat the throng, improvements were not made in the clubhouse section. However, those who visit this section of Churchill Downs this Derby Day, will experience one of the most pleasant surprises imaginable, for the improvements are not only of the type that will add to the convenience of visitors, but satisfy their artistic sense.

The years of the depression retarded improvements to the extent that many of the buildings gathered dust and dirt and suffered from the ravages of the weather. Today, all of Churchill Downs buildings are clothed in purest white paint, trimmed with green, lending a beautiful picture to the scene, with a background of nature's hills in the offing.

Additional seats and boxes have been erected whereby one will be better able to view the running of the races and at the same time, add to their improvement.

Below: Horses begin leaving the paddock to emerge from under the grandstand to the strains of "My Old Kentucky Home" and the parade to the post for the 1938 Derby.
Opposite: Matt Winn's office, 1940.

FROM MATT J. WINN IN *DOWN THE STRETCH*, PAGE 238

Each new year, more and more people wanted to see the running of the Derby. When we had built as far up the track as we thought we then should go, we made some additions on the other side of the grandstand — toward what is now the clubhouse turn. When we had gone a considerable distance in that direction, we realized that the site where the clubhouse stood was about as desirable as any — and that the clubhouse wasn't seating anybody, so far as viewing the race was concerned. So we tore down the clubhouse, put a section in there, and that provided more seats.

FROM "'NINE OLD MEN' OF THE DOWNS," *THE LOUISVILLE TIMES*, 15 APRIL 1937

In recent years, with racing revived in Texas, Florida and California, the Kentucky Derby has assumed a place as something national and not of local interest, though the "nine old men" have allowed nothing to happen which would mar local pride in any way. The Derby belongs to the Nation. Churchill Downs belongs to the Americn Turf Association but the "nine old men" belong to Kentucky. They are of us and they are ours. [Note: Those pictured were Johnson N. Camden, A. J. Carroll, Samuel A. Culbertson, Maurice Galvin, Polk Laffoon, Charles F. Price, William H. Shelby, Daniel E. O'Sullivan, and Matt J. Winn.]

Early in 1937, Churchill Downs and Latonia were officially merged into a single operating unit. Churchill Downs-Latonia, Inc. had been formed to weather the Depression and the tracks probably had been tied together informally for several years.[17]

According to Matt Winn, Washington Park was sold by the American Turf Association in 1935, the same year he said that the turf association abandoned the Lexington track and the operation at Douglas Park ceased. The Lexington track did finally close and its plant was dismantled in 1935, but it had not been owned by the Kentucky Jockey Club since 1923, when it was sold to a Lexington group which reorganized the old and famous Kentucky Association.[18] As for Douglas Park, it was never used for racing after being purchased by the Kentucky Jockey Club in 1918. Its structures were left stripped by salvage wreckers in 1939 and it was abandoned as a training track in 1957.[19]

Thus, two decades after the formation of the Kentucky Jockey Club in 1919, only Churchill Downs, Latonia, and Lincoln Fields had survived and still remained under Matt Winn's thumb.

FROM "BUCK" WEAVER, "PLANS MADE FOR CHANGES AT CHURCHILL," *THE LOUISVILLE TIMES*, 21 MAY 1937

A Churchill Downs capable of accommodating 100,000 Derbyites, or more, began to take form Friday as Col. Matt J. Winn revealed plans to further enlarge, beautify and modernize the old plant, which was built originally for a capacity of 2,500.

The 1937 flood, the city's worst disaster, reportedly caused $8,000 damage at Churchill Downs.

FROM *THE COURIER-JOURNAL*, 30 OCTOBER 1936

Time was when the extra day of racing furnished funds for charity, but as the need declined, officials concluded to give the extra day of racing to the cause of building up Kentucky's No. 1 spectacle, the Derby. Proceeds of today's racing will go to the Kentucky Derby Festival Committee for the purpose of drawing more people to the Derby of 1937.

By April 1937, the old pari-mutuel arcade (see page 178) had been replaced, exposing a pavilion of the red brick grandstand which was painted white by Derby time. The twin spires received painted decoration that year as did the judges' pagoda in the infield. The space between the old grandstand and clubhouse had been filled by a structure with contrasting classical detailing, partially visible at right.

The immediate program as mapped out by the maestro of the greatest show in American racing, calls for a terraced infield, a tunnel under the track, a new paddock, new racing secretary's office, new cafeteria, new judges' pagoda, additional betting sheds, more terrace seats, new entrances, and additional gardens, just to mention a few of the outstanding features....

The proposed terrace in the infield, reclaiming, as he styles it, 150 feet from the Derby starting point to the wire, will afford at least 10,000 a birdseye view of the classic they come miles to see. This can be extended as the occasion demands and will be readily accessible through a tunnel at the eighth pole.

Entrance to the latter, which will be a two-way affair of eight "lanes" each, will be at the mouth of the shed in front of the general offices....

The new paddock will be located just to the west of the present one or along the present grandstand entrance to the clubhouse. It will be designed after that at Lincoln Fields, being of single stalls only. While it will be considerably narrower, it will be almost 100 feet longer, extending the full length of the new grandstand addition. [Note: The planned paddock was not erected. The existing one was moved northward in 1941.]

FROM AN INTERVIEW WITH THOMAS DADE LUCKETT II, 20 OCTOBER 1993

The smallest D. X. Murphy & Brother ever got was in 1933 when Mr. J. C. and D. X. both died, and the Depression was on. I was pulled into the firm, and there was Mr. Baldez and Mr. Piatt, a mechanical engineer, Will O'Toole, who was a designer, and a Dane by the name of Peterson, who was a structural engineer.

In my early days, Will O'Toole was the one dealing with Churchill Downs.[20] He was president of the firm when he died in 1956, and I bought his share from his estate. All the other older people had passed away.

The infield work started out with discussions between Will O'Toole and Tom Young. They would do a little bit here and a little bit there. They would say they needed three more toilets out in the infield, so we would build them three more toilets. They never did get enough. I have heard that women have gotten so desperate, they went in the men's john.

I remember when the tunnel was built. Will O'Toole did the tunnel. The chief thing that Will O'Toole did that you still see is the presentation stand in the infield. I think they just told him to do something and he did it.

Above: Infield tunnel under track during its construction in the summer of 1937.

FROM MARION PORTER, "MILLIONAIRE AT DERBY TO FIND REST AND QUIET IN ROOM 20," *THE COURIER-JOURNAL*, 29 APRIL 1939

With that ostentatious simplicity that is supposed to appeal to the ultra rich, the new room at Churchill Downs will be called Room Twenty. [Note: The room was 100 feet by 28 feet, carpeted, mirrored and decorated with paintings of Derby winners.[21]]....But the cards of admission...have been sent to exactly seventy-five rich and well-placed persons in the United States who have either had a Derby winner or done their bit toward promoting racing....Nary a woman will be admitted."

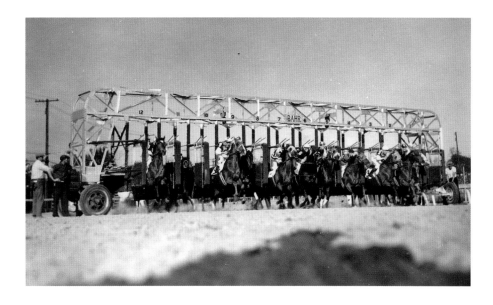

FROM *THE COURIER-JOURNAL*, 7 APRIL 1940

Right: When the Bahr starting gate was first used in the 1940 Derby, its innovative feature, electronically controlled doors both front and back, had been removed and assistant starters were again required on the track. The Bahr gates were fully operational when Whirlaway set a new track record in the 1941 Derby pictured. Below: the "new electronic odds board" was erected in 1938 in anticipation of "a totalizator" that was to be installed the next year. The judges' pagoda and presentation stand was open on the ground level so the winning numbers could be displayed. The lighted board required 3,648 bulbs, and for the first time, patrons could see the approximate odds without venturing to the pari-mutuel rooms.

The Colonel [Matt J. Winn] was discussing the Bahr electrical starting gate, which will have its first test on Kentucky tracks this spring, starting with the Keeneland meeting next Thursday. The Colonel recently purchased at Chicago one of the improved type gates for his Churchill Downs and Latonia plants, after first seeing it at Hialeah and other tracks. Derby visitors will see its inaugural in the Downs classic on May 4.

There are several types of the new electrical gates, but the Bahr pleases the Colonel most because it shows more of the horses. Its major improvements over the old web barriers and later mechanical gates is that it is electrically operated and stalls are closed at both ends, thereby preventing restless mounts from backing or lunging out, thus causing post delays and sometimes injuries to horses and jockeys.

New clubhouse entrance off Central Avenue, 1941. The roof of the jockeys' quarters appears just above the balustrade.

"You can say for me that the spectators are going to like the new gate much better than any of the old ones," the Colonel declared. "And they've got to be very alert not to miss the start, for the average post delay since it was put in operation last year is less than a half minute as compared to an average of three to four minutes under the old systems." [Note: Newsreel film of the 1940 Derby shows that the front gates actually remained opened when the horses were loaded. The gates were opened electronically for the first time in 1941 Derby.]

FROM *THE COURIER-JOURNAL*, 30 APRIL 1941

One of the many innovations brought into the picture by Colonel Winn was the use of publicity.

"Tell 'em about it," he'd say, "and tell 'em again. And again. And again."

Another "must" on his program was the continual improvement of the track, of the grounds, of the facilities for the racegoer's comfort. And with those improvements came the necessity for continual enlargement of the racing plant to handle the fast-growing crowds.

This year, for instance, one of the most striking and beautiful of the many added features is the new clubhouse entrance at the street car gate. Developed by Colonel Winn primarily to handle the huge Derby Day crowds, the smartness and simplicity of design of this new entrance is enhanced by the free use of amber-stained glass and represents a dignified beauty reminiscent of an old Southern mansion. It is finished in shiplap and painted a gleaming white.

The jockeys' quarters in 1930 was connected to the paddock by a balustraded overhead walkway (also see page 197).

In addition to facilitating the handling of the clubhouse traffic, this beautiful structure houses the offices of the racing secretary and his assistants and the jockey's quarters are on the second floor. A new odds board also has been erected between this entrance and the paddock.

Another of the many improvements this year is the location of the paddock some seventy feet nearer the grandstand section. This will give more persons an opportunity to see the horses better before each race. The moving of this structure, which in itself was no mean engineering feat, was carried out under direction of Track Superintendent Tom Young, and is one of the vast number of things he has done to add greatly to the beauty and symmetry of design of this area.

Press box facilities have been increased again this year to a point where there will be seating room for more than 200 of the Nation's crack sports writers and radio commentators.

Aerial picture made during 1937
Derby. Central Avenue is at top.
Inset: Grandstand garden with jockeys gathered on the arcade leading
from their quarters to the paddock,
just out of picture at left, 1939 Derby
day.

FROM *THE COURIER-JOURNAL*, 30 APRIL 1941

Picturesque Col. Daniel E. O'Sullivan recently was promoted from resident manager at Churchill Downs to assistant to President Matt J. Winn, at the age of 82....

When the conflict [WWI] ended, Colonel Dan returned to Louisville and, in 1924, when the time neared for the Golden Jubilee running of the Kentucky Derby, Colonel Winn asked Colonel Dan to get out the souvenir program. In 1926, when Colonel Andrew Vennie, resident manager of Churchill Downs, died, Colonel Dan succeeded him.[22]

FROM LOUIS J. HERRMANN, SR., "AS FOR SEATS, THE DOWNS IS SITTING PRETTY,"
THE COURIER-JOURNAL, 4 MAY 1941

The Downs system of box distribution circumvents most ticket scalpers. Each boxholder now owning a box has the privilege of renewing it from year to year. If the boxholder should sell his box he also sells his claim to it the next year. The purchaser can establish priority by showing a track official last year's stubs.

Then, too, most boxholders are reluctant to sell their boxes. Bids of $1,000 for a box on Derby Day have been refused. Families hand down many of the boxes from one generation to the next. Not merely a horse race, the Derby has a personal friendliness lacking at other sports gatherings. People with adjoining boxes have struck up friendships which they renew every Derby Day....

The price of a box at Churchill Downs ranges from $65 to $125, depending on the location. This price will include six admissions to the grounds and clubhouse, six box seats and all taxes. The clubhouse boxes are divided into sections. One section may be composed chiefly of persons from St. Louis and Chicago, another section holds the Kentucky and Southern aggregation, and another the Eastern delegation made up of horse owners and socialites such as the Whitneys, the Wideners, the Peabodys, the Woodwards and the Vanderbilts.

The dividing lines followed in the distribution of boxes are not that clear-cut, but it is true that most of the Eastern visitors are seated south of the finish line, while the Western and Southern groups are north of the finish line, with the directors. A box north of the finish line is always reserved for the Governor of Kentucky, the Mayor of Louisville, and the United States Cabinet officers.

Lawrence L. Jones, 81, principal owner of Frankfort Distilleries, died on 21 October 1941. He was a director of the Kentucky Jockey Club and the American Turf Association, as well as Churchill Downs, Inc. His brother was Saunders P. Jones.[23] Two days later, Henning Chambers, whose brokerage firm had merged with W. L. Lyons and Co. in 1939, died at 68. He had also been influential in banking affairs and a director of the American Turf Association since its formation. According to his obituary, he "arranged a trusteeship for the association so that Kentucky's outstanding institution would not fall into hands of 'strangers' and there would always be a Derby at Churchill Downs."[24]

Churchill Downs Resident Manager Dan E. O'Sullivan (left) and Matt Winn, *ca.* 1935.

FROM MATT J. WINN IN *DOWN THE STRETCH*, PAGE 230

Mr. and Mrs. [Henning] Chambers and their friend, Mrs. Blandina Babcock, had greenhouses on their estates in Kentucky, and the custom which the three of them originated years ago is still continued by Mrs. Chambers and Mrs. Babcock.[25] Each day during our race meetings at Churchill Downs they ship a truckload of flowers to my office, and then the two of them, sometimes assisted by my daughter Ollie (Mrs. Louis J. Herrmann) transform the room into a bower of the finest flowers that grow in the soil of Kentucky.

Above: Far turn, site of original clubhouse, 1940 Derby. Structures, at left, line west side of Fourth Street. Right: View toward grandstand and stadium from greenhouses, 1937.

James William Wyatt, Sr., took charge of the greenhouses in 1924. He had started as a laborer in 1912. A 1961 article stated that "for more than ten years he has planted approximately 15,000 new tulip bulbs." Wyatt was succeeded by Donald Lord, the grandson of a gardner and son of an English tulip expert. He began planting his 7,500 yellow, pink and red tulips 8 inches deep instead of the traditional 16 inches to delay premature blooming.[26]

FROM AN INTERVIEW WITH WARNER L. JONES, JR., 19 OCTOBER 1993

I came on the board in 1941 when I was twenty-five years old. I replaced my stepfather, Henning Chambers. My uncle Lawrence Jones had also been on the board. My grandfather, Saunders P. Jones, had also been on the board, and I am distantly related to Meriwether Lewis Clark, the track's principal founder, as well as to the Churchills.[27] Colonel Winn was a great friend of my stepfather, Henning Chambers, and my uncle, Lawrence Jones, and when my stepfather and uncle died, I guess he volunteered to make me a director. He knew me and he would come out to their house for dinner. We used to have the directors' meeting in Chicago, and we would go up on the train the night before.

I was probably eight or ten when I went to my first Derby. My mother would take me to the track. My mother would go to the track with Blandina Babcock. They would go out there and have lunch every day of the world, and they would bet. I would go out with them and you would get corned beef and cabbage and damn good lunches. Later I couldn't go so much because I was out here [at Hermitage Farm] driving a team of

Cars and crowd arriving at the Longfield Avenue (south) entrance to the clubhouse, 1940 Derby day.

mules, working. We used to mow this with mules; now we can hardly get it done with tractors. I bought Hermitage Farm in 1936 when I was twenty years old.[28]

I sold my first yearling at Saratoga in 1937 for $6,000. There was a man from Pleasureville, Kentucky, who ran the bank up there, named W. S. Threlkeld. He was a great friend of my stepfather, Henning Chambers, who was in the banking and brokerage business. Henning Chambers got Mr. Threlkeld to help me lay out the farm. He was the one who suggested putting these barns in a row up through here and all that. And he found this mare, named Sweeping Queen, that I bought for $1,500. She was in foal to a stallion named Bull Dog. We took the yearling to Saratoga where Mr. Threlkeld had already been selling and we got $6,000 for the first yearling I ever sold. It sounded easy. Of course, it wasn't.

There was a big demand for horses back then because there were only four or five thousand foals born a year versus fifty thousand a couple of years ago. It has dropped off now to between thirty-five and forty thousand. We would go to Saratoga and take the yearlings up there on the train, and there were gambling joints up there, and we could get our check from the sales company the next day, and a lot of times I would come home with two or three times what my yearlings brought. And sometimes I would come home with damn near nothing.

The next year I had probably two yearlings and the next three or four, and then probably in 1941, I topped the whole Saratoga sale. I sold a colt of Bull Dog to Ogden Phipps, who is a friend of mine, for $10,000.

When the war came along, we couldn't get transportation for the yearlings to Saratoga, so we started a sales company, called the Breeders Sales Company, here at Keeneland. We sold under a tent. It was a cooperative,

Whirlaway established a new track record easily winning the 1941 Derby when attendance exceeded 100,000 for the first time. It was Eddie Arcaro's second of five Derby victory rides, and Whirlaway would become the fifth horse to win the Triple Crown.

and we would rebate ourselves the difference between a five percent selling cost we would charge ourselves and the actual selling cost which was about three and a half percent, so we would get one and a half percent back. We kept on doing that, and I forget when Hal Price Headley, who was the guiding light at Keeneland and was awful smart, wanted to merge the Breeders Sales Company into Keeneland. They had a big meeting and I was the only one who got up and was against it. Here we had a going-concern sales company. Keeneland now sells $400-million worth of horses a year, which times five percent is $20 million. Their expense couldn't conceivably be by the highest imagination over $5 million. There must be $15 million profit. They have continued to charge us five percent and they have added on fees.

FROM "LATONIA SALE OPTION GIVEN," *THE LOUISVILLE TIMES*, 13 JANUARY 1942

Climaxing negotiations intermittently recurring for five years, Churchill Downs-Latonia, Inc. today confirmed a report that it has optioned its Latonia race track at Covington for sale to an oil refinery....Its Latonia Derby, run continuously from 1883 to 1937, was ranked second only to Churchill Downs' Kentucky Derby...Sale and abandonment of racing at the mile oval would leave Kentucky, traditional home of the thoroughbred, with but three tracks—the Downs, Keeneland at Lexington, and Dade Park, near Henderson.

The sale of the Covington track site was reflected in the corporate name changes on 24 April 1942 from Churchill Downs-Latonia, Inc. to simply Churchill Downs, Inc. [29]

Twenty-three horses were spread across the track when the largest field in Kentucky Derby history broke from the starting gate for the hundredth running in 1974. The crowd of 163,628 also was record-setting.

PART FIVE

Churchill Downs, Inc.

From "Nonresidents Return Fourth Of Derby Boxes,"
The Courier-Journal, 23 April 1943

A fourth of the 400 boxes sold this year to out-of-town patrons of the Kentucky Derby have been returned and resold to Louisville customers, the Churchill Downs management revealed yesterday....

Box reservations were sold to out-of-town customers before the Office of Defense Transportation asked that travel to the Derby be limited. Col. Matt J. Winn, Derby impresario, said yesterday he has "absolutely no way of knowing" how many of the out-of-town holders of box seats will be at the Derby.

"But I do know that many people who paid for their boxes will not attend the Kentucky Derby, having sent the boxes, with their compliments, to friends in the Louisville area," his statement added.

Colonel Winn had been asked by *The Courier-Journal* for a list of box-holders. To make one public, he said, would be an injustice, explaining:

"In other years Churchill Downs has supplied to the newspapers about two weeks before the running of the Derby, a list of the boxholders,

The infield had been converted for three days (28-30 October 1942) before the regular fall race meeting into a bivouac housing 400 motorized cavalrymen from Fort Knox. Tanks and other armament were spread around the grounds, as Churchill Downs raised $120,000 for the Louisville War Fund. Race tracks around the country were committed to raise $2 million for war relief.

assuming that such persons, with their guests, would occupy the boxes. Churchill Downs can not do that this year because of the possible injustice to boxholders outside the Louisville area whose names would appear as boxholders.

"The fact that 300 out-of-town boxholders have their tickets does not mean that those persons will attend the Derby. Many made the purchases so as to perpetuate their names on the list of boxholders, thus giving them a right to the box in future Derby years."[2]

FROM *THE COURIER-JOURNAL*, 20 JANUARY 1944[3]

Col. Matt Winn, a young fellow of 83 just starting out on a new career...has just taken over the job of running Empire City in New York and Laurel in Maryland, on top of his old spots at Churchill Downs and Chicago's Lincoln Fields....About a year and a half ago, he got the operators of several tracks together at a meeting in his quarters in Chicago, and from that huddle the Thoroughbred Racing Association was organized.[4]

FROM BOYD MARTIN, "THE REVIVAL OF OUTDOOR CONCERTS RECALLS OLDTIMERS," *THE COURIER-JOURNAL*, 15 JULY 1945

The idea of Summer Night Music at the Downs, which the Louisville Philharmonic Society is to inaugurate July 23 with Joan Davis as guest star, has long been a popular one in Louisville, and in the past has proved a delightful form of entertainment....

It was [Johnny] Kurkamp, we seem to remember, who was one of the maestros who brought bands to Churchill Downs during 1903 when Charles F. Grainger, then the Mayor of Louisville, introduced band concerts on a shell built especially for the purpose right behind the grandstand, a modest unit of the present huge structure. Perhaps the most vivid picture of Kurkamp, at least to a small boy, was the one in his snow-white uniform, elaborately embroidered in highly burnished gold braid.

We remember well the refreshments served there because we were allowed, as a special privilege, a very choice summer drink—claret lemonade....

The Louisville Philharmonic Society's scheme for Churchill Downs seems to follow the general idea of the old formula. Instead of a continuous season, however, five musical programs will be given for five consecutive weeks, three programs each week, beginning July 23. Tables for parties, or comfortable individual chairs, promise audiences an informal, cool setting for the music. An added touch, very Continental in flavor, will be refreshments served during the concert.

I went to Hawthorne during the war. We could not run at Lincoln Fields because of the war travel restrictions. Lincoln Fields was in Crete, Illinois, and quite a distance from Chicago by car. They could go by trolley and buses to Hawthorne. So they negotiated a contract with the Hawthorne race track to run the Lincoln Fields dates. I think they did that for two years. I was still with Humphrey Robinson at that time doing monthly payroll work.

—FROM AN INTERVIEW WITH KENNETH A. COYTE, 29 DECEMBER 1993

FROM *THE COURIER-JOURNAL*, 22 AUGUST 1945

They wanted swing at Churchill Downs last night and, by golly, they got it. Starting at an easy pace, the "Summer Nights" final entry, Benny Goodman, crossed the Downs wire in a red-hot heat....

Even the Philharmonic showed it wasn't averse to jam. When the symphony orchestra accompanied Goodman on "Dizzy Fingers," more than one person was heard to remark, "The Philharmonic is strictly in the groove."

It was music that made you want to dance. In fact a few couples did some impromptu stepping on the outer edges of the courtyard lawn where just a few minutes before sedate concert-goers sat....

Knowing that the last of the "pops" concerts would be a sell-out, fans jammed the gates at 6 p.m. for the final "Summer Nights" fling. Baskets chock full of chicken, ham and other preconcert palatables accompanied many, who had dinner as well as music "under the stars."

FROM DONALD MCWAIN, "ODD LOTS," *THE COURIER-JOURNAL*, 4 MARCH 1947

Discussion in financial circles that American Turf Association directors this week will receive a formal offer for purchase of Lincoln Fields was a factor yesterday in a rising demand for the Association's stock. A bid of 18 1/2 was reported for American Turf actual shares in the local over-the-counter market. Offerings were scanty.

The story in financial circles was that a group of Chicago men Thursday would place their bid before the directors of American Turf.

Above: Street cars at the entrance during 1944 wartime Derby. Right: Arcades were being reconfigured in late 1945 around frame building housing the racing secretary's office and the jockeys' quarters in anticipation of moving the paddock and erecting a more sophisticated tote board (out of picture at left).

Derby day, 1946. The paddock had been moved from the end of the stone walls to create adequate space for the gigantic totalisator board that would "automatically register the punting of Churchill Downs patrons...in minute and a half cycles." The system was later computerized and new equipment was installed by United Tote in 1993, linking Churchill Downs with other tracks in Kentucky.

Any sale of capital assets, such as Lincoln Fields, would further fatten the already lush cash position of American Turf.[5]...

Holding only Kentucky property, the Association management well might consider liquidating American Turf Association, now a Delaware corporation, and incorporating its Kentucky assets into a Kentucky corporation.

FROM AN INTERVIEW WITH KENNETH A. COYTE, 29 DECEMBER 1993

We used to have big wooden boxes, maybe six feet long and four or five feet deep and we would take two or three of those and we would take all our records up there with us—all the books and all the records of the company. We sort of transferred the office up there from Louisville and operated out of the Lincoln Fields office. The meeting was some thirty days up there.

FROM LARRY BOECK, *THE COURIER-JOURNAL*, 25 APRIL 1948

"We had our biggest crowd of over 100,000 last year," [Russell Sweeney] said, "but even then we had room. Of course, that's standing room, principally in the centerfield. We've been getting the centerfield area in shape—putting up mutuel boards, benches, garden, and so on. So, actually, practically everyone who really wants to see the Derby can. That is, if he isn't too particular and doesn't want a reserved seat or box."

Sweeney himself has seen every Derby, except one, since 1924. That year, he did a jack-of-all-trades stint at Latonia and in 1925 took over as manager of the Illinois track along with Juarez near El Paso, Texas. "It was in 1925 I missed the Derby," said Sweeney. "Mrs. Sweeney was in ill health so we decided to spend the time in Mexico and Texas." Mrs. Sweeney, formerly Julia Winn, died in 1941. She was the daughter of Colonel Matt Winn, now 87, who built the Derby into the world's most famous horse race.... Until Colonel Winn sold Latonia and Lincoln Fields, Sweeney also managed those tracks.

It had been eleven years since *The Louisville Times* profiled and pictured the "'Nine Old Men' of the Downs." They were almost all gone by 1948, except one—eighty-seven-year-old Matt J. Winn. He had retired from Laurel and Empire City, sold off Fairmount Park, Washington Park, Latonia, and Lincoln Fields. He had run a conservative operation and Churchill Downs was left with cash reserves, but no direction for the future. Winn had trained no protégé who could step in and reinvigorate the operation. He had built the Kentucky Derby into an institution and he wanted that legacy and the historic site where it had been run since 1875 to live on in perpetuity. On 22 November 1948, the directors of the American Turf Association appointed a committee to study a proposal that called for a foundation to purchase Churchill Downs and operate it as a non-profit entity, with all earnings going to the University of Louisville School of Medicine. Three weeks later, Samuel A. Culbertson, 86, chairman of the board of Churchill Downs, died.[7]

The sale plan would subsist until 1960 when the city of Louisville was approached to purchase Churchill Downs by issuing revenue bonds. The property would be controlled by a bipartisan commission that would lease its operation; profits would as before support the University of Louisville, then still a municipal institution. Religious groups voiced opposition and the proposal was withdrawn from consideration.[8]

FROM "DOWNS DIRECTORS APPROVE SALE PLAN," *THE COURIER-JOURNAL*, 3 APRIL 1949

American Turf Association directors yesterday approved the sale of Churchill Downs to a nonprofit corporation....Previously mentioned as the purchaser was the Churchill Downs Foundation, a nonprofit organization incorporated in 1946. Previously mentioned as the chief and perhaps only beneficiary was the School of Medicine of the University of Louisville.

Citation won the 1948 Kentucky Derby as well as the Triple Crown. The bay colt's owner, trainer, and jockey as a team are unmatched. Horses of Warren Wright (left), owner of Calumet Farm, won the Derby four times; trainer Ben A. Jones held a horse's bridle in the winner's circle five additional times. Jockey Eddie Arcaro won five times.

When this picture of a Brink's armored truck being loaded was taken in 1950, the spring meet's handle was $12,603,020 for 19 days of racing.

Matt J. Winn, 88, died on 6 October 1949. He was president of both Churchill Downs and its parent corporation, the American Turf Association. His obituary mentioned: "In recent times, Winn had been a backer of a still-pending plan to convert Churchill Downs to a nonprofit concern." William H. Veeneman, a Louisville capitalist, was named chairman of the corporate entities as well as CEO.[9] Respected columnist and radio commentator Bill Corum, 54, was selected over U. S. Congressman Tom Underwood, George "Brownie" Leach, and John H. Clark (president of Hialeah Park) and others to succeed Winn.[10] And before the year 1949 was out, the proposal to sell Churchill Downs to a foundation had been shelved.[11]

FROM *THE COURIER-JOURNAL*, 4 APRIL 1950

In an action not related to the profit trend, the stockholders voted yesterday to dissolve the [American Turf] association. This will eliminate a no-longer-needed stockholding company. Churchill Downs will not be affected. Association stockholders will exchange their shares for those of Churchill Downs, Inc., one for one. [Note: Articles of Incorporation were amended to authorize 383,292 shares of common stock instead of the previously specified 40,000 shares. There were 32,242 shares outstanding worth $1,289,680, or $40 per share. The new value was $3.36 per share.[12]]

FROM "DOWNS PLEASED, SO TV CAN SHOW DERBY IN '53,"
THE LOUISVILLE TIMES, 5 MAY 1952

This year's race was the first to be televised "live" over a national network and...the Downs president conceded that TV "certainly didn't hurt" Saturday's turnout.

The Kentucky Derby had been televised locally in 1949, but Bill Corum estimated that 5,000 people had stayed home to watch and the new Churchill Downs president was reluctant to continue the experiment. By 1994, over 7-million American households and countless others in foreign countries would view the race.[13]

FROM GRADY CLAY, *THE COURIER-JOURNAL*, 3 MAY 1953

Alfred Gwynne Vanderbilt—by all rights the most disappointed man at Churchill Downs yesterday—advanced toward his old friend, Harry F. Guggenheim. They shook hands, two men 12 years apart in age, but each representing pinnacles of wealth, social position, and sportsmanship in America. "I'm glad it was you," Vanderbilt repeated, his disappointment hidden behind a friendly smile.

The scene was the long string of rooms atop the north wing of Churchill Downs' grandstand—the apartment of Downs president Bill Corum. Here, every year, a lavish buffet supper of meats, caviar, and salads, and a bar are set up for a small circle—the favored few winning and losing owners and trainers and their friends. [Note: Vanderbilt's highly favored horse, Native Dancer, lost to Guggenheim's Dark Star, bred by Warner L. Jones, Jr., at Hermitage Farm.]

FROM MIKE BARRY, *THE COURIER-JOURNAL & TIMES*, 28 APRIL 1974

The vintage year, though, must be 1957, when three of the best horses in the history of the Derby were in the field. Strangely enough, all three were beaten—Gallant Man second, Round Table third, Bold Ruler fourth. And Iron Liege, the horse who beat all three, never beat a single one of them again....

If you saw the 1957 Derby, you saw the best field that ever ran in the race. When will you see a better one? We should all live so long.

Bill Corum, 63, president of Churchill Downs and long-time columnist for *The New York Journal-American*, died on 16 December 1958. He was succeeded by Wathen R. Knebelkamp, 58, a former baseball and Schenley Distillers executive. Stanley F. Hugenberg, Sr., 66, executive vice president and director, retired in 1960. During his 23-year tenure handling Churchill Downs' money, Derby Day betting rose from $1.5 million to over $4 million, and the annual take from $5.7 million to $24.5 million.[14]

FROM AN INTERVIEW WITH KENNETH A. COYTE, 29 DECEMBER 1993

The meetings were held at the old Drake Hotel in Chicago. I was young and just brand new in the organization, and they took me along for one reason or another. I started working at Churchill Downs in 1945. I was doing work for their accountants, Humphrey Robinson and Company. In 1949, I was hired full time by the Churchill Downs corporation. I was secretary-treasurer when I retired in 1984, right before Tom Meeker came on board. Lynn Stone was still president.

When Winn was here, he had his own way of doing things and he hardly ever brought to the board of directors any ideas. He just went ahead

Opposite top: Part of the grandstand garden was converted into a TV studio on Derby day, pictured in 1953. The clubhouse garden in the foreground had been walled in. Opposite bottom: Also shown in 1953, the administrative offices and president's apartment above, were at the end of the grandstand where the tunnel entrance to the "Centerfield" is still located. Above: Jockey's quarters in 1954.

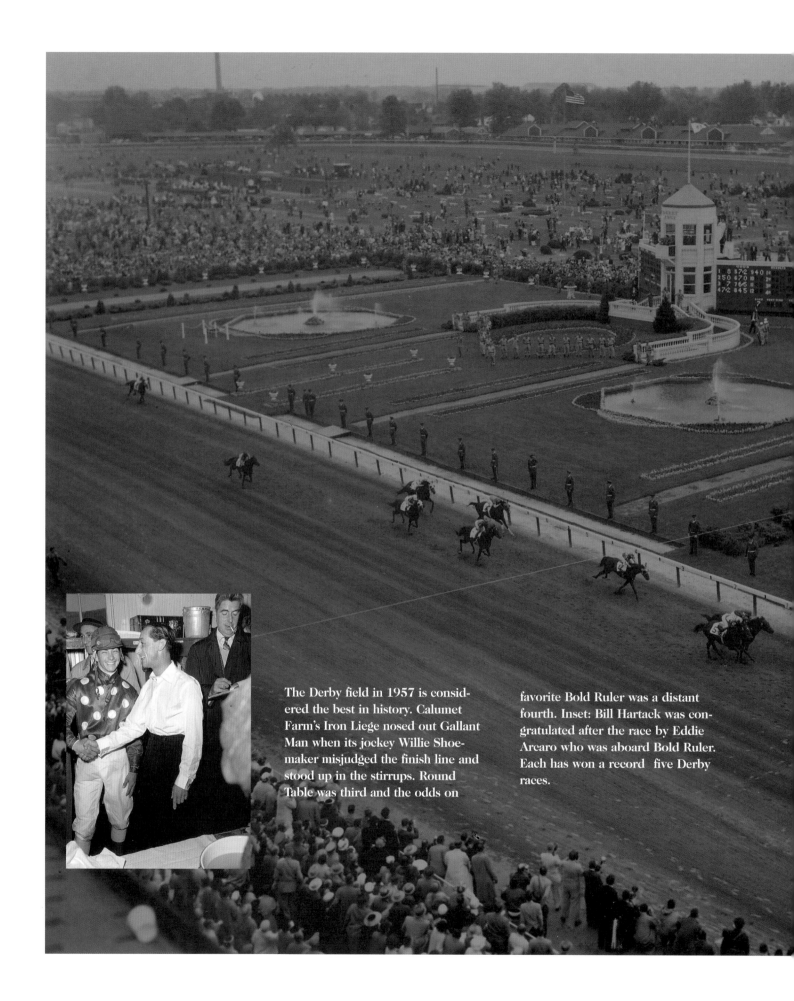

The Derby field in 1957 is considered the best in history. Calumet Farm's Iron Liege nosed out Gallant Man when its jockey Willie Shoemaker misjudged the finish line and stood up in the stirrups. Round Table was third and the odds on favorite Bold Ruler was a distant fourth. Inset: Bill Hartack was congratulated after the race by Eddie Arcaro who was aboard Bold Ruler. Each has won a record five Derby races.

Matt Winn was ever present in the 1959 staff portrait which included (l to r): Kenneth Coyte, Russell Sweeney, unidentified woman, Henry Watermann, Wathen Knebelkamp, Tom Young, Katherine Huber, Stanley Hugenberg, Sr., and George B. "Brownie" Leach.

and did them. He may have asked for $100,000 for expenditures prior to the Derby. They always built something new. But the board didn't have too much control over that situation.

Bill Corum was more of a figurehead than anything else. He didn't want to get involved too much in the operation of the plant. He was a businessman and a writer, so the operation was left to Stanley Hugenberg, Sr., who was my mentor. He was a very special kind of person.

When Hugenberg had charge and Knebelkamp and then Stone, these men preferred to talk to everybody — other race tracks and anybody who could come up with ideas. They would talk to Tom Young and Danny Parkerson and would ask, what do we need. Then they would shuffle through this information and make recommendations to the board. These recommendations are in the minutes. I tried to list all the anticipated improvements. These would go to the board with dollar amounts. And they would be approved. Starting with Hugenberg and up to today, that's the way it is done.

FROM "DOWNS PLANS MUSEUM OF RACING BY FALL," *THE COURIER-JOURNAL*, 15 DECEMBER 1960

Churchill Downs visitors next fall should find a nostalgia-loaded racing museum to browse through between races. Downs directors yesterday voted $50,000 for a one-story free museum at the Central Avenue main entrance. And a call went out to attic-searchers and collectors to contribute historic racing mementos.

"We will try to uncover things that will reflect the history of racing in Louisville and the history of the Kentucky Derby," said Brownie Leach, public-relations director.

Construction will start after the spring Derby and an effort made to complete it before the fall racing season. The idea of a museum had been discussed for 10 or 12 years, but other improvements had to come first, Leach said. The money became available this year.

An assortment of museum objects that have gathered dust around the track for years will be enshrined. Among the historic items are one of the first 1875 stock certificates issued for the Downs and a picture of the late jockey Jimmy Lee, who rode every one of the six winners on the card on a spring day in 1909. Old pictures, winning silks, and trophies of past years will be welcome, Leach said. [Note: The Churchill Downs museum was opened in the spring of 1962.[15]]

FROM *THE COURIER-JOURNAL*, 31 AUGUST 1961

Lynn Stone, 35, assistant vice-president in charge of marketing at Liberty National Bank, was named resident manager of Churchill Downs, replacing Russell Sweeney, 58, who retired because of ill health. Stone had been president of the Louisville Colonels baseball team.

FROM CAROL SUTTON, "ODDS AGAINST CRITICS URGING NEW RACING PLANT," *THE COURIER-JOURNAL*, 13 MAY 1962

Does Churchill Downs need a new lease on life? Should the sprawling, aging structure be torn down and replaced with a shiny new plant? A few visiting sportswriters raise these questions each year at Derbytime when they refer to the plant as "ramshackle...unattractive...a monstrosity of a

The sun was shining bright for this 1959 Derby aerial providing a contrast that helps define the intricate construction pattern connected to the expanse of seating.

The State Racing Commission retained the Aetron group of Covina, California, to prepare a restoration program in 1961. The proposed construction, pictured above, was designed to "emphasize the original architecture." It was estimated to cost $10,000,000 and to have been completed by 1971.

woodshed."…Churchill Downs is a structure that has been in almost constant transition since it was started in the past century.…This continually changing situation apparently is destined to go on. Long-range plans announced last year call for clearing out the area behind the main entrance that now houses the old mutuel plant and offices and extending the second-floor grandstand area to make more room for betting and restroom facilities.

Tom Young, 76, superintendent of Churchill Downs since 1911, died in 1963. He was also involved in Empire City, Lincoln Fields, Washington Park, and Douglas Park. He made his first rounds on a mule and in later years by car. Young was succeeded by his assistant, Thurman Pangburn, who had had a similar position at River Downs.

FROM EARL RUBY, "$20,000,000 IDEA TO PUT KENTUCKY AHEAD IN RACING," *THE COURIER-JOURNAL*, 22 DECEMBER 1963

A major program of construction and expansion of racing facilities aimed at helping Kentucky maintain its position as undisputed leader in the Thoroughbred-breeding industry is being pushed by members of the State Racing Commission.

Part of the plan calls for establishment of a nonprofit Kentucky Racing Association patterned after the highly successful New York Racing Association.

The new organization would be financed through revenue bonds and would have as primary purposes the purchase of Churchill Downs, Keeneland and possibly other race tracks within the state, rebuilding the Downs stands, "all but the steeples," and completing the modernization of Keeneland.

The Racing Commission is expected to meet this week to begin moves calculated to clear the way for quick action, should an early agreement among all groups develop. Up to the time this was written no official action had been taken by directors of either track, and none had been asked. Individual comment has ranged from warm approval to reserved questioning.[17]

FROM EARL RUBY, "NEW VIP BOXES ON ROOF ARE INCLUDED IN FIVE-YEAR
PLAN AT CHURCHILL DOWNS," *THE COURIER-JOURNAL*, 23 MARCH 1965

A sign just outside the Central Avenue entrance to Churchill Downs reads, "Churchill Downs Museum." Three tourists who followed the arrow came to a halt at the gates. Before them was a scene of what appeared at first glance to be utter devastation. A large section of the brick walkway was torn up. The old general office building was gone. Where it had once joined the grandstand was a dark gray patch against the white siding.... "Looks more like an archeological excavation than a museum," said one of the visitors....

The steel-and-concrete building replaces a rotten frame one which included an apartment once occupied by Winn and later used for the annual Derby winner's party....

We drove under the track to the infield. Looking back at the stands, the white-haired president [Wathen Knebelkamp] said, "Our next big change, we hope, will be to build VIP boxes from one end of the roof to the other, except for the middle section which frames the historic spires. The boxes will be for 10 persons each, will be carpeted, and have separate dining facilities like the few boxes we have up there now." The press box, he said, would be torn out and a new one built atop a section of the roof boxes.

Opposite: A fire was quickly extinguished at the end of the clubhouse stands on Derby day in 1965. Right: Grandstand seating in 1965 before a massive structural reworking was initiated to increase the number of floors, shown below in a 1969 view.

FROM MIKE BARRY, *THE COURIER-JOURNAL*, 7 MAY 1967

In capital improvements alone, this is what [Wathen Knebelkamp] has asked for: 1959, $128,000; 1960, $162,000; 1961, $328,000; 1962, $453,000; 1963, $408,000; 1964, $456,000; 1965, $420,000; 1966, $1,016,0000.

Knebelkamp's rebuilding program has covered both the track and the people who work there. Churchill Downs has group insurance, hospitalization, a pension plan, and union contracts with the majority of its employees....

He has gotten younger men, too. "When I came here," Knebelkamp said, "this place looked like the shuffleboard courts at St. Petersburg. In one major department the head man was 76—and his assistant 75!"

Now the No. 2 man at the track, resident manager Lynn Stone, is 41. Track superintendent Thurman Pangburn is 47, chief of security Al Schem 40, and director of public relations Kelso Sturgeon a downy-cheeked 27. Knebelkamp himself is 66.

FROM ROD WENZ, "7 HORSEMEN INCREASE OFFER IN DOWNS FIGHT," *THE COURIER-JOURNAL*, 14 MARCH 1969

The battle for control of Churchill Downs intensified yesterday as National Industries' offer to buy all the race track's stock at $35 a share moved within hours of expiring.[18]...The Kentucky Derby Protection Group, made up of seven prominent horsemen, raised its bid $500,000 — to $35 a share — to make its move to head off National's competition.[19]

FROM AN INTERVIEW WITH WARNER L. JONES, JR., 19 OCTOBER 1993

James Cox Brady, Nick Brady's father, who was chairman of the Jockey Club, and chairman of the NYRA, the New York Racing Association, was a close friend of mine, and he told Bull Hancock and me while playing golf that National Industries was thinking about taking Churchill Downs over in a proxy fight. Arnold Hanger[20] and John Galbreath were down at Hialeah. I had played polo with John Galbreath, so I told him about what we had been told about the takeover. He didn't have any stock in Churchill Downs at that time, but he was for racing and he wasn't for that bunch taking over a big race track.

So we formed the Kentucky Derby Protection Group, and John Galbreath was its backbone. John Tarrant was our lawyer. The stock was selling on the open market for $22 a share. We kept bidding the stock up against one another and we finally had to give $35 a share for it to keep National Industries from taking us over. I borrowed the money to buy I think 8,500 shares. Bull Hancock and I bought the same amount. That would be 85,000 shares now because of the 10 for 1 split.[21] If it hadn't been for John Galbreath, National Industries would have taken us over.

FROM "128,571 DOWNS SHARES BOUGHT," *THE COURIER-JOURNAL*, 18 APRIL 1969

The Kentucky Derby Protection Group, with its goal of heading off National Industries' bid for control of Churchill Downs accomplished, apparently will cease to function as a unit.

The organization, which has added five members to its original group

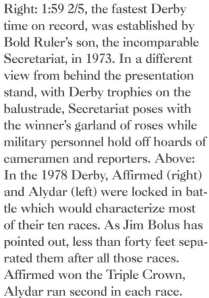

Right: 1:59 2/5, the fastest Derby time on record, was established by Bold Ruler's son, the incomparable Secretariat, in 1973. In a different view from behind the presentation stand, with Derby trophies on the balustrade, Secretariat poses with the winner's garland of roses while military personnel hold off hoards of cameramen and reporters. Above: In the 1978 Derby, Affirmed (right) and Alydar (left) were locked in battle which would characterize most of their ten races. As Jim Bolus has pointed out, less than forty feet separated them after all those races. Affirmed won the Triple Crown, Alydar ran second in each race.

of seven prominent horsemen, yesterday accepted 128,571 shares of Downs stock at $35 per share. The total cost of this stock is just under $4.5 million....

John Tarrant, attorney for the horsemen's group, said its members will own their shares individually and will not work as an organized bloc. The shares purchased yesterday represent about one-third of the track's total stock. Many members of the group had held Downs stock previously.

At the end of 1969, Wathen Knebelkamp retired as president and was succeeded by Lynn Stone, 44, who had come to Churchill Downs as resident manager in 1961.[22] In the meantime, William H. Veeneman, Sr., 78, chairman of the board since 1949, had died and former U. S. Senator Thruston Ballard Morton had taken his place.[23] John W. Galbreath of Darby Dan Farm, a real-estate developer and owner of the Pittsburgh Pirates, succeeded Morton in 1980.[24]

In late 1981, Lynn Stone disclosed plans for a new $5-million Kentucky Derby Museum. The old Churchill Downs museum would be torn down. Warner Jones, Stanley Hugenberg, and Joe Rodes were instrumental in establishing the new nonprofit entity with its own operating board of directors. The J. Graham Brown Foundation would fund the replacement containing "electronic exhibits, animated displays, Derby artifacts and

Model of the proposed Kentucky Derby Museum, 1983.

other items."[25] In writing about the new museum proposal *Courier-Journal* Sports Editor Billy Reed noted: "Churchill always must understand that its No. 1 product isn't horse racing, but tradition." The $7.5 million museum with a multi-projector slide program in the great hall opened on 28 April 1985.[26]

FROM JIM BOLUS, *THE LOUISVILLE TIMES*, 21 DECEMBER 1982

Churchill Downs continues to take on a new look. The historic track, which began using computerized pari-mutuel betting this fall and has approval to race during the summer next year for the first time in its history, now plans to add grass racing to its program.

The track's board of directors today approved the construction of a grass course, pending a favorable outcome of an appeal that Ellis Park has made in connection with the granting of a summer meeting at Churchill Downs....If Ellis Park wins the appeal and there is no summer racing, the grass course won't be built. The cost of the course will be $1.6 million.

The course, which will be seven furlongs and 165 feet in length, will be built on the inside of the existing one-mile dirt track....

Warner L. Jones, a director, has been a strong advocate of grass racing at the Downs. "I'm one hundred percent in favor of it," Jones said in a recent interview before the directors' meeting. "I made as strong an argument as I could at the last directors' meeting."

At that meeting on June 1, the directors reconsidered their plans and decided to delay construction of a grass course, which originally had been approved by the board a year ago....

Jones pointed out that a grass course would put Churchill Downs in a position of serving as the host track for the Breeders' Cup Series, a one-day program of seven championship races, including two on the turf.

We now water the track and irrigate the turf with well water. For a spring meet, we use five and a half million gallons. We used city water up until 1985 when we built the turf course. We are pumping water ninety feet. There is an unlimited supply at that depth, but because of the cost to pump it, it might not be as cheap as people think.

You can hit water twenty-five feet down. Our Longfield tunnel is sitting on the aquifer. For years, the track superintendents before me had trouble with the track settling in that turn. When I put the turf course in, I found out why. That corner was sitting on water. We had to put extra concrete in the tunnel there and some is actually sitting in water. We raised the tunnel so the water is about a foot below the roadway. We have pumps on it just in case the water comes up and needs to be pumped out.

We have found some old wells around the course. There was one near the two old greenhouses up by the bank. It was twenty-five feet deep and brick lined. There was one over by the grandstand. It was just covered with a dome. It's a wonder somebody hadn't fallen through it. We filled it in, but it's still there.

—FROM AN INTERVIEW WITH BUTCH LEHR, 24 MAY 1993

Right: Tunnel under the Longfield corner being constructed in July 1985. It can accommodate a semi-tractor trailer. Below: The turf course was also under construction in July 1985.

Summer racing at Churchill Downs led to large financial losses in 1983. Earnings dropped from $5.03 a share to $1.06. This spurred Brownell Combs II of Spendthrift Farm in Lexington to offer a 10-year, $100 bond bearing 10 percent interest for each share in a takeover bid in April 1984. The son of Leslie Combs II, a large stockholder in Churchill Downs, thought the track could be operated more profitably. This tender prompted two Minneapolis investors to offer $110 a share in cash for stock that had been selling for half that amount. At Churchill Downs' annual shareholders' meeting in July, four measures were adopted that general counsel Thomas H. Meeker had prepared to discourage takeover attempts. At the board of directors meeting, Warner L. Jones was elected chairman to replace John W. Galbreath, who had been sidelined by a heart attack. The board also made major changes in its executive committee, naming younger directors to it as well as J. David Grissom as its chairman.[27] The losses from the two years of extended spring-summer race meets prompted the resignation of track president Lynn Stone in August.

FROM SANDRA DUERR, "BIG PROFITS IN RACING? DON'T BET THE FARM," *THE LOUISVILLE TIMES*, 1 SEPTEMBER 1984

Many horsemen were particularly displeased with the way Downs management handled summer racing during the regime of Lynn Stone, who resigned as track president Aug. 7....

Enter Thomas H. Meeker.[28] A Louisville lawyer who had been representing Churchill Downs, Meeker stepped in as acting president following Stone's resignation. Meeker is a no-nonsense man who expects results, and under his direction the operation at the Downs has taken on a fresh, positive approach.

A more centrally located and visible 20-stall paddock was nearing completion in conjunction with a new tote board in September 1986. The 1924 paddock was converted into a beer garden pavilion. It had become too small and potentially dangerous. The new tote board with a huge television monitor was built some eighty feet behind the 1946 tote board which was razed.

Patrons have a much better view of horses in the 70'x180' walking ring placed in front of the paddock, pictured on Derby day 1987.

The employees, frequently criticized for their indifference, suddenly have become friendlier. The fields now are fuller. Management has begun promoting with enthusiasm....

Business has picked up considerably at the Downs during the past two weeks, and the track's board of directors has requested a third summer meeting for 1985. Horsemen are hoping that the third time will turn out to be a charm for summer racing. It was the horsemen, after all, who wanted summer racing at the Downs in the first place. Racing fans certainly never clamored for summer racing. Neither did the Downs management, although it applied for the dates.

The two-year experiment with summer racing was disappointing enough to bring about its early demise, and Churchill Downs' financial picture dramatically turned around in 1985 aided in part by major improvements to the track's accommodations.[29] Earnings continued to increase, and as attendance and pari-mutuel revenue reached local market saturation, management began experimenting with inter-track wagering.[30] However, at the same time Kentucky voters approved a lottery and the floodgate of land and riverboat casino gambling was opening as well.

Through the efforts of Churchill Downs and others to sustain pari-mutuel betting, legal gambling had been horse racing's domain. Suddenly the gaming wraps were off, as states and local governments viewed proceeds from gambling as windfall substitutes for tax increases or as economic stimulus packages.[31] The stakes were high as Tom Meeker formulated both offensive and defensive strategies to keep Churchill Downs and horse racing effectively positioned in the fast and furious gaming tug of war.

FROM SANDRA DUERR, "DOWNS PLANS $6.5 MILLION INTERTRACK BETTING CENTER," *THE COURIER-JOURNAL*, 22 FEBRUARY 1991

The decision to build an ITW complex clearly signals that Churchill Downs is embracing intertrack wagering, Meeker said, but that decision is not by choice. "I'm enough of a pragmatist to know that this will be with us," he said, "and as our board said, 'If we go with ITW, we want the best possible operation.'"

ITW is a form of betting in which one track transmits races from another via satellite. The Downs now accommodates patrons for such showings in the existing clubhouse area, which features "10-foot ceilings and smoke-filled corridors" and is spread out on different floors, Meeker said.

The planned two-story, 70,000-square foot building — to be situated about 60 feet from the track [on the first turn] — will seat about 2,700 people, including about 630 in an upscale sports bar, Meeker said. A total of 3,300 to 3,400 people could be accommodated.

However, instead of building a betting parlor at Churchill Downs as planned, the enclosed grandstand at Louisville Downs was transformed into the Sports Spectrum. Churchill Downs had looked upon Louisville Downs since 1984 as a possible source of stable space and for a training area to relieve track congestion. The 90-acre trotting track off Poplar Level Road had opened in 1966, but the recent advent of intertrack wagering had reduced both its attendance and handle. In August 1991, a purchase agreement was announced. The $5.7 million indoor facility was Churchill Downs' initial venture into off-site wagering. Simulcasting of out-of-state races was viewed as one way to offset the increasing threat to Thoroughbred racing from land-based casinos and riverboat gambling.[32]

FROM AN INTERVIEW WITH WARNER L. JONES, JR., 19 OCTOBER 1993

I see twelve or fifteen big race tracks in this country and the rest of it telephone betting at home and television betting where you can bet on credit and punch in a race at Belmont or wherever. That money you bet goes into the mutuel pool at Belmont so that the purses will go way up, and the price of horses will go up. There won't be as many race tracks to survive or owners to survive, trainers or breeders or broodmares to survive. It will all be ITW and OTW.

In the horse industry, the owner is putting on the show. If it wasn't for the owner, Wayne Lukas wouldn't have the horses to train, Pat Day wouldn't have the horses to ride, the breeders wouldn't have anybody to

Patrons view other tracks' races at the Sports Spectrum, which was opened on 29 November 1992.

sell their horses to, and the race tracks couldn't put on the races. If we could do anything at Churchill Downs, I would raise the purses of the owners, because the business is running out of owners. The plight of the owner is tough. Of the 90,000 horses that ran two or three years ago, only 6,000 earned $25,000 — and that is what it costs to keep one horse in training for a year. The rest of the owners are losing money.

FROM JENNIE REES, "FOR WANT OF A HORSE...," *THE COURIER-JOURNAL*,
21 FEBRUARY 1993

But the equine athletes being conceived now won't be ready to replenish race tracks until 1996. And the estimated 36,000 babies being born now, the result of last year's matings, will constitute the smallest thoroughbred crop in 13 years, reflecting a decrease of about 30 percent from the 1986 peak of 51,293.

The decline in racing stock is just one result of the sudden downturn in foal numbers as ownership lost popularity because of several factors, including less favorable tax laws and a worldwide recession.

The impact has been felt on the backsides of race tracks across the country and in support industries and groups — everything from equine insurance companies to the Breeders' Cup and Jockey Club....

"The reality is, no matter what happens to simulcasting, we aren't going to have the horses...," said Nick Nicholson, vice president of the Jockey Club, the registrar of North American thoroughbreds....

From a peak of 82,726 races in North America in 1989, there were 77,711 last year. That's partly because of the lack of horses, but also because of competition from other forms of gambling, such as lotteries, casinos and video-poker machines.

FROM RIC MANNING, "UNDER MEEKER, GREEN HAS BEEN A WINNING COLOR,"
THE COURIER-JOURNAL, 1 MAY 1993

Under Meeker's management, revenue doubled from $25 million in the 1984 fiscal year to $52.8 million last year. Profits rose even more, from a dismal $407,000 when Meeker arrived to a record $5.4 million for fiscal 1992, when the track served as host for the Breeder's Cup....

"In the past 10 years, Churchill Downs has executed a tremendous corporate turnaround," said Eugene Christiansen, a New York consultant to the gaming industry. He credits the success to a three-pronged approach: emphasis on customer service, capitalizing on the world-class status of the Kentucky Derby and exploiting intertrack wagering....

Meeker said that electronic wagering accounts for about 30 percent of Churchill Downs' revenue. And he can imagine a day when it might contribute half.

A new strategic business plan being developed at Churchill Downs looks at three broad options: Export [transmit electronically] more live races...Import more races...Acquire new markets. Meeker would love to run off-track betting systems in other states, which would give Churchill Downs new outlets for its races. But most states require companies that operate off-track betting also to operate a race track.

FROM KEN BERZOF, "DOWNS TO KEEP STRATEGY FOCUSED ON RACING,"
THE COURIER-JOURNAL, 22 OCTOBER 1993

Despite the current rage over riverboat gambling, Churchill Downs intends to keep placing its biggest bets on horse racing. "Our basic strategy is to become the pre-eminent racing center in the country," said Thomas Meeker, president and chief executive officer of the Louisville-based race track. "But more and more we'll be involved in other gaming operations."...

Over the next two or three years, Meeker said, Churchill Downs will become more development-oriented as it looks for other opportunities.

FROM JACALYN CARFAGNO, "CHURCHILL IS MOVING EARLY, OFTEN TO EXPAND,"
LEXINGTON HERALD-LEADER, 10 OCTOBER 1993

Churchill is a leader in an industry that often feels under siege these days. With video lottery terminals, casinos and Indiana gaming facilities popping up all over, many people in racing predict a dismal future of the sport that once had a virtual monopoly on legalized gambling.[33]

Not so with Churchill. A world of expanding casinos presents an opportunity to [Tom] Meeker, not a problem. "I have never been more optimistic about our industry than I am today," he said....

"We're going to have to address this issue of casinos," Meeker said. "On the horizon, I don't see too many alternatives other than getting in the business."...[34]

The expansion of gaming is the major movement in his industry now, Meeker said, and "we've got to position ourselves to be part of that."[35]

Churchill Downs' plant and surrounding area on 10 February 1994. Corner of Fourth Street and Central Avenue is in the foreground.

ENDNOTES

THE BACKGROUND ERA

1. The first local victim of the Epizootic, belonging to commission merchant B. C. Levi, was reported in *The Daily Louisville Commercial* on 31 October 1872.

Alexander Harthill (1849-1921) was a native of Glasgow, Scotland, and a graduate of the Ontario Veterinary College, Toronto. He specialized in racehorses, and was well known on Louisville tracks and at Latonia. His son, Dr. Henry C. Harthill (1882-1939), was a veterinarian as is his grandson, Dr. Alex Harthill. The youngest Harthill graduated from Ohio State University and immediately became the veterinarian for Calumet Farm. According to Jim Bolus's "The Alex Harthill story," which took up an entire page of the 1 September 1972 *Courier-Journal*, he attended Citation, winner of the 1948 Derby, and a host of others including Dancer's Image. The winner of the 1968 Derby was disqualified three days later after tests revealed an illegal medication had been used. Despite this and other controversies, Dr. Harthill's services were much in demand.

2. United States Census of Agriculture records for 1870. *The Courier-Journal*, 23 November 1872. "The Horses," *The Daily Louisville Commercial*, 27 November 1872.

3. United States Census of Agriculture records for 1945.

4. "Fast Driving," *The Courier-Journal*, 8 November 1872.

5. William Ransom Johnson (1782-1849) was a North Carolina native, but after he married Mary Evans of Petersburg, Virginia, whose father's place was called Oakland, he moved there. He was active in politics, but was better known for his turf activities which included training horses as well as putting on match races with regional overtones. He was known as "The Napoleon of the Turf."

6. *Louisville Public Advertiser*, 2 October 1822. It is not known when the first Louisville Jockey Club was formed or by whom. John Funk's statement was reprinted in "Nancy Pope and Havoc," *The Turf, Field and Farm*, 18 April 1879.

7. *The Focus*, 2 October 1827. Henry McMurtrie, *Sketches of Louisville And its Environs* (Louisville, 1819), 127. For additional information, see J. Stoddard Johnston, *Memorial History of Louisville* 2 (1896), 323-324; Melville O. Briney, "The Sport of Kings the Sport of Louisvillians, Too," *The Louisville Times*, 29 October 1953; and George H. Yater, "There's Always Been a Horse Race," *Louisville* 29 (April 1978): 14-15, 17, 19, 21, 25.

8. John D. Wright, Jr., *Lexington: Heart of the Bluegrass* (Lexington, 1982), 41.

9. A copy of the 12-page pamphlet was given to The Filson Club in 1927. The stockholders are also listed.

10. Samuel Churchill (1779-1863), according to his death notice in *The Louisville Daily Journal* on 5 January 1863, "had served as a legislator and as a judge of the county court of this county at various times."

11. James Silk Buckingham (1786-1855) was a prolific English travel writer, who having just retired from Parliament in 1837, toured America for nearly four years.

12. Although the Woodlawn (National) Race Course was established in 1858, the property was not purchased until 12 April 1859 (Jefferson County Deed Book 104, p. 98). The subscribers to the association listed in the deed included: Thomas H. Hunt, Richard Atchison, William B. Reynolds, Benj. J. Adams, James K. Duke, R. A. Alexander, A. Throckmorton, Thomas J. Martin, Gerald B. Bate, John Burks, James A. Grinstead, A. Buford, E. Eagle, Robert A. Bell, W. D. C. Whipps, "and others."

13. The stock certificates are in the Woodburn Farm files.

14. The reference may be to Richard Atkinson, a commercial merchant whose home was on the southeast corner of Fourth and Walnut streets. He soon died. Thomas H. Hunt had come from Lexington and was in the rope and bagging business. He lived in New Orleans after serving in the Civil War. His brother was A. D. Hunt.

15. "Oakland Course. Four of the fastest Pacers and several of the most celebrated Trotters in the world are entered for the following stakes and purses..." *Louisville Daily Courier*, 4 June 1852. Regular trotting races were scheduled at Woodlawn in the fall of 1862 when the war caused an indefinite postponement. See *Louisville Daily Journal*, 15 and 21 October 1862.

16. Kent Hollingsworth, *The Kentucky Thoroughbred* (Lexington, 1985), 30-32. "The Death of Lexington," *The Turf, Field and Farm*, 9 July 1875.

17. "The Woodlawn Meeting," *The Turf, Field and Farm*, 19 May 1866. "The Late Woodlawn Meeting," *The Turf, Field and Farm*, 16 June 1866. "The Woodlawn Fall Meeting," *The Turf, Field and Farm*, 4 August 1866.

18. "Death of Mr. Robert A. Alexander," *Louisville Daily Journal*, 3 December 1867.

19. *The Turf, Field and Farm*, 8 April 1881. "Bramble the Victor," *The Courier-Journal*, 27 September 1878. "The Woodlawn Vase," *The Turf, Field and Farm*, 25 September 1885. *Laurel/Pimlico '93 Media Guide*, 61.

20. *The Courier-Journal*, 10 and 13 June 1872. A subdivision plat was filed in Jefferson County Deed Book 166, p. 639. For subsequent information see John C. Scheer, *The History of Woodlawn Park, Kentucky*, 1977.

21. Letter from Harry F. Allmond to Allen E. Allmond, 7 January 1956. The Filson Club. For information about a conflict in the lease arrangement which led to its demise as a track, see "Over Wilder Park," *The Courier-Journal*, 16 April 1890. For subdivision plat, see Jefferson County Deed Book 393, p. 639.

22. *The Courier-Journal*, 10 February 1890.

23. "A Magnificent Enterprise," *The Courier-Journal*, 25 May 1872. "Grand Central Exposition and Villa Park," *The Courier-Journal*, 28 June 1872. "Grand Central Exposition and Villa Park," *The Daily Louisville Commercial*, 17 November 1872.

24. "The Falls City Association," *The Courier-Journal*, 27 May 1872. "Racing Ground," *The Courier-Journal*, 29 June 1872.

25. "Louisville (Ky.) Gossip," *The Turf, Field and Farm*, 12 December 1873. "Gossip from Louisville," *The Turf, Field and Farm*, 3 April 1874. "The Villa Park Sale," *The Courier-Journal*, 31 May 1880.

26. "Death of Gen. M. Lewis Clark," *The Courier-Journal*, 29 October 1881.

27. Information from the family Bible, courtesy of Nathaniel Tyler III, Dorset, Vermont. Before being razed, the brick house carried the address 2412 Mount Claire Avenue which is southwest of Preston Street and Eastern Parkway. The property had been assembled by Armistead Churchill, Jr., father of Samuel Churchill.

28. "Effort Is Made To Save Church," *The Courier-Journal*, 15 April 1912. "Death of Major John L. Martin," *The Louisville Daily Journal*, 18 October 1854. "The Martin Estate," *The Courier-Journal*, 19 September 1874. "Dead And Alone," *The Courier-Journal*, 1 August 1892.

29. Kent Hollingsworth wrote that Darley was purchased after "Ten Broeck formed a syndicate including prominent Kentucky horsemen General Abe Buford, Junius R. Ward and Captain Willa Viley." Dr. Warfield accepted their offer of $5,000 as well as the condition that Darley's name be changed to Lexington. Hollingsworth provided no citations in his excellent and informative book, *The Kentucky Thoroughbred* (Lexington, 1985). However, when Lexington died, "Egnus" wrote *The Courier-Journal* (16 July 1875) to clarify some points made by the newspaper earlier.

The writer of the aforesaid article alleges that "Lexington was first known upon the turf by the name of 'Darley.'" This, I think, is a common error. Dr. Warfield, Mr. Ten Broeck and myself were the only persons present when the purchase of the horse was made (it was not consummated until the next day), and I very well remember that the Doctor said he intended to call the horse 'Darley,' as he was descended from the Darley [blank], and had, like him, four white feet and a white nose.

After leaving Dr. Warfield's, and on our way to Lexington, Mr. Ten Broeck suggested the name of Lexington as the best name for the horse, for the reason that he was born and bred in this town, and was to represent the State of Kentucky at the races. This name was accordingly adopted. Now if the horse had run under the appellation of "Darley," it would have been so announced, either when the entry for his first race was made or afterwards in the report of the race. Before his second contest on the turf, Lexington had changed hands, and came into the possession of Mr. Ten Broeck, who would certainly have published this fact. I have seen no such statement in print, but the author of the article for *The Courier-Journal* is on the spot and has an opportunity to examine the records and ascertain the truth of the matter.

For a contemporary evaluation of Lexington see "Development of the American Race-Horse," *The Turf, Field and Farm*, 24 November 1876.

30. It might be noted that although Ten Broeck raced American horses in England, he favored the English method of pacing them for the finish of a race instead of the American style of running "end to end." (See "The Recollections of a Jockey [Gil Patrick]," *The Turf, Field and Farm*, 7 May 1875.) For Ten Broeck, see "He Lived Too Long," *The Courier-Journal*, 6 August 1892.

31. "Death of Orville M. Anderson," *Louisville Daily Courier*, 7 March 1857.

32. Georgie B. Cooper to Nettie Oliver, 15 December 1987, The Filson Club.

33. "Death of Mrs. Ten Broeck," *The Courier-Journal*, 28 March 1873. Ten Broeck was wounded in an altercation on 8 August 1894 after stepping off a train near Hurstbourne. Genl. Walter C. Whitaker had taken offense to a remark Ten Broeck made, and in the ensuing tussle, a bullet from Whitaker's revolver grazed Ten Broeck's head, prompting reports of his death. See *The Courier-Journal* and *The Daily Louisville Commercial*, 9 August 1874. An in-depth biographical sketch prepared for the *New York World* was reprinted in *The Daily Louisville Commercial* (18 August 1874).

Ten Broeck then married Mrs. Mary Cornelia Smith Newcomb (1848-1905), widow of Horatio Dalton Newcomb (1809-1874) who made a fortune in Louisville as a liquor and grocery merchant, in a Cannelton, Indiana, cottonmill, and coal mines, and finally with the L & N Railroad which he presided over. She was Newcomb's second wife. The Ten Broecks went to live in England, and when he retired from racing, they bought a small ranch at San Mateo, California, but near the end of his life she left him and tried to have him committed (see "Richard Ten Broeck Insane," *The Courier-Journal*, 16 November 1889). For a description of Ten Broeck's Louisville operation see "Hurstbourne," *The Courier-Journal*, 8 September 1884.

34. T. H. Bird, *Admiral Rous and The English Turf* (London, 1939), 199-202.

35. Richard Ten Broeck, "Some Personal Reminiscences, Incidents And Anecdotes," *The Spirit of the Times*, 27 December 1890.

36. A journal of the trip kept by fourteen-year-old Rogers Clark Ballard recorded they encountered others from Louisville including the Henry Wattersons, William and Morris Belknap, and H.D. Newcomb. The journal is in the R.C. Ballard Thruston Coll., The Filson Club. For a contemporary view of French racing, see "The French Turf," *The Courier-Journal*, 10 September 1882.

37. His obituary (*The Courier-Journal*, 23 April 1899) stated he studied the turf systems of England and France "for several years;" however, his first child, John Henry Churchill Clark, was born in Louisville on 15 August 1874. Another obituary (*The Louisville Commercial*, 23 April 1899) reported he had been in the tobacco business twice before becoming president of the Louisville Jockey Club. There is no substantiation of that assertion.

38. The preceding letter responding to the 27 May 1874 article appears as a single response signed by J. Richard Barret. For clarity, they have been separated. John Richard Barret (1825-1903) was a native of Green County, Kentucky, but moved to St. Louis where he studied and practiced law and became active in politics. He was for many years president of the St. Louis Agricultural Society, which may explain the reason M. G. Kern laid out the grounds surrounding the Falls City Association track. Barret was first mentioned as manager of the project in *The Turf, Field and Farm*, 17 November 1871. He moved to New York and died there. See "Once Prominent In Kentucky Politics," *The Courier-Journal*, 3 November 1903.

39. The author of this intriguing idea is not known; *The Commercial* piece was unsigned. He mentions having received a park plan by Joseph Paxton "that has been laid away for several years waiting for an opportunity to use it." The writer may have been Major John Throckmorton (1816-1881) who owned much of the designated property and who had visited Europe before the Civil War. Louisville would have been fortunate to have had its first large, formal park designed by the eminent English gardener and architect, Sir Joseph Paxton (1801-1865). He had been superintendent of the gardens at Chatsworth before designing the Crystal Palace. Robert Ross, who was then superintendent of Cave Hill Cemetery, trained under Paxton at the Duke of Devonshire's estate, Chatsworth.

LOUISVILLE JOCKEY CLUB AND DRIVING PARK ASSOCIATION

1. The list of officers and directors, which may not be complete, is based upon information from Jefferson County Corporation Book 1, p. 374; *The Daily Louisville Commercial*, 1 and 4 July 1874 and 22 October 1874; Louisville Jockey Club and Driving Park Association Minute Book, 1874-1894. *Kentucky Live Stock Record*, 19 March 1875; *The Turf, Field and Farm*, 7 January 1876; *The Courier-Journal*, 14 May 1889; *The Kentucky Jockey Club* (1920); and Frank G. Menke, *Down the Stretch* (1945), 32-33.

2. Articles of Incorporation were filed on 20 June 1874 and recorded in Jefferson County Corporation Book 1, pp. 374-375. The incorporators were: E.H. Chase, M. Lewis Clark, Jr., R. A. Newhouse, John E. Green, James Graves, A.V. du Pont, W.H. Henderson, Miller Stuart, A.A. Wheeler, F. S. Carrington, Isaac W. Tyler, Roman A. Browinski, and A.B. Schell.

3. Charles Donald Jacob (1838-1898) was in one of his unprecedented four terms as mayor of Louisville. The son of John I. Jacob, who was considered one of the richest men in the city, he was educated at Cambridge and Harvard, and in 1869, married Addie Martin, daughter of Thomas J. Martin, a commission merchant and one-time president of the L & N Railroad. Her brother was on the Louisville Jockey Club board, and Jacob's sister was married to Col. R. A. Johnson, a prominent member, and her son by a previous marriage to D. W. Johnson would become its secretary. Mayor Jacob's secretary was Joel M. Womack, an influential director of the track. Jacob was later responsible for Iroquois Park and in that administration, M. Lewis Clark was hired as his chief of parks. Also see, "Notable Characters Memorable To Louisville," *The Courier-Journal*, 5 March 1916.

4. Louisville Jockey Club and Driving Park Association Minute Book, 1874-1894, p.1. The 9"x14" leatherbound book is owned by Ken Grayson, Lexington, Kentucky. A. D. Hunt (1809-1885) was a lawyer before becoming a cotton goods manufacturer in Lexington and moving in 1860 to Louisville where he was principally identified with the banking firm A. D. Hunt & Co. In addition, see "Dead At Seventy-Six," *The Courier-Journal*, 25 May 1885. William Preston's letter of introduction is in the manuscript collection of The Filson Club.

5. "John Andrewartha," *Louisville Daily Ledger*, 18 September 1873, and research file of Samuel W. Thomas.

6. J. Jacobs *vs*. The Louisville Jockey Club and Driving Park Association, Louisville Chancery Court case 28694. Included were various depositions as well as the contract specifications for the projects. Plans and elevations from the case papers were transferred to Churchill Downs by an agreement with the Kentucky Department of Finance, dated 24 May 1971, and copies were made to replace them in the court files.

7. The old clubhouse appears in a Kentucky Derby Museum photograph dated 10 May 1910. Reportedly, it was moved off site and reused as a residence into the 1950s. See Barry Irwin, "Creeping Sprawl and Rise of Derby Seating At Downs," *The Blood-Horse*, 25 April 1970. It may have been confused with the turn-of-the-century clubhouse of the Louisville Bicycle Club at 3854 Southern Parkway that was razed in 1952. See *The Louisville Times*, 21 November 1952.

8. Charles F. Price in his *ca.* 1909 booklet, *Churchill Downs: A Brief History of the Famous Course*, credits W. H. Thomas with loaning the club funds to complete the grandstand. Based upon the cost figures available in court suit depositions and supporting documents, this often-repeated story is doubted. Perhaps William Hinton Thomas (1825-1908), who was a dealer in fine whiskies, helped pay for the grandstand's enlargement in 1882. For Thomas, see "Full Of Years," *The Courier-Journal*, 7 October 1908.

9. Greenland's revival for trotting was certainly undertaken in concert with the Louisville Jockey Club as Robert A. Johnson was one of its charter members. Rachel Johnson Macauley was an actress and the wife of Barney Macauley (1837-1886), who in 1873 had just built Macauley's Theatre, which his brother John T. Macauley took over and made successful.

10. Matt Winn, who became part of the new management of Churchill Downs in 1902, is quoted in *Down the Stretch: The Story of Colonel Matt J. Winn*, as making the point that pari-mutuels did not appear at Churchill Downs until 1878. However, they were there from Derby day, 1875.

11. Barak G. Thomas (1826-1906), a law graduate of Transylvania University, was subsequently a civil engineer, planter, newspaper publisher, banker, and sheriff of Fayette County before devoting his energies exclusively to horse breeding and racing. In 1892, the confederate veteran bred Domino, a most successful money winner for James R. Keene. For additional information see, Kent Hollingsworth, *The Kentucky Thoroughbred* (Lexington, 1985), 55-73. Also, "Major Barak G. Thomas Is Dead," *The Thoroughbred Record*, 19 May 1906.

12. In 1908, Hamilton C. Applegate went to Paris and interviewed Joseph Oller about the system of wagering he had devised and his acounting machines. Oller told Applegate that pari-mutuel machines had first been sent to Louisville in 1867. "Oller Talks Of Pari-Mutuels," *The Courier-Journal*, 27 September 1908. Modern references to the inventor of the French pools call him Pierre Oller. This may hark back to Matt Winn's reference to Pierre Oller in *Down the Stretch* (1945), 26. Richard Sasuly's *Bookies And Bettors* (New York, 1982) states that "a Frenchman known as Professor Drommel" installed four of Oller's machines at Churchill Downs in 1878. This was taken directly from Winn's 1945 account, so perhaps Pierre is an off-handed recollection of Winn or a misidentification by Frank Menke, his recorder.

13. Peter Chew in his centennial book, *The Kentucky Derby* (Boston, 1974), 5, relates the story that the Earl of Derby and his friend Charles Bunbury "tossed a coin to decide whether the new race would be called the Derby Stakes or the Bunbury Stakes." The Derby Stakes was at a distance of one mile until 1784 when it was lengthened to a mile and a half. Bunbury's Diomed won the first Derby in 1780, and later was brought to America. Lexington was a descendant. See "The Louisville Derby," *Kentucky Live Stock Record*, 23 April 1875.

14. Leonard Stansfield Sutcliffe's collection of photographic negatives and company records has been acquired by Lexington insurance executive Ken Grayson, who graciously supplied the print of Aristides used here. It is similar in appearance and pose to Henry Collins Bispham's 1876 painting of Aristides owned by William Price McGrath, Jr., of Richmond, Virginia. (Bispham [1841-1882], a native of Philadelphia who studied in Paris and worked in New York, frequently exhibited cattle paintings.) The painting appeared in the *Richmond News Leader* on 4 May 1956, when it was in the possession of his grandfather, Richard A. McGrath, Jr., the great-nephew of the owner of the first Kentucky Derby winner, H. Price McGrath, Jr. For information about Sutcliffe, see "Death Takes Famed Horse Photographer," *The Courier-Journal*, 1 July 1937.

15. Mary Martin Anderson Clark died on 28 August 1934 in Washington, D.C., where she had lived for thirty-four years. She was survived by two daughters: Mrs. Nathaniel Tyler and Miss Mary Barbaroux Clark. Her son, John Henry Churchill Clark, died in 1915. Caroline Anderson Clark had married Nathaniel Tyler, Jr., in 1901. Two of their children survived: Nathaniel Tyler III and Orville Anderson Tyler. In 1935 the latter married Frances Smith, the interviewee.

The fact that Mary Martin Anderson was raised by her aunt, Pattie Anderson (Mrs. Richard Ten Broeck), is confirmed by family papers belonging to the late Kate Helm Buckner.

16. Benjamin Gratz Bruce, founder and editor of the *Kentucky Live Stock Record*, was most certainly knowledgeable about horse lineages, but his account was not precise when he reported that Aristides was bred by Henry Price McGrath at McGrathiana on the Newtown Pike, now part of Coldstream Farm. Leamington, Aristides' sire, was standing at Aristides Welch's Erdenheim Stud near Chestnut Hill, Philadelphia, from 1872 until he died there in 1878. McGrath's mare

Sarong was shipped to Philadelphia and returned to Lexington to foal the first Kentucky Derby winner.

On the same page that *The Spirit of the Times* (12 April 1890) announced the death (on 9 April) of Aristides Welch in Philadelphia, it reported the upcoming sale of Erdenheim yearlings. The farm was being reestablished after the dispersal sale brought on by the death of Commodore N. W. Kittson, who had purchased it in 1882. Welch had also been a navy man. His farm was well established when described in *Sportsman's Oracle and Country Gentleman's Newspaper*, 6 January 1866. In the same issue was a detailed history of Leamington who was standing for that season at Abe Buford's Bosque Bonita. Also see Susan Rhodemyre, "Aristides of Pennsylvania," *The Thoroughbred Record*, 23 January 1980.

George D. Widener died at Erdenheim Farm in 1971 at the age of 82. He also owned the old Kenney Farm in Lexington. His uncle was Joseph E. Widener (1872-1943), also of Philadelphia, who once controlled Belmont Park and built Hialeah, which his son Peter A. B. Widener took over. *The Courier-Journal* on 11 January 1925, carried a long report of Joseph E. Widener and George D. Widener's day of inspecting their horses at Churchill Downs, before departing for Joseph's Elmendorf Farm in Lexington. Erdenheim Farm is now owned by Widener relative Fitz Eugene Dixon, Jr.

17. "A Burgoo at McGrathiana," *The Turf, Field and Farm*, 20 September 1872. "Lexington," *The Courier-Journal*, 15 May 1877. For a sketch of Bobby Swim on the occasion of his funeral, see "Autumn Leaves Gathered In Kentucky," *The Turf, Field and Farm*, 25 October 1878.

18. Ansel Williamson has been referred to, incorrectly, as Ansel or Andy Anderson in media guides and anniversary books commemorating the Kentucky Derby. "Death Of Ansel Williamson," *Kentucky Live Stock Record*, 25 June 1881. Williamson was "some seventy-five years of age….He did not long survive his old master Mr. A. Keene Richards, to whom he was greatly attached, which was fully reciprocated by the noble and generous proprietor of Blue Grass Park."

H. Price McGrath (1814-1881) was born near Keene in Jessamine County, but growing bored as a tailor in Versailles, traveled to New Orleans in 1852 and began to accumulate wealth as a gambler. *The Louisville Commercial* (6 July 1881) commended: "It was here that pool-selling in America was originated, and the honor of the originality belongs to Price McGrath." He then went to work for the gambling house in New York operated by Morrissey, Chamberlain & Co. Reportedly, he withdrew winnings of $250,000 in 1865, returning to Kentucky to establish McGrathiana. Not only did he race horses, but he became involved with hemp manufacturing through Calvin C. Morgan, whose partner and brother, John Hunt Morgan, had been killed in the Civil War.

"Tom Bowling and Uncle Ansel," *The Daily Louisville Commercial*, 7 June 1874. "Price McGrath," *The Courier-Journal*, 6 July 1881. "The Death of H.P. McGrath," *The Turf, Field and Farm*, 8 July 1881. "Henry Price McGrath, "*The Spirit of the Times*, 9 July 1881.

19. Although Louisville Jockey Club President Clark reportedly would move into the clubhouse, which was on the east side of the track, apparently this cottage was on the west side. It does not appear on the 1892 Sanborn map of the track buildings. Capt. James T. Larkin was a native of Frankfort. He was a deputy warden at the Frankfort reformatory and a patrolman at the Capitol before moving to Louisville. He died in 1931 at the age of 74. See *The Courier-Journal*, 20 August 1931.

20. The writer of the letter was identified mistakenly as Miss Grundy. Christina Johnson is first listed as a dressmaker in the 1866-67 directory. She married George Grunder and was listed in 1875 as

Mrs. C. Grunder. Eventually she became Madame G. Grunder and was quite well known locally. She died at age 74 in 1920.

21. Jerome Park was opened on Leonard W. Jerome's estate, Fordham, on Long Island in 1866.

22. C. C. Rufer's well-known hotel was on the east side of Fifth Street south of Main. He briefly served on the board of directors of the Louisville Jockey Club (see *Kentucky Live Stock Record*, 19 March 1875).

23. *The Daily Louisville Commercial* reported on 7 May 1875 that "Kitts & Werne have just completed the gentleman's cup for the Kentucky Derby, and have placed it on exhibition." Because of this ambiguous wording, official media guides for the Derby for some years incorrectly described the gentleman's cup as the trophy awarded to the first and subsequent Derby winners.

Alexander Keene Richards (1827-1881) began purchasing Thoroughbreds in 1853, establishing Bluegrass Park near Georgetown in his native Scott County. Edward Troye's 1857 painting of Glencoe shows a Gothic barn in the background. Richards made four trips to Europe and was a friend of Richard Ten Broeck. See *Kentucky Live Stock Record*, 26 March 1881. A. Trigg Moss worked in the hardware store of Moss and Semple.

24. The 1876 Louisville Cup was won by Ten Broeck, ridden by the African-American jockey, William Walker.

25. The Louisville Cup, a two-and-a-quarter-mile race for all ages was run between 1875 and 1887.

26. Whitley has been credited with building the first brick house west of the Alleghenies as well as the state's first race track. According to *The Kentucky Encyclopedia* (Lexington, 1992): "Having an aversion to anything English, he used clay instead of turf for the surface of the race track that he laid out in 1788, and he raced the horses in a counterclockwise direction. To this day, all American sports using oval tracks, race counterclockwise." While practically none of the English courses were ovals, or flat, there is still no universal direction for the horses to run. The Derby at Epsom Downs, near London, is run counterclockwise.

27. Frank Harper's uncle, Adam Harper, was shot and killed defending Nantura from marauders in 1864; his aunt, Elizabeth, and uncle, Jacob, were murdered in their beds in 1871. See *The Courier Journal*, 7, 12, 13, and 15 March 1873.

28. "Woodford County," *The Courier-Journal*, 10 September 1882. "The Harpers and the Departed Glories of Nantura," *The Courier-Journal*, 3 March 1901. "Old School," *The Courier-Journal*, 9 April 1905. "Cradle of Kentucky Race Horse History Today But Tottering Ruins of Faded Fame," *Louisville Herald*, 23 December 1924.

29. "The American Turf," *The Courier-Journal*, 8 July 1878.

30. "Frank Harper Passes Away," *The Courier-Journal*, 5 April 1905. Woodford County Will and Inventory and Appraisement Book 6, pp. 170, 332, 532 and 571 and Book 8, pp. 332 and 398.

31. Heggy Dent, "Brothers Prize Cup Ten Broeck Won In Match Race," *The Courier-Journal*, 4 January 1939. The descendants who inherited the bowl believed that fact until the inscription was inspected in 1993.

32. "The Races," *The Daily Louisville Commercial*, 24 September 1876. "7:15 3/4," *The Daily Louisville Commercial*, 28 September 1876.

33. "3:27 1/2!" *The Courier-Journal*, 30 May 1877.

34. For a historical perspective of comparative times, see "Time–Why

It Should Be Abolished," *The Spirit of the Times*, 12 January 1878.

35. Theodore "Black T" Winters (1823-1894) was the acknowledged owner of Mollie McCarthy, although in a published interview in *The Courier-Journal* (29 September 1885), fellow Californian, Elias Jackson "Lucky" Baldwin (1828-1909) indicated that he was the owner at the time of the race. Evidently, Baldwin purchased Mollie McCarthy soon after the race through his son-in-law Budd Doble. See *The Courier-Journal*, 7 July 1878; and Robertson, *The History of Thoroughbred Racing In America* (1964), 120-123. Baldwin had gone to California in 1853, starting out as a brick maker. Eventually he traded in mining stocks and accumulated a fortune. *The Courier-Journal* (10 May 1887) quoted Baldwin about the town he was starting called Arcadia, and about the seven ranches he owned comprising 56,000 acres, the home place being called Santa Anita. For additional information on Lucky Baldwin see Pat McAdam and Sandy Snider, *Arcadia* (Arcadia, 1981). This is partially based upon Snider's thesis, a copy of which is in the Keeneland Library.

36. When Frank B. Harper died, Susan Stafford was a principal beneficiary of his estate. She had worked for Edward Blackburn at Equiria. His son, Luke Pryor Blackburn, M.D. (1816-1887), was governor of Kentucky from 1879 until 1883. After Dr. Blackburn's first wife died, he married Julia Churchill, sister of John and William Henry Churchill. He served on the board of the Louisville Jockey Club.

37. "The Races," *The Louisville Daily Commercial*, 5 July 1878. "The Very Latest Phase," *The Courier-Journal*, 7 July 1878. *Blue Grass Clipper*, 12 July 1878. Also see "The Cause of It" and "Race Reflections," *The Turf, Field and Farm*, 12 July 1878.

38. "Ten Broeck's Jockey," *The Louisville Daily Commercial*, 11 July 1878. William Walker (1860-1933) was born on the Harper farm, Nantura, and first raced at Jerome Park when he was eleven. He rode in the first two Kentucky Derbys before winning in 1877 on Daniel Swigert's Baden-Baden, trained by Edward Brown. At that meeting, he was given a purse by the Louisville Jockey Club for being the best-behaved rider. Billy Walker became a trainer in 1884 and later served as an advisor to John E. Madden. The sage was an authority on blood lines as well as racing history. See "Sidelights On Running of Kentucky Derby of 1877," *The Courier-Journal*, 5 March 1916; and "The Rider of the Derby Winner of 1877," *The Thoroughbred Record*, 13 May 1922.

39. The engraving is owned by Martin F. Schmidt and reproduced in his *Kentucky Illustrated* (Lexington, 1992), 192.

40. *Rules and Regulations of the Louisville Jockey Club* (Louisville, 1874), 23-24. Frank G. Menke stated in *The Story Of Churchill Downs And The Kentucky Derby* (1940), 16: "In truth, the fall of the flag was the official gesture that started the race, and also gave the timekeepers the signal to start clocking, while the drum was beaten so that the jockeys, who might have been too busy with a fractious horse to see the flag fall, would hear the starting signal." However, this would not explain why the tap of the drum was discontinued in 1880. Menke did also note that "the starting drum of 1875 eventually fell into the hands of Samuel S. Brown, of Pittsburgh, who gave it to Col. Matt J. Winn in 1929, but some years ago it disappeared from Colonel Winn's office." However, Capt. Brown died in 1905.

41. On 4 July 1878, *The Courier Journal* called the race the richest in America, "the winner taking the Woodlawn Challenge Vase." In 1879, the race winnings included the Louisville Jockey Club vase, but from 1880 to 1889, when the great American Stallion Stakes was discontinued, no vase was presented.

42. Louisville Jockey Club Minute Book 1, pp. 52 and 54.

Kentucky Live Stock Record, 14 and 28 August 1880. "T. G. Moore Reinstated," *The Courier-Journal*, 29 September 1880. The former steamboat captain and native of Ireland died on 1 April 1887 in Crab Orchard at the age of 70. He had been writing a history of the turf, but it evidently was never published. See the *Interior Journal* (Stanford), 1 April 1887.

43. "Bar Privileges," *The Courier-Journal*, 9 May 1879. H. and W. Israel vs. The Louisville Jockey Club and Driving Park Association, Jefferson Court of Common Pleas case 23099. The Israels had paid $1,258 for bar privileges at each meet.

44. "Fleetwood Stock Farm," *Kentucky Live Stock Record*, 29 January 1876. "Hunt Reynolds Dead," *The Courier-Journal*, 23 September 1880. "Col. Hunt Reynolds," *The Courier-Journal*, 24 September 1880. *Kentucky Live Stock Record*, 25 September 1880. "New Associate Judge," *The Courier-Journal*, 2 May 1889. Family materials belonging to Christine Stephens of Fort Thomas, Kentucky, and burial records for the Hanna mound in the Frankfort Cemetery. The relationship of Murphy and Mrs. Reynolds is described in *The Courier-Journal*, 15 May 1890.

45. "D. W. Johnson's Funeral Today," *The Courier-Journal*, 11 March 1936. C. J. P. Lucas, "Kentucky Takes Bow…," *The Herald-Post*, 3 May 1934.

46. Architecture files of Samuel W. Thomas. Levy's would transform the old Turf Exchange into its annex. See *The Courier-Journal*, 18 September 1904.

47. *The Courier-Journal* reported on 19 May 1882 that J.T. Williams purchased the Stull paintings of Virgil, Hindoo, and Foxhall. The Kentucky Derby Museum acquired the Stull paintings, both signed and dated 1882, of Hindoo and Checkmate from Jane Ellen Hardy, Lexington. Stull's earlier exhibition at the Galt House was reported in *The Daily Louisville Commercial*, 1 October 1879. Green B. Morris was the co-owner and trainer of Apollo. Jockey Isaac Murphy was first brought in January 1875 "to the Louisville track then being built," by trainer Eli Jordan who was engaged by J.T. Williams and Richard Owings. See "Isaac Murphy. A Memorial," *The Thoroughbred Record*," 21 March 1896.

48. *The Courier-Journal*, 19 May 1882. For information on Stull, see W.S. Vosburgh, "The Late Mr. Stull," *The Thoroughbred Record*, 29 March 1913; and Frederick M. Burlew, "A Glow Of Silver," a research study and inventory presented to the Keeneland Library. According to Burlew, Stull also painted Luke Blackburn for Williams. For illustrations of Stull's later work, see Turner Reuter, Jr., "Precision Painter," *Spur*, 30 (January and February 1995): 42-46.

49. Charles Kerr, ed., *History of Kentucky* 3 (1922), 570. Williams lived in Louisville for some years to educate his children (*The Courier-Journal*, 7 March and 14 November 1892). He resided at 1136 Fourth Street.

50. "The Dead Virgil," *The Courier-Journal*, 16 September 1886.

51. Jim Bolus, *Run For The Roses* (New York, 1974), 15. Michael F. Dwyer (1846-1906) and brother Philip J. Dwyer (1843-1917) were the dominant characters on the American turf prior to 1890, when they went their separate ways. They were butchers from Brooklyn who returned to the Kentucky Derby in 1881 with the winner, Hindoo. Their Runnymede, favored the next year, finished second. They owned Bramble, purchased Luke Blackburn from J. T. Williams, and won a fortune with Hanover. Philip handled the horses, Mike the betting. They were active in New York jockey clubs as well as in the ownership of local race tracks, including Gravesend and Aqueduct.

52. "Sam Says He Didn't," *The Courier-Journal*, 4 March 1888.

53. "Drops The Matter," *The Courier-Journal*, 6 March 1888.

54. A steeplechase was inaugurated at Jerome Park in 1869, but Pimlico did not hold one until the fall meeting of 1873. See Roger Longrigg, *The History of Horse Racing* (New York, 1972), 232.

55. "Capt. Brown In Lexington," *The Kentucky Farm and Breeder*, 23 March 1905. Two other articles on Brown appear in the same issue. "Peacefully," and "Capt. Brown's connection with Churchill Downs," *The Courier-Journal*, 12 December 1905. "Capt. S. S. Brown," *The Thoroughbred Record*, 16 December 1905. "Estate Dwindles," *The Courier-Journal*, 7 February 1907. For photographs of Senorita, see Knight and Greene, *Country Estates of The Blue Grass* (1904).

56. The Clark family Bible carries the entry: "Lewis left the house on Friday, Sep. 7, 1883. Trial separation Wednesday Oct. 24, 1883." According to family recollection, Mary Martin Anderson Clark had been embarrassed and requested that her husband leave their house. She moved to Europe, but no divorce was ever sought. At some point, Col. Clark took up residence at Churchill Downs.

57. There is no deed record that the land was purchased, and the lake and driving park were never made.

58. Price's comment was in an unidentified newspaper clipping in the Price papers, Kentucky Derby Museum. For Ridgely, see "For Burial Here," *The Courier-Journal*, 14 October 1908. Matt J. Winn in *Down the Stretch*, 25.

59. "Louisville Track Pioneered In Using Of Straightaway," *The Cincinnati Enquirer*, 12 February 1956.

60. Clark had convened a "Turf Congress" five years before, but "nothing definite was determined on." See *The Courier Journal*, 21 May 1878.

61. "Col. Robert Johnson," *The Courier-Journal*, 16 March 1886.

62. Such legislation was reiterated in an act to amend the charter of the Louisville Jockey Club approved by the legislature on 10 May 1884.

63. After Edward Corrigan (1832-1924) and his family made a fortune building the street railway system in Kansas City, he turned to the turf, not only as an owner of race horses, but race tracks as well. His establishment of Hawthorne in Chicago and City Park in New Orleans were in opposition to existing tracks and brought on "turf wars." His filly, Modesty, won the Kentucky Oaks in 1884, and Riley, the Longfellow colt, won the Derby in 1890. In 1902 he brought English horses back to establish Freeland Stud near Lexington. McGee was the sire of Exterminator and In Memoriam. See "Death of Edward Corrigan," *The Thoroughbred Record*, 12 July 1924.

64. Daniel Swigert died at age 79 in 1912 at the home of his daughter, Mrs. Leslie Combs, in Lexington. He had bred Kentucky Derby winners, Hindoo and Apollo, and owned Baden-Baden, winner in 1877. He also bred Firenzi and Salvator. See "Dan Swigert Dies," *The Courier-Journal*, 26 May 1912. He was a long-time vice president and director of the Louisville Jockey Club.

65. Haggin had horses entered in the 1887 Derby, but withdrew at the last minute. See "The Derby Starters," *The Courier-Journal*, 8 May 1887. Betty Earle Borries, *Isaac Murphy: Kentucky's Record Jockey* (Berea, 1988), 68. Interview of Jim Bolus, "The Run For The Roses," 1994 video by Decade Productions, Inc. For an analysis of Haggin's breeding operation see Robertson, *The History of Thoroughbred Racing In America* (1964), 143-145.

66. The pooling privilege for 1887 was sold to Anderson M. Waddell, who was in partnership with Joseph Burt. Twenty-three bookmakers agreed to pay them $100 each per day. See "Derby Day," *The Courier-Journal*, 11 May 1887.

67. The formation of a new jockey club was earlier noted in *The Thoroughbred Record*, on 12 November 1887.

68. A photograph of the graveyard for Ten Broeck and Longfellow appeared in *The Courier-Journal*, 4 January 1939. For Ten Broeck's marker, see J. Winston Coleman, Jr., *Historic Kentucky* (Lexington, 1967), 180.

69. Cathcart followed the legendary pool seller, Doc Underwood.

70. According to a paper delivered by Andrew Cowan (in the Temple Bodley papers in The Filson Club), M. Lewis Clark had been appointed "Chief of Parks with a salary of three thousand dollars a year, and Manlius Taylor, Assistant, at fifteen hundred." Taylor was also superintendent of the Louisville Jockey Club. See "Derby Day," *The Courier-Journal*, 14 May 1886.

71. Grand Boulevard, now Southern Parkway, was extended to Jacob (Iroquois) Park in 1889. The project was encouraged by Mayor Charles D. Jacob, an early director of the Louisville Jockey Club. M. Lewis Clark would have been involved in the making of the boulevard, which was not completely improved until 1893. "Knocked Out," *Louisville Commercial*, 3 May 1889 and "Rich Men Of The East," *Louisville Commercial*, 25 May 1890.

72. The act was approved on 18 April 1890, but evidently without the changes Clark expected. The association would erect Douglas Park for harness racing. It was purchased by the Kentucky Jockey Club in 1918 and used for a training track.

73. It is interesting to note that when the New Louisville Jockey Club took over Churchill Downs in 1894, the major stockholders were W. E. Applegate, who with Enright owned The Suburban, Emile Bourlier of the Turf Exchange, and Charles F. Bollinger and Henry Wehmhoff of The Ascot, who both served as treasurer.

74. The jockeys decided to strike unless Col. Clark allowed their valets. See "Jockeys Will Strike," *Louisville Commercial*, 14 May 1891. The United Brotherhood of Valets was formed at Latonia in 1906 when the American Turf Association declared that valets had to wear uniforms. See *The Thoroughbred Record*, 25 August 1906.

75. "Honored Life Ended," *The Courier-Journal*, 28 December 1891.

76. "Richard Ten Broeck Insane," *The Courier-Journal*, 16 November 1889. "Richard Ten Broeck," *The Spirit of the Times*, 4 January 1890. "Richard Ten Broeck Dead," *The Turf, Field and Farm*, 5 August 1892. "Mrs. Ten Broeck Dead," *The Courier-Journal*, 29 July 1905. Also see John K. Ward, "The Colorful Richard Ten Broeck," *The Thoroughbred of California* 76 (November 1985): 9-13. He is buried in Cave Hill Cemetery along with his second wife and their son.

77. "Sudden Death," *The Courier-Journal*, 24 September 1891. "Sudden," *The Kentucky Leader*, 24 September 1891. *The Lexington Transcript*, 24 September 1891. *History of Fayette County, Kentucky* (Chicago, 1882), 564-565. For information about his publishing ventures, see "A Tale of Two Brothers," *Hoofprints of the Century* (Lexington, 1975). Letter of Daniel E. O'Sullivan to Charles F. Price, 17 July 1908, Charles F. Price papers, Kentucky Derby Museum. Newspaperman Ben Ridgely had been considered, but O'Sullivan rallied support for Price.

78. *The Courier-Journal*, 7 March 1892. "Garfield Park," *The Courier-Journal*, 2 August 1892. *The Thoroughbred Record*, 10 September 1892. For a description of the Indiana Racing Association's track at Roby, see

The Courier-Journal, 19 September 1892. Roby is in the northwest corner of Hammond which absorbed it in 1897. Not only was a race track established there in 1892, although evidently not as elaborate as predicted, but also a gambling casino and a boxing arena. Two other tracks followed, but in 1905 the Indiana General Assembly outlawed betting on horse races. See Powell A. Moore, *The Calumet Region* 39 (Indiana Historical Bureau, 1959): 109-113.

79. In the same issue, *The Critic* also commented that bond holders of Kentucky Union Railroad were left "to hold the bag, including M. Lewis Clark, who gives up $10,000 without so much as a protest."

NEW LOUISVILLE JOCKEY CLUB

1. *The Courier-Journal*, 2 September 1894 and 1 October 1902. *The Kentucky Jockey Club* (1920). Frank G. Menke, *Down the Stretch*, 37.

2. Deed agreement dated May 1912, Matt J. Winn papers, Kentucky Derby Museum. *The Kentucky Jockey Club* (1920).

3. When he died, Emile Bourlier (1842-1898) was secretary of the fire department and "recognized as one of the shrewdest politicians in Louisville or in Kentucky," as *The Courier-Journal* pointed out in its obituary on 5 November 1898. He had been a clerk at the Galt House before forming a partnership with his brother, Al Bourlier, in a stove and tinware company that evolved into cornice and roofing work. He was connected with the pool-selling firm of Hughes, Watts & Cathcart and had stock interests in the Latonia track and Oakley near Cincinnati, as well as the New Louisville Jockey Club, where he served as vice president.

William Edward Applegate (1851-1928) was a native of Georgetown, Kentucky, who came to Louisville with his family about 1869. He is first listed in his father's wholesale liquor firm, W. H. Applegate & Sons, in 1871. His father died in 1885, and he took over and turned to producing whiskey. He also had interests in both the Latonia and Oakley tracks before becoming entrenched at Churchill Downs and ending up as its principal stockholder. Applegate was a horse breeder and racer, and was co-proprietor of the Suburban Pool Room before it was taken over by Emile Bourlier (see "Bought It Up," *Louisville Commercial*, 31 July 1892). He died on 13 May 1928 at the age of 76. See "Death Summons Turf Veteran," *Louisville Herald-Post*, 14 May 1928.

Jerome C. "Billy" Boardman (1846-1918) "for many years conducted the restaurant and cafe at Churchill Downs and Douglas Park race tracks." His obituary in *The Courier-Journal* on 27 November 1918 also pointed out that "thirty years ago, [he] was one of the best-known bookmakers on the Western turf."

4. *The Evening Post*'s headlines included the fact: "The Racing Will Be Held at Thompson's Tract." E.V. Thompson, Sr., owned the contiguous property to the south of Churchill Downs which was later a part of Oakdale.

5. Stock and bond broker William Graves Osborne (1853-1926) was also the only member of the board of directors of the Louisville Jockey Club to function in the same capacity for the New Louisville Jockey Club. He had been a *Courier-Journal* reporter. See "William Osborne, Broker, Is Dead," *The Courier-Journal*, 12 January 1926.

6. Henry Wehmhoff was proprietor of the old Turf Exchange and in real estate after he retired. He died on 15 August 1920 at the age of 59.

7. The incorporators of the New Louisville Jockey Club were Emile Bourlier, Henry Wehmhoff, and W. E. Applegate. The hundred shares of stock worth $10,000 was divided thus: Bourlier, Wehmhoff, and Applegate with 20 shares each; W. F. Schulte and C. J. Bollinger 15 shares each; and W. S. Simonton, 10 shares. All resided in Louisville except Simonton, who lived in Cincinnati. A copy of the papers filed in Jefferson County Corporation Book 9, p. 70 on 24 November 1894 was delivered to Kohn, Baird & Spindle, attorneys for the New Louisville Jockey Club, on 29 October 1901. An article in *The Courier-Journal* on 28 April 1901 included George Gaulbert, Buck Schell, and M. Lewis Clark in a list of purchasers.

8. The lease of 80 plus acres for ten years, dated 9 August 1894, was filed in Jefferson County Deed Book 437, p. 321. The previous lease for ten years required a monthly payment of $1,250. Although effective on 1 June 1884, it was not dated until 30 December 1886 and then recorded in Jefferson County Deed Book 297, p. 463.

9. "Paul Jones President," *The Courier-Journal*, 7 August 1894.

10. "Our Trotting Track," *The Courier-Journal*, 22 May 1895. "Ready To Score," *The Courier-Journal*, 4 September 1895.

11. James J. Douglas had been an incorporator of the Falls City Running and Trotting Club in 1890 (see "Col. Clark's Eagle Eye," *Louisville Commercial*, 15 April 1890). The legislature approved the corporation on 18 April 1890. An earlier organization, the Louisville Driving Park Association, although supported by many prominent Louisvillians, apparently had not gotten off the ground either. See "Going To Work," *The Courier-Journal*, 16 November 1887.

12. Jefferson County Corporation Book 11, p. 573, dated 30 October 1901.

13. "Douglas Park Track To Be Put To Grass Like Old Race Horses," *The Courier-Journal*, 16 March 1958.

14. Bourlier Cornice and Roofing Company was partially owned by New Louisville Jockey Club investor Emile Bourlier.

15. First known as the Chicago Driving Park, but later called Garfield Park, the track was located about ten blocks west of the downtown, adjacent to Central Park, which was laid out by F. L. Olmsted in 1869. M. Lewis Clark had been presiding judge there for many years. The Chicago Historical Society does not have an illustration of the Garfield Park track, which went out of existence in 1892. Professor Steven A. Reiss of Northeastern Illinois University, who has researched Chicago horse racing, is not aware of any extant illustrations.

16. "Improvement At The Asylum," *The Louisville Times*, 1 April 1895, contains a drawing of the Lakeland spires. "Designer of Downs Grandstand, Other Landmarks, Joseph D. Baldez, Dies," *The Courier-Journal*, 23 October 1957.

17. James S. Green was superintendent, according to city directories, from 1892 until he left in 1896 to run Wathen's Stock Farm.

18. Lyman H. Davis, Sr., worked at Latonia and at the Worth track near Chicago before coming to Churchill Downs in 1903 as assistant secretary and handicapper. He was appointed racing secretary in 1905 and could have lived in the old clubhouse in 1906 and 1907, according to city directories. However, son Fountain C. Davis is not aware of his having resided there. Davis died in 1941 at the age of 71. See "Fall Fatal To Former Race Official," *The Courier-Journal*, 15 June 1941.

19. J. W. Hunt Reynolds was a vice president of the Louisville Jockey Club, and after he died in 1880 at the age of 34, his widow continued the operation of their farm Fleetwood. She later married racing official Lew P. Tarlton, who wrote an authoritative memorial

of Isaac Murphy for *The Thoroughbred Record*, 21 March 1896.

20. Recollection of Capt. J. T. Larkin in the *Louisville Herald-Post*, 13 May 1928.

Murphy was born Isaac Burns. The story of his youth and name change was related by trainer Eli Jordan in "Turf Talk," *The Courier-Journal*, 17 February 1896.

21. The earlier policy of free admission to the infield had been eliminated by the new owners.

22. The account did not mention the use of a barrier at the start. However, according to Frank G. Menke, *The Story of Churchill Downs and the Kentucky Derby* (1940), 15-16, a barrier technique was first used in the 1897 Kentucky Derby. George B. "Brownie" Leach in *The Kentucky Derby Diamond Jubilee* (Louisville, 1949), 73, says it was first used in the 1903 Derby. A machine is mentioned in *The Courier-Journal* account of the 1901 Derby.

23. Starter Jack Chinn And The New Machine," *The Louisville Times*, 9 May 1896. An earlier version of the machine was described in *The Spirit of the Times* on 2 January 1892. See Steve Haskin, "They're In The Gate," *The Thoroughbred Record*, September 1989.

John Pendleton "Jack" Chinn (1849-1920) was a Harrodsburg native who named his Mercer County farm, Leonatus, after the Longfellow colt which he co-owned won the 1883 Kentucky Derby. He was a state senator when appointed chairman of the first State Racing Commission in 1906.

24. According to "Starting Machine O.K.," in *The Courier-Journal*, 7 May 1896, the Dill machine had been tried "in a great many cities and has been unanimously declared the best in existence."

25. Harry D. "Curly" Brown owned a cafe in Cincinnati and had a checkered turf career. In 1899 when he was racing horses at Newport, instead of starting them, he was ruled off the track for life for fighting (see *The Courier-Journal*, 11 November 1899). He later built race tracks in Chicago (Arlington), in Mexico (Tijuana), in Maryland (Laurel), and Oriental Park in Havana, as well as others. He died in California 4 May 1930 at the age of 67. See *The Thoroughbred Record*, 10 May 1930.

26. William Frederick Schulte operated a haberdashery in his native Louisville before becoming involved in horse racing. When elected the first president of the New Louisville Jockey Club, he was president of the American Turf Congress which controlled racing in the south and west. Schulte bred and raced horses and also served as a steward at several tracks including Havana's. His wife died in 1910; he died at the age of 60 in 1918. See "William F. Schulte, Turfman, Dies," *The Louisville Herald*, 26 April 1918.

27. Jockey Willie Simms (also spelled Sims) won the Kentucky Derby in both 1896 and 1898. He died in 1927 at the age of 47 in Asbury Park, New Jersey. See *The Thoroughbred Record*, 5 March 1927.

28. "Taken To His Home," *The Memphis Commercial Appeal*, 24 April 1899. It was recalled by those knowledgeable of early Tennessee history that Meriwether Lewis (1774-1809), who had conducted the first exploration to the Pacific with Col. Clark's grandfather, had ended his life in similar fashion.

29. "Reminiscences Of Col. Clark," *The Thoroughbred Record*, 6 May 1899. Meriwether Lewis Clark, Jr., was buried in Section A, lot 699 in Cave Hill Cemetery on 24 April 1899. He was 53 years old. His son was working for the L & N Railroad in Chicago; his estranged wife and two daughters were living in Europe. Churchill Downs, without his influence or that of his uncles, would not be the same.

30. For additional information about these families, see William H. P. Robertson, *The History Of Thoroughbred Racing In America* (Englewood Cliffs, 1964).

31. Telegram from W. E. Applegate to C. F. Price, dated Memphis, 27 April 1899, Charles F. Price papers, Kentucky Derby Museum. Also see *Louisville Commercial*, 28 April 1899. Des F. Dressen was named acting or temporary secretary. General John B. Castleman of Louisville and Charles Alcock of Liverpool, England, were appointed associate judges. See *The Courier-Journal*, 3 May 1900. Price's son blamed ownership's avarice for the change. See Clarence F. Price's letter of 26 April 1900 in Charles F. Price papers, Kentucky Derby Museum.

32. Winkfield was greatly disappointed at not winning his third consecutive Kentucky Derby. Pat Dunne, who owned the favorite, Early, claimed that Winkfield did not follow his instructions. Winkfield went to Russia the next year. The story surrounding his exodus is described by Roy Terrell, "Around The World In 80 Years," *Sports Illustrated*, 8 May 1961.

The Louisville Herald on 3 May 1903, after the ill-fated Derby ride, commented that Winkfield "is one of the last great colored riders. The colored jockey is passing out and but a few representatives are left. Winkfield is twenty-three years old and a product of Lexington." He died in Paris, France, at the age of 91. See "Jimmy Winkfield, Jockey, Dies; Rode 2 Derby Winners in a Row," *The New York Times*, 25 March 1974.

33. The following year (1902), Jacob J. "Jake" Holtman, "the best starter that has ever manipulated the barrier," was brought in from Hawthorne. He had also worked in San Francisco where Charles F. Price was general manager. See *The Courier-Journal*, 25 May 1902.

34. William Withers Douglas (1869-1912) was the first sports editor of *The Courier-Journal*. He died on Derby Day 1912, having covered the previous fifteen races for the newspaper. According to his obituary in *The Courier-Journal* on 12 May 1912, "he had been a prime factor in the advancement of baseball and horse racing in Louisville."

35. Andrew Vennie (1859-1926) was connected with a New York company dealing in silks, satins, and tailor finishings when he met Matt Winn in 1893. They became close friends, and Vennie was also made a colonel by Governor J. C. W. Beckham. After Charles F. Grainger died in 1921, Col. Vennie became resident manager of Churchill Downs, where he and Matt Winn shared an apartment they had constructed over the general offices. See "Col. Vennie Falls Dead At Downs," *The Courier-Journal*, 21 May 1926.

36. Saunders Paul Jones (1857-1916) was a native of Lynchburg, Virginia, where his grandfather was a manufacturer and banker. His father, Warner Paul Jones was killed in the Civil War. S. P. Jones moved to Louisville in 1888 and was the senior member of the Paul Jones Distilling Company and had other business interests including the Paul Jones Building (afterwards named the Marion E. Taylor Building). He was survived by four children, Warner L. Jones, Mrs. John Churchill, Saunders P. Jones, Jr., and Barnett Jones, and by his brother, Lawrence Jones. See "Death Summon For S. P. Jones," *The Courier-Journal*, 20 March 1916.

Louis Seelbach (1852-1925) came to Louisville from Germany when he was 17 years old and started as a bellboy at the Galt House. His first restaurant was at Tenth and Main streets; he then expanded at Sixth and Main an establishment later known as the Louisville Old Inn. He opened the Seelbach Hotel with his brother, Otto, in 1905. Louis Seelbach was very active in the development of the Louisville parks system. He was survived by three children, including Louis, Jr., a lawyer, whose daughter, Harriet, married

Warner L. Jones, Jr. See "L. Seelbach, Sr., Is Dead At Hotel," *The Courier-Journal*, 19 March 1925.

In 1901, Frank Fehr consolidated most of the remaining Louisville breweries, including his own, founded by his father in 1872, into Central Consumers Company, which not only produced beer, but also owned many saloons. He started up another brewery bearing his name after repeal of prohibition. Fehr had graduated from Notre Dame where he played on its first football team. He died in 1962 at 92 years old. See "Frank Fehr, Brewery's Ex-President, Dies," *The Courier-Journal*, 16 August 1962.

37. Frank G. Menke also collaborated with Gene Tunney, James J. Corbett, and Ty Cobb on their autobiographies. He was a native of Cleveland and started there as a journalist before moving to New York. In addition, he published the *Encyclopedia of Sports* and the *All-Sports Record Book*. When Matt Winn hired George B. "Brownie" Leach in 1946 to bolster public relations, Menke resigned. He died in 1954 at the age of 68. See "Frank G. Menke, Sports Columnist," *The New York Times*, 14 May 1954.

38. The articles of incorporation of the New Louisville Jockey Club were amended on 24 October 1902 to reflect this involvement. "Article III. The business to be conducted is a Jockey Club, Race Course, and Amusement Garden for the profit, where racing of horses will be conducted according to the law and where spectacles, concerts and amusements of all kinds will be provided for the entertainment of the public, and where refreshments of all kinds will be prepared and served for the benefit and convenience of its patrons." Jefferson County Corporation Book 12, p. 395.

39. Interestingly, Matt Winn and Billy Boardman had entered into a contract on the day of all the changes providing them with catering privileges for seven years. They were to receive 25% of the net profits from catering during meets and 50% for "amusements features" and catering during other times. Contract signed by W. E. Applegate, vice president, and Charles Bollinger (position not specified), dated 1 October 1902, is owned by Hugh Elkins, Louisville. Boardman already had restaurant and catering experience at Churchill Downs (see *The Courier-Journal* 10 May 1897). Winn was a tailor. But more importantly, he was Col. Applegate's tailor, according to Jean Tower Rennie, daughter of Bessie Applegate Tower and granddaughter of Col. Applegate. She was interviewed by Samuel W. Thomas, 11 August 1993.

40. W. E. Applegate had a bare majority of stock in 1903 and along with his son and Charles Bollinger still controlled 82% according to figures in the Charles F. Price papers, Kentucky Derby Museum. Matt Winn had less than 1%. At the end of 1918, Applegate held 27%, Winn 21%. When the articles of incorporation were again amended on 20 November 1916, H. C. Applegate attested as secretary. Jefferson County Corporation Book 25, p. 560.

41. The Latonia Jockey Club track opened on 9 June 1883 to mixed reviews in the next day's *Courier-Journal*. The track, named for a resort springs, was slow, and "there is a painful dearth of trees, shrubbery, or grass of any kind on the grounds." But the prospects for improvement and success were enhanced under the leadership of the Cynthiana whiskey distiller, Thomas J. Megibben (see *The Cincinnati Enquirer*, 25 June 1933). Col. Applegate revealed his syndicate's purchase of the track in *The Louisville Times* on 18 March 1895. Ed Hopper would remain as racing secretary.

According to a 1971 research paper by Howard Hodge, a student at Thomas More College, Applegate lost control of the track in 1902 when he defaulted on purchase payments. Unfortunately, the Kenton Circuit Court case 6334 (1903) that recorded the legal wrangling has been lost. Several years later, Applegate was able to regain

control and improvements were made (see photograph of track structures in *The Courier-Journal*, 13 May 1906). Congressman Joseph L. Rhinock replaced Cincinnati Mayor Julius Fleischmann as president in 1907. Rhinock would later have an interest in Fairmount Park.

42. For examples, see John O. Humphreys, *American Racetracks...* (South Bend, 1966); and Nancy Stout, *Great American Thoroughbred Racetracks* (New York, 1991).

43. David Lowe, *Lost Chicago* (Boston, 1975), 86.

44. Photographs by Edward Klauber accompanied the article. *The Louisville Times* on 30 April 1903 published a sketch of the clubhouse, headed: "Will Be the Scene of Social Activity During The Races."

45. The article was actually a caption for a panoramic photograph of the improvements.

46. Although steeplechases were very popular when initiated at Churchill Downs in the spring of 1882, by 1890 they had been abandoned because M. Lewis Clark considered them too easy to fix.

47. *Goodwin's Annual Official Turf Guide*, (New York, 1903), 375.

48. "Winkfield's Sad Story," *The Louisville Herald*, 3 May 1903. "Winkfield, 91, 2-time Derby winner, dies," *The Courier-Journal*, 25 March 1974.

49. This evidently was a simple structure that lacked permanency. D. X. Murphy & Bro. drew up plans, dated 28 December 1903, for an elaborate band shell. This was erected behind the grandstand and is pictured in an early postcard, but it does not appear on the 1905 Sanborn map.

50. George F. "Doc" Wohlgamuth was listed in the city directories as superintendent from 1896 until 1904.

51. "Fall Fatal To Former Race Official," *The Courier-Journal*, 15 June 1941. He may have resided in the old clubhouse during 1906-1907.

52. Winn stated in *Down the Stretch*, p. 52, that he took over before the spring meet in 1904.

53. This organization of race tracks is not to be confused with the holding company that came into existence in 1928 and owned Churchill Downs.

54. In 1901, Churchill Downs was a member of the Western Jockey Club, which may be the organization Winn refers to in *Down the Stretch*, p. 54, as the Western Turf Association. In a series of undated articles on Matt Winn by Henry Simmons, contained in a scrapbook owned by Winn's grandson Louis J. Herrmann, Jr., the American Turf Association was referred to as the American Jockey Club.

55. "Negotiations Are Called Off," *The Courier-Journal*, 18 April 1905. "To Talk Over The Situation," *The Courier-Journal*, 20 April 1905.

56. Winn was appointed to the board on 25 March 1904 (see "Appoints," *The Courier-Journal*, 26 March 1904). A photograph of the board was published in *The Courier-Journal* on 23 April 1905. His obituary and other biographical information later referred to his position as director of safety, and his obituary incorrectly stated that he received his colonelship from A. O. Stanley, who was governor from 1915 until 1919.

57. Columbus "Lum" Simons was a partner of J. J. Douglas and Jacob Gast before establishing his own real estate firm. He died on 17 February 1921. Louis A. Cella was about 50 years old when he died in 1918. See "Owner of Racetracks Answers Last Summons," *The Courier-Journal*, 30 April 1918.

58. Matt J. Winn papers, Kentucky Derby Museum.

59. "Peacefully," *The Courier-Journal*, 12 December 1912. "Turf Loses Big Man, S. S. Brown," *The Courier-Journal*, 12 December 1905. "Deep Regret Over Death," *The Courier-Journal*, 13 December 1905. "Disposes of $2,500,000," *The Courier-Journal*, 15 December 1905. Malcolm Patterson, "Cradle Of The Turf," *Lexington Herald-Leader*, 12 January 1941.

60. See "Winn Off For New Orleans," *The Courier-Journal*, 8 March 1906. For background see George H. Yater, "Growing Up with the Downs," *Louisville* 38 (April 1987): 36-39; and Barbara N. Bishop, *Oakdale: An Early Twentieth Century Suburb* (Louisville, 1989).

61. George Barry Bingham, Sr. (1906-1988) was an influential journalist and owner of *The Courier-Journal* and *The Louisville Times* as well as the WHAS radio and television stations. Ensuring that his money was well placed on a Kentucky Derby horse was an early spring ritual for him.

62. Leach, *The Kentucky Derby Diamond Jubilee*, 51. "George J. Long, Capitalist, Turfman Dies," *The Courier-Journal*, 16 January 1930.

63. "Negro Ex-Deputy Sheriff Dies," *The Courier-Journal*, 18 August 1948.

64. Louis A. Cella, the St. Louis race track and theater owner, had recently purchased Douglas Park, obviously intending to compete with Churchill Downs. But as Ed Corrigan asserted in *The Courier-Journal* on 12 December 1905: "It cannot be a serious consideration in opposition to Churchill Downs. When the latter track is going, they can't get enough people at Douglas Park to carry on a good crap game." Cella would make considerable improvements to the track plant with the hope of proving Corrigan wrong.

65. "An act to regulate the racing of running horses in the Commonwealth of Kentucky and to establish a State Racing Commission" was approved 23 March 1905. The governor appointed J. P. Chinn of Harrodsburg, Ezekiel Field Clay of Paris, Milton Young and Louis des Cognets of Lexington, and Charles F. Grainger of Louisville.

66. Douglas Park was named for James J. Douglas, who built the original trotting track in 1894. The "prince of sports" died on 2 January 1917. He lived on the old Womack farm that had a track called Highland on it. The site is now Douglas Hills near Middletown.

The name, Castleton Jockey Club, did not stick for very long, if at all. *The Courier-Journal* on 13 May 1906 did refer to the "Castleton Race Track." Breckinridge Castleman (1874-1912) was the son of Gen. John B. Castleman and was associated with his father as an insurance agent. He attended Harvard and M. I. T., and was an orator as well as a grand commander of the Knights Templar. His health, however, was poor. See "In Bathhouse," *The Courier-Journal*, 5 April 1912.

67. Curiously, Winn recalled in *Down the Stretch*, p. 56, that Douglas Park went head to head with Churchill Downs in the fall of 1906, and "after the meetings were finished, Cella and John Hachmeister, his general manager, dropped in and admitted defeat."

68. In a novel approach, the betting shed at Douglas Park was enclosed and incorporated in an arcade at the rear of the grandstand. See photographs in *The Courier-Journal*, 9 September 1906.

69. A signed agreement, dated May 1912, is in the Matt J. Winn papers, Kentucky Derby Museum.

70. Affidavit of Hamilton C. Applegate, dated 17 November 1924, is in the Matt J. Winn papers, Kentucky Derby Museum. "Revival of Racing at Beautiful Douglas Park," *The Courier-Journal* magazine, 8 September 1912.

71. "James Butler Dies In Eightieth Year," *The New York Times*, 21 February 1934.

72. On 27 March 1908, *The Courier-Journal* reported: "Paris Mutual Machines Here." They had all come from New York. However, Matt Winn in *Down the Stretch* said four were found around Louisville and Phil Dwyer found two in New York and shipped them to Churchill Downs.

73. Democrat Paul C. Barth had been elected to succeed Grainger in 1905, in an election marked by fraud and overturned by the Kentucky Court of Appeals in 1907. Robert Worth Bingham served as interim mayor until Grinstead was elected in November 1907 as Louisville's second Republican mayor. Winn believed that Grinstead was retaliating against Grainger for waging "a bitter political fight" against his candidacy.

74. Photographs of the Indianapolis Speedway under construction appeared in *The Courier-Journal* on 4 July 1909.

75. Acts passed by the legislature on 10 May 1884 and 25 March 1886 also permitted such pool selling.

76. A copy of Grainger's report is in the Matt J. Winn papers, Kentucky Derby Museum. In contrast, however, Grainger did not vote with the State Racing Commission to bar bookmakers from Kentucky tracks. See "Racing Commission Refuses To Allow Bookmaking At Tracks," *The Courier-Journal*, 15 October 1908.

77. Various institutions have been combed or contacted in France about Joseph Oller, but to no avail.

78. Hamilton Clarke Applegate (1879-1960) was a major stockholder in the Louisville Racing Association and in Churchill Downs itself. His father, W. E. Applegate, was still Churchill Downs' largest stockholder. The younger Applegate was also in the distillery business and had a racing stable entwined with his father's. Old Rosebud, named for an Applegate & Sons brand, won the 1914 Kentucky Derby.

79. Alexander C. Schuman, according to the 1907 city directory, was a manufacturer of mathematical and philosophical instruments. Matt Winn and Charles F. Price went to Europe before the 1913 Kentucky Derby to study racing and in particular the pari-mutuel system in Paris. In *Down the Stretch*, Winn recalled meeting a Pierre Oller, whom he assumed was the son of Pierre Oller, the inventor of the system. Applegate referred to him as Joseph Oller.

80. Kent Hollingsworth, *The Kentucky Thoroughbred*, 64-68.

81. *Down the Stretch*, 78-104. "John G. Follansbee Dead," *The New York Times*, 16 December 1914. "Racing Gossip of Mexico Meeting," *The Courier-Journal*, 30 November 1909. "Ready For Flag Fall At Juarez," *The Courier-Journal*, 24 November 1912. Greyhounds now run at the Juarez track. It has been renovated by new Mexican owners and they have no record or other history of the track's origin.

82. When the State Racing Commission barred bookmakers, Col. Milton Young proposed to take over the race meeting at Latonia and operate it without bookmakers. However, the offer was not accepted by Joseph Rhinock's group, and they defied the commission's ruling.

83. Glenn Hammond Curtiss (1878-1930) was a pioneer in speed and flight, working his way from bicycles to dirigibles, airplanes, and hydroplanes. After his NC-4 made the first transatlantic flight in 1919, he was active in aircraft manufacturing and directing a chain of flight services and schools.

84. "Downs 'Fixture' Tom Young, 76, Dies," *The Courier-Journal*, 2 June 1963. "Superintendent Tom Young Enters 50th Year At Track," *The Courier-Journal*, 3 May 1961. "Downs' Tom Young Has Nursed Horses, Gardens, Track, and Lonely Ash Tree," *The Courier-Journal*, 30 April 1961. "Tom Young Came To Landscape Downs In 1911, Stayed 44 Years," *The Courier-Journal*, 8 May 1955.

85. Architecture files of Samuel W. Thomas.

86. Price McKinney moved to Cleveland and married the daughter of Stevenson Burke, a prominent lawyer with interests in rail and steel companies, including the steel firm of Corrigan, Ives & Co., which McKinney rescued in 1909. It became the Corrigan, McKinney Steel Co. and he remained in partnership with James W. Corrigan not only in steel but in horse racing. They bought many of the horses in the James R. Keene dispersal sale and established Wickliffe Stud. The operation was successfully run by Elizabeth Dangerfield, until McKinney retired from the turf in 1918. When Corrigan ousted McKinney as head of the steel company, McKinney committed suicide at the age of 63 on 13 April 1926. See "Price McKinney Kills Himself," *Cleveland Plain Dealer*, 14 April 1926. Corrigan dropped dead at age 47. See *The New York Times*, 24 January 1928.

87. J. A. D. McCurdy was renowned for his 1910 flight from Key West to Havana.

88. "The American Turf," *The Courier-Journal*, 4 July 1878.

89. A floor plan prepared by Grainger & Co., dated May 1912, for 18 private boxes on top of the clubhouse with a walkway leading to the grandstand is in the Kentucky Derby Museum.

90. For the exact location of the big stable, see the 1905 Sanborn map.

91. "Death Comes To Wife Of Col. Matt J. Winn," *The Courier-Journal*, 16 August 1912. Matt J. Winn was listed in the city directories until 1915 as president of M. J. Winn & Co. (Inc.) at 628 Fourth Street. In 1915 he is noted as general manager of the New Louisville Jockey Club. For a contemporary biography, see "Matt J. Winn," *The Thoroughbred Record*, 29 March 1913.

92. *The Evening Post*, 26 October 1912.

93. "Fine Exhibition By Giant Cars," *The Courier-Journal*, 28 October 1912.

94. August Belmont, Jr. (1853-1924), the son of a successful international banker and the grandson of Commodore Matthew Perry, added to his family fortune by financing the New York City subway system after the Vanderbilts and Whitneys rejected the venture. Among other interests, he was a director of the Louisville & Nashville Railroad Company.

Belmont, along with William C. Whitney, re-established the Saratoga Race Course and then built Belmont Park. He had taken over his father's Nursery Stud at Lexington in 1891. It was there that Man o' War was foaled in 1917, but he was sold to Samuel D. Riddle long before becoming a legend.

After Belmont's first wife died, he married actress Eleanor Robson in 1910. See "August Belmont Stricken In Office," *The New York Times*, 11 December 1924. Kent Hollingsworth, *The Kentucky Thoroughbred*, 112-119.

95. Thomas Patrick Hayes was a tobacco farmer in Fayette County when he entered the race horse business. He owned four other Kentucky Derby horses. The colt he trained for Mrs. Silas B. Mason is probably best remembered for its spirited second place finish to Brokers Tip in 1933. Hayes died the following August at the age of 68. See *The Thoroughbred Record*, 2 September 1933. Three of his scrapbooks are in the Kentucky Derby Museum.

96. "Tom Young Came To Landscape Downs In 1911, Stayed 44 Years," *The Courier-Journal*, 8 May 1955.

97. The revival of racing in Maryland is covered in an article on the Lexington track in *The Courier-Journal*, 18 December 1922. *Laurel/Pimlico '93 Media Guide*, 5. Also *Down the Stretch*, 110-112.

98. H. P. Whitney (1872-1930) was the son of William C. Whitney who had amassed the family's fortune, mainly from New York City's street railway system. The younger Whitney developed mining interests with Daniel Guggenheim, but maintained a sportsman's interest in polo and racing. He led the winning owners' list seven times, while his son, C. V. Whitney, topped it on five occasions.

99. Fillies Genuine Risk (1980) and Winning Colors (1988) have subsequently won.

100. Matt J. Winn papers, Kentucky Derby Museum.

101. This account is based upon Matt Winn's recall in *Down The Stretch*, 128-131. He sold his stock in New York race tracks, including Jamaica, but retained his interest in Laurel.

102. "Brown's Life Spectacular," *The Louisville Times*, 25 October 1940. J. B. Brown, Banker, Dies At 68," *The Courier-Journal*, 25 October 1940. Robert Fugate, "The BancoKentucky Story," *The Filson Club History Quarterly* 50 (January 1976): 29-46. Jim Brown had come to Louisville as a young man, and as a member of the Whallen political machine, he was elected tax receiver and then was appointed to head the Sinking Fund Commission by Mayor Robert W. Bingham. From there he moved into banking. In 1919, Brown created the city's largest financial institution, the National Bank of Kentucky, through the consolidation of three Louisville banks. Eventually he organized a huge holding company, Banco-Kentucky Corporation. In the meantime, for political expression, he also merged the old Louisville dailies, the *Herald* and the *Post*. However, in 1930, Brown's empire collapsed from the sheer weight of bad investments.

103. Veteran Tobacco Man Dies In City," *The Louisville Times*, 19 October 1935. Hanlon was 67 when he died.

KENTUCKY JOCKEY CLUB

1. The list of officers and directors is based upon information from *The Kentucky Jockey Club* (1920). Frank G. Menke, *Down the Stretch*, 132. *The Louisville Post*, 15 January 1923.

2. The articles of incorporation were filed on 21 February 1919. The purchase, for one dollar, was recorded on 13 March 1919 in Jefferson County Deed Book 907, p. 148.

3. Sam H. McMeekin would become steward and secretary at Churchill Downs. He had been sports editor of *The Courier-Journal* as well as publicity director for the track before devoting full time to Churchill Downs after 1923. He was the city of Louisville's director of safety from 1937 until 1941. McMeekin would also serve in various capacities at other tracks, and he was a director of Churchill Downs and the American Turf Association. He died in 1965 at the age of 76 and was survived by his wife, Isabel McLennan McMeekin, a prolific Louisville author. See "Men Behind The Kentucky," *The Courier-*

Journal, 30 April 1950, and "Ex-Downs Official, McMeekin, Dies," *The Courier-Journal*, 21 July 1965.

4. "A. T. Hert Drops Dead," *The Courier-Journal*, 8 June 1921.

5. Also see "Mayor Says Hospitality of Hert Open-Hearted, Sincere," *The Louisville Times*, 28 June 1921. Hurstbourne had been owned by Joseph L. Harris, a wealthy resident of New Orleans, but a native of Kentucky. The farm was managed by his son Norvin T. Harris. Both served as directors of the Louisville Jockey Club. See "Hurstbourne," *The Courier-Journal*, 8 September 1884.

6. Young E. Allison, "My Old Kentucky Home, The Song and The Story," *The Courier-Journal*, 10 April 1921.

7. Advertisements for Lemon & Son in *The Courier-Journal*, 19 May 1923 and 11 May 1924. "Untarnished," *The Louisville Times*, 30 April 1979. The drawings made by George Louis Graff were given to the Kentucky Derby Museum by his granddaughters in 1986.

8. The movie, *Garrison's Finish*, was based upon the novel by W. B. M. Ferguson. It was reviewed in *The New York Times*, 28 May 1923.

9. Robert W. Bingham papers, Library of Congress.

10. "James B. Brown Buys Louisville Herald, As Galvin Sits In On Deal," *The Courier-Journal*, 18 January 1924.

11. John Ed Pearce, *Divide and Dissent: Kentucky Politics 1930-1963* (Lexington, 1987), 26-27.

12. After Verney Sanders left *The Louisville Times* in 1930, he continued to produce material for racing publications. He had worked on the *Louisville Commercial* and *The Courier-Journal* and also had been "publicity man" for the American Turf Association. Sanders died in 1936 at the age of 67. See "Verney Sanders, Turf Writer, Dies," *The Courier-Journal*, 29 March 1936.

13. The McKinney cottage was probably owned or leased by Price McKinney when he was active on the track at Churchill Downs with James W. Corrigan.

14. The Kentucky Derby was run on a weekday until 1908. Work weeks were commonly six days and fifty hours or more before 1910, so Saturday races were no more convenient than weekdays. It has been run continuously on a Saturday since 1911 and on the first Saturday in May since 1938 (except 1945). The Preakness was not run exclusively on Saturdays until 1931. It was a week later than the Derby until 1956 when the intervening period was set at two weeks.

15. A photograph of the Douglas Park paddock and other structures appeared in "Revival of Racing At Beautiful Douglas Park," *The Courier-Journal*, 8 September 1912.

16. "Downs Will Be In New Dress For Derby Jubilee," *The Louisville Times*, 15 December 1923.

17. Photographs of these improvements made for the fiftieth anniversary appeared in *The Courier-Journal* on 17 May 1924 and in the *Herald-Post* on 15 June 1924.

18. The Louisville Film Company owned by William E. Carrell later became the Falls City Theatre Equipment Co. These films were reportedly destroyed in a fire. Pathé newsreel coverage of the Kentucky Derby began as early as 1914. See Randy W. Ray to Howard W. Hays, UCLA Film Archives, 1 January 1986, Kentucky Derby Museum. The earliest newsreel clip on display in the Kentucky Derby Museum is 1928.

19. "C. Bruce Head, Steward At Churchill Downs, Dies," *The Courier-Journal*, 18 July 1945.

20. Frank G. Menke, *Down the Stretch*, 167-170. "Revival Of Racing At St. Louis Today Has Able Guidance," *The Louisville Herald*, 26 September 1925.

21. An elevation of the clubhouse by D. X. Murphy & Bro., also architects for Churchill Downs, is in the Matt J. Winn papers, Kentucky Derby Museum. Plans for the buildings are in the files of D. X. Murphy & Bro's. successor firm, Luckett & Farley. According to Fairmount Park's track announcer, John Scully, who did research on the track some years ago, there are no extant records about its conception or the Kentucky Jockey Club's takeover.

22. *Down the Stretch*, 170-172. Stuyvesant Peabody, Sr., a Yale University graduate, headed the Peabody Coal Company. He died on 7 June 1946 at the age of 58. See "Stuyvesant Peabody, Sr.," *The New York Times*, 8 June 1946. "Lincoln Fields Race Meeting Gets Auspicious Start; Fields of Class," *Herald-Post*, 10 August 1926. Subsequent history was provided by Ray Garrison, an attorney and former member of the Illinois Racing Board.

23. *Down the Stretch*, 172-174. Unidentified newspaper clipping in Charles F. Price papers, Kentucky Derby Museum. Interview with Thomas F. Carey II, 29 October 1994.

24. Joseph E. Widener, who had recently succeeded the late August Belmont as president of the Westchester Racing Association, visited Churchill Downs while traveling to his Lexington farm, Elmendorf. For Widener, see "J. E. Widener Dies," *The New York Times*, 27 October 1943.

25. "Col. Vennie Falls Dead At Downs," *The Courier-Journal*, 21 May 1926. "Dan O'Sullivan, 88, Dies, Managed Downs 15 Years," *The Courier-Journal*, 13 April 1946.

26. Frederick Mosley Sackett (1868-1941) was a Harvard-educated lawyer who moved to Louisville and married Olive Speed, daughter of J. B. Speed. He sat on various boards, and after serving in the U. S. Senate (1925-1930), he was appointed ambassador to Germany.

27. Bardstown educator and lawyer John Crepps Wickliffe Beckham (1869-1940) was lieutenant governor when Gov. William Goebel was assassinated. He also served in the U. S. Senate (1915-1921), but was defeated seeking re-election.

28. "Ex-Senator Camden, Financier, Dies at 77," *The Courier-Journal*, 17 August 1942. Walter E. Langsam and William Gus Johnson, *Historic Architecture of Bourbon County, Kentucky* (Paris, 1985), 62. Elizabeth M. Simpson, "Runnymede With Its Golden, Lyric Beauty Is Historic Soil," *Lexington Herald-Leader*, 11 September 1938.

29. Robert F. Sexton, "The Crusade Against Pari-Mutuel Gambling In Kentucky: A Study Of Southern Progressivism In The 1920s," *The Filson Club History Quarterly* 50 (January 1976): 57.

30. "Gambling," *The Courier-Journal*, 18 May 1908. The Rev. E. L. Powell of the First Christian Church again defined the opposition's attack in 1908 and he was still prominent in the anti-pari-mutuel gambling movement in the 1920s, when the Rev. M. P. Hunt, prominent in Baptist church circles, joined the fray. They were supported by Patrick H. Callahan, an active Catholic. See "War On Gaming At Race Tracks," *The Louisville Post*, 10 May 1921, and "Betting At Race Track Target Of Pastors Sunday," *The Louisville Times*, 11 May 1921

AMERICAN TURF ASSOCIATION

1. *Louisville Herald-Post*, 18 May 1930; Frank G. Menke, *Down the Stretch*, 175; *The Courier-Journal*, 4 April 1933.

2. Jefferson County Corporation Books 37, p. 641 and 46, p. 149; Matt J. Winn papers, Kentucky Derby Museum.

3. 1940 Kentucky Derby souvenir booklet.

4. According to an unidentified newspaper clipping of 25 March 1929 in the Charles F. Price papers, Kentucky Derby Museum, the 51 per-cent interest in Hawthorne was "obtained when the Jockey Club assisted the Hawthorne organization in getting out of reported finan-cial difficulties. The "organization" must have been the Chicago Business Men's Racing Association that leased the track from the Carey family which owned it.

5. Samuel A. Culbertson (1862-1948) was a native of New Albany, Indiana, who moved to Louisville in 1897 and was listed in the city directories simply as a capitalist. Dinner dances in the Culbertsons' Third Street home were elegant affairs, and he was noted as a meticu-lous dresser who wore spats, white gloves, and a derby. See "Culbertson, Downs Ex-President And Old-School Gentleman, Dies," *The Courier-Journal*, 12 December 1948.

6. Papers were filed on 18 January 1928. Jefferson County Corporation Book 37, p. 641.

7. James Butler, Price McKinney, and Matt Winn had bought H. D. "Curly" Brown's track at Laurel, Maryland, in 1913, and Winn remained as vice president of the operation until he became chairman of the board in 1944 (see *Down the Stretch*, 110, 288-289). The Butler estate sold Laurel to the Maryland Jockey Club in 1947.

8. Bingham family papers, The Filson Club. Also see Robert F. Sexton, "The Crusade Against Pari-Mutuel Gambling In Kentucky...," *The Filson Club History Quarterly* 50 (January 1976): 47-57.

9. The last board of directors meeting of the American Turf Association that Camden attended was in December 1940. He died at the age of 77 (see *The Courier-Journal*, 17 August 1942).

10. William Burke "Skeets" Miller had won a Pulitzer Prize for *The Courier-Journal* for his on site coverage of the failed rescue of Floyd Collins from a cave in Edmonson County, Kentucky, in February 1925. See "'Skeets' Miller dies...," *The Courier-Journal*, 1 January 1984.

Graham NcNamee (1888-1942), radio announcer for NBC for 19 years, was known for "his colorful descriptions and his vivid narra-tives." He was a pioneer in sportscasting, and recalled Earle Sande's third Kentucky Derby victory in 1930 as one of top eleven sporting events he had covered. See *The New York Times*, 10 May 1942.

Charles L. "Clem" McCarthy (1882-1962), first described the Derby in 1928. He remained with NBC from 1929 until 1947 and then called three Derby runs for CBS. In a gravelly voice he was known "for delivering exciting machine-gun accounts of horse races." He held binoculars in one hand and the microphone in the other. See *The New York Times*, 15 June 1962.

11. Edward Britt "Ted" Husing (1901-1962), who joined CBS in 1927, also covered news events, but his knowledge of sport, conveyed with a "dramatic, resonant voice," made him one of the best announcers. See *The New York Times*, 11 August 1962.

12. Charles W. Bidwill operated the Hawthorne track for the Chicago Business Men's Racing Association and then directly for the Carey family, its owners. His Chicago printing company produced pari-mutuel tickets for Churchill Downs for which he received his initial stock. Bidwill was a member of the Chicago group which helped Matt J. Winn get Lincoln Fields started, and Bidwill's wife took two of Winn's daughters to Europe. Letter of Charles W. Bidwill, Jr., to Samuel W. Thomas, 3 January 1994.

13. Maurice L. Galvin, 68, general counsel for the American Turf Association and secretary and treasurer of Churchill Downs-Latonia, Inc., died on 25 August 1940. The Covington native was an active Republican and former publisher of the *Frankfort State Journal*. He had been a founding director of the Kentucky Jockey Club on whose behalf he lobbied the General Assembly.

14. Thomas P. Hayes scrapbook, Kentucky Derby Museum.

15. Thomas Patrick Hayes died on 28 August 1933 at the age of 68. He had also trained Head Play, which was beaten by Brokers Tip but won the Preakness in 1933 and ran in Matt Winn's "World's Fair American Derby" at Washington Park on 3 June 1933.

For additional information on Walker see "William Walker, Jockey Star of 70's, Dies At 73," *The Courier-Journal*, 21 September 1933.

16. The present run of festival activities was initiated in 1956.

17. Matt J. Winn in *Down the Stretch*, 175, stated they were merged in 1935, but the incorporation papers recorded in Jefferson County Corporation Book 46, p. 149 are dated 28 January 1937.

18. Matt J. Winn in *Down the Stretch*, 175. "Sells Track At Lexington," *The Louisville Post*, 15 January 1923. "Old Kentucky Association Track Passes Out of Existence," *The Lexington Herald*, 30 October 1936. Malcolm Patterson, "Cradle Of The Turf," *The Lexington Herald*, 12 January 1941.

19. "Race Track Given Legion For Use As Country Club," *The Louisville Times*, 28 September 1922. "Wreckage Marks Douglas Park Site," *The Louisville Times*, 17 February 1939. "Douglas Park Track To Be Put to Grass Like Old Race Horses, *The Courier-Journal*, 16 March 1958.

20. William G. O'Toole (1898-1956) was an exceedingly gifted archi-tect, educated at St. Xavier High School and University of Louisville, and in architecture at Harvard University. He won a fellowship to study in Europe and taught at Georgia Institute of Technology before joining D. X. Murphy & Bro. Besides his work at Churchill Downs, he designed the Federal Land Bank, the Security Bank, part of Norton Infirmary, St. Agnes Church, and the city-county Board of Health.

21. In 1953, pari-mutuel machines replaced messengers who placed bets for the hundred or so men issued membership cards in Room Twenty, which was named the Matt J. Winn Room after his death. It was located on the third floor of the clubhouse behind section G.

22. Matt J. Winn's son-in-law, Russell Sweeney, became general man-ager in 1941 when Daniel E. O'Sullivan retired because of ill health. See "At the Downs, It's Tell It to Sweeney," *The Courier-Journal*, 25 April 1948. Also, "Dan O'Sullivan, 88, Dies, Managed Downs 15 Years," *The Courier-Journal*, 13 April 1946.

23. *The Courier-Journal*, 22 October 1941.

24. *The Courier-Journal*, 24 October 1941.

25. Blandina Griffiths Babcock was an active and charter member of the Glenview Garden Club. She died on 26 July 1949 at the age of 58. Her husband, George W. Babcock, Sr., was president of the Puritan Cordage Mills and a founder of the River Valley Club. Their home, Rockledge, overlooks Upper River Road.

26. *The Courier-Journal*, 3 May 1961. Wyatt died at the age of 71, see *The Courier-Journal*, 7 December 1965. "Lord Of The Tulips," *The Courier-Journal*, 7 May 1967.

27. Warner L. Jones, Sr., married Mina Breaux Ballard in 1914. Her great-grandmother, Mary Eliza Churchill Thruston (1804-1842), was a sister of John and William Henry Churchill as was Abigail Prather Churchill who married Meriwether Lewis Clark, Sr.

28. Hermitage Farm is located on U. S. Highway 42 in Oldham County, near Goshen. The brick home was built (1832-1836) by Philip Telfair Henshaw although he did not live to see it completed. His daughter, Lucy Mary Jane Henshaw, married Richard Waters, and their son, Philip Edmond Waters, died there in 1927. His family sold it to Warner L. Jones, Jr., in 1936.

29. Jefferson County Corporation Book 49, p. 13.

CHURCHILL DOWNS, INC.

1. 1946 Kentucky Derby souvenir booklet; *The Courier-Journal*, 30 April 1950, 29 May 1982, and 12 March 1985.

2. Until WWII ended in 1945, the "Street-Car Derbies" continued, as transportation into Louisville was restricted. The 1945 Derby was delayed until June 9th.

3. Before coming to Churchill Downs in 1945, Kenneth A. Coyte (1919-1995) worked seven years for its accounting firm, Humphrey Robinson and Co. Also see "Kenny Coyte, Former Churchill official, dies," *The Courier-Journal*, 17 February 1995.

4. For a sketch of Winn's early career see "Matt J. Winn," *The Thoroughbred Record*, 29 March 1913. The Thoroughbred Racing Associations of the United States, Inc. was founded in 1942. Early in 1994, it named its first commissioner, J. Brian McGrath, who is to "showcase the industry and to utilize his marketing experience to promote the sport and make it more fan friendly." See Rick Bozich, "First race-track commissioner is a fan, and that's a plus," *The Courier-Journal*, 18 January 1994.

5. Lincoln Fields was sold to a group headed by Edward J. Fleming. "Syndicate Buys Lincoln Fields," *The Courier-Journal*, 6 March 1947. The sale price was approximately $1.75 million.

6. Russell Sweeney, resident manager of Churchill Downs, retired because of ill health in 1961. "Sweeney, Former Downs Manager, Dies," *The Courier-Journal*, 6 July 1966.

7. "Downs Operators Order Study Of Plan For Civic Use of Profit," *The Courier-Journal*, 23 November 1948. *The Courier-Journal*, 12 December 1948. "How Would Downs Stockholders Fare in the Trade for New Bonds," *The Courier-Journal*, 12 June 1949.

8. "City Is Due Downs-Sale Proposal," *The Courier-Journal*, 2 January 1960. "Proposal To Buy Downs Dropped," *The Courier-Journal*, 13 January 1960.

9. *The Courier-Journal*, 11 October 1949.

10. *The Courier-Journal*, 25 and 27 October 1949.

11. *The Courier-Journal*, 30 December 1949.

12. Jefferson County Corporation Book 70, p. 293.

13. "Corum and Head of WHAS Will Debate 'Live' Derby TV," *The Courier-Journal*, 25 April 1950. Churchill Downs' files.

14. *The Courier-Journal*, 17 December 1958. *The Courier-Journal*, 12 March 1959. *The Courier-Journal*, 7 May 1960.

15. A photograph of the $50,000 museum under construction appeared in *The Courier-Journal* on 12 October 1961.

16. *The Courier-Journal*, 2 June 1963. *The Courier-Journal*, 19 September 1962.

17. The undated pamphlet, *Churchill Downs Restoration Program*, was prepared by Aetron of Covina, California. The intent of the takeover was to better the track's facilities and lengthen race meetings in order to stimulate attendances and increase revenues, which would be used to produce larger purses and encourage breeding operations to remain in Kentucky. The proposal languished.

18. National Industries, Inc. was the largest publicly held industrial company based in Louisville. Founded in 1963, the conglomerate had been fashioned through mergers and acquisitions by Stanley R. Yarmuth, son-in-law of Bank of Louisville head, Samuel H. Klein. "From Conglomerate to Multi-Industry Company," *Louisville* 23 (July 1972): 40.

19. The seven members were John W. Galbreath, Columbus, Ohio; William Arnold Hanger and A. B. "Bull" Hancock, Jr., of Lexington; Warner L. Jones, Jr., of Goshen; Frank McMahon, Vancouver, British Columbia; and John C. Clark of Binghamton, New York. See *The Courier-Journal*, 25 March 1969. The number of members in the group was later doubled.

20. William Arnold Hanger was head of the Mason & Hanger-Silas Mason Company that built tunnels, dams, and treatment plants. He donated his family home, Arlington, to Eastern Kentucky University; books and photographs to the Keeneland Library; and funds to establish the University of Kentucky School of Medicine. He was a large stockholder and director of Churchill Downs. He died at 80 in 1976. "William Hanger, Turfman, Builder," *The New York Times*, 2 June 1976.

21. See *The Courier-Journal*, 21 June 1991. The 10-for-1 stock split took effect on 16 August 1991. *The Courier-Journal*, 17 August 1991. The price per share before the split was $270.

22. "Lynn Stone Named To Downs Post," *The Courier-Journal*, 31 August 1961. *The Courier-Journal*, 5 December 1969. "Stone Luckiest Man," *The Courier-Journal*, 17 December 1969.

23. *The Courier-Journal*, 4 December 1968.

24. "Darby Dan Farm owner to lead Downs board," *The Courier-Journal*, 4 June 1980.

25. Billy Reed, "Churchill Downs museum to be replaced," *The Courier-Journal*, 3 November 1981. James Graham Brown (1881-1969) was a successful Louisville entrepreneur with hotel and other real estate and business interests. He enjoyed racing horses and was a large stockholder in Churchill Downs. He created a foundation to manage his estate and earmarked the dividends from his track stock for the Churchill Downs Foundation to improve the museum which he considered a valuable educational and civic asset. The Churchill Downs Foundation was established in 1946 (see Jefferson County Corporation Book 55, p. 91). However, a nonprofit museum entity, divorced from Churchill Downs, had to be established and the land donated before the J. Graham Foundation could provide funding for the project. E. Verner Johnson of Boston was the Kentucky Derby Museum architect. The exhibits were designed by Gerald Hilferty & Associates of Athens, Ohio.

26. "Downs gambling new president can lead track into winner's circle," *The Courier-Journal*, 29 September 1984. Bob Deitel, "Kentucky Derby Museum," *The Louisville Times*, 13 March 1985.

27. "Spendthrift Farm making run at buying Churchill Downs," *The Courier-Journal*, 27 April 1984. "Combs defends offer for Churchill Downs," *The Courier-Journal*, 1 May 1984. "Galbreath may lose job as chairman of Downs," *The Courier-Journal*, 16 July 1984. "Downs board appoints W. L. Jones as chairman," *The Courier-Journal*, 18 July 1984.

28. The Oklahoma native and 13-year Marine Corps veteran, Thomas H. Meeker, graduated from Northwestern University and the University of Louisville School of Law. He joined the firm of Wyatt, Grafton & Sloss in 1977. It subsequently merged with the firm that

included John Tarrant and formerly Charles Dawson, attorneys for Churchill Downs.

29. Jennie Rees, "Attendance, handle show an increase at Churchill Downs," *The Courier-Journal*, 28 June 1986.

30. Sandra Duerr, "New management guides Downs to winner's circle," *The Courier-Journal*, 4 November 1988.

31. Dave Koerner, "Challenges loom from competition for money, fans," *The Courier-Journal*, 29 April 1990.

32. Greg Otolski, "Meeker says Churchill Downs hopes to expand simulcasting," *The Courier-Journal*, 18 June 1993. John Bowman, "Churchill reportedly to seek more simulcasting," *Business First*, 14 February 1994.

33. For a state by state compilation of gaming, see Robert T. Garrett, "Competition gallops toward horse industry," *The Courier-Journal*, 5 September 1993.

34. Meeker had remained ambivalent about pushing track-based casinos, believing a constitutional amendment could not be passed and worrying what harm it might do to the image of the Kentucky Derby. See Robert T. Garrett, "Downs takes no stand yet on casinos," *The Courier-Journal*, 28 July 1993.

After a University of Louisville study concluded that Kentucky's horse industry could best survive "if the state's race tracks get in on the casino games themselves," Churchill Downs supported efforts in the Kentucky General Assembly to get the issue of legalizing casino gambling, requiring a constitutional amendment, brought to a statewide referendum. The proposal was opposed by the Kentucky Thoroughbred Association and the Keeneland track, even though casino revenues would be used in part to increase racing purses. The proposition died when it appeared that casinos could not be the exclusive franchise of the race tracks. See Kirsten Haukebo, "Tracks' study backs casinos to save racing," *The Courier-Journal*, 27 January 1994. Kirsten Haukebo, "Most oppose casino gambling," *The Courier-Journal*, 16 February 1994. Al Cross and Kirsten Haukebo, "Stumbo says ballot would not limit casinos to tracks," *The Courier-Journal*, 4 February 1994.

35. In July 1993, Churchill Downs in partnership with Promus Cos. made one of three proposals for a riverboat complex at Jeffersonville, Indiana, but defeat of the gambling referendum on 2 November 1993 made any selection moot. See Scott Wade, "Churchill joins gambling giant to launch proposal for riverboat," *The Courier-Journal*, 23 July 1993.

In April 1992, Churchill Downs agreed to invest in the development of a Thoroughbred and harness-racing track in Indiana stimulated by a new law permitting establishment of up to four off-site betting locations. See Judith Egerton, "Churchill Downs proposes track in Indianapolis," *The Courier-Journal*, 23 April 1992. When a track site could not be obtained, Churchill Downs became involved with Anderson Park Inc., forty miles northeast of Indianapolis. Eventually it took over full control of the harness-racing track and proposed to introduce Thoroughbred racing when its four off-site betting parlors were open. Called Hoosier Park, the facility opened on 1 September 1993, and shortly thereafter, Churchill Downs was awarded a license for a betting parlor near Chicago. If a proposed competing Thoroughbred track does not open southeast of Indianapolis, Hoosier Park is ready to resurface its track for that type of meet. Pari-mutuel horse racing had returned to Indiana, a hundred years after being made illegal. See Mary Dicter, "History made as track opens in Indiana," *The Courier-Journal*, 2 September 1994.

In July 1993, Churchill Downs announced it wanted to build a $56-million race track in Virginia Beach, Virginia. Support was forthcoming from the local city council as well as a regional bonding agency, but desirable OTB parlors in Arlington and Alexandria were denied by referendum. Ultimately, the Virginia Racing Commission approved a competing application for its first Thoroughbred track. See Kirsten Haukebo, "Churchill loses bid for Virginia track," *The Courier-Journal*, 13 October 1994. In the meantime, a development department was created "to expand the Downs' management and ownership interest in the racing and gaming industries." See Sheldon Shafer, "Churchill Downs hires 3 to focus on expansion," *The Courier-Journal*, 5 March 1994.

CREDITS AND SOURCES

Unless credits and sources are given in captions, they are provided below. When multiple illustrations per page: (a) = above; (bw) = below; (t) = top; (m) = middle; (bm) = bottom; (l) = left; (r) = right.

ABBREVIATIONS

CD   Churchill Downs, Inc.
C-J   *The Courier-Journal*, Louisville
C&S   Caufield & Shook, Inc., Louisville
FC   The Filson Club Historical Society, Louisville
KC   Kinetic Corporation, Louisville
KDM   Kentucky Derby Museum, Louisville
KHS   Kentucky Historical Society, Frankfort
KL   Keeneland Library, Lexington
LC   Library of Congress, Washington, D.C.
L&F   Luckett & Farley, Architects, Louisville
LFPL   Louisville Free Public Library
UKKL   University of Kentucky, Margaret I. King Library
ULPA   University of Louisville Photographic Archives

FRONT MATTER

End paper: L&F. 1: FC. 2-3: George B. Leach Coll., ULPA. 4-5: by Royal Photo Co., *Herald-Post* Coll., ULPA. 5: by Royal Photo Co., *Herald-Post* Coll., ULPA. 6-7: by Royal Photo Co., KDM.

BACKGROUND ERA

10: (inset map) by John Foster. 10-11: *Every Saturday*, 29 April 1871, p. 397. 12-13: F.H. Verhoeff Coll., FC. 14: R.G. Potter Coll., ULPA. 19: J.B. Speed Art Museum, Louisville. 20: LC. 21: LC. 22: (both) Dr. A. J. Alexander, Lexington. 25: Paul Mellon Coll., Virginia Museum of Fine Arts, Richmond. 26: KDM. 27: FC. 28: (inset) by Joseph Krementz, Mrs. John Cody Coll., ULPA. 28-29: by Wm. C. Coghlan, UKKL. 31: FC. 32: *The Courier-Journal*, 25 August 1918, courtesy of Mary Jean Kinsman, Louisville. 33: J.B. Speed Art Museum, Louisville. 34: FC. 35: (b) KDM.

LOUISVILLE JOCKEY CLUB

38-39: FC. 40: KDM. 41: (both) KDM. 43: Samuel W. Thomas. 44-45: R.G. Potter Coll., ULPA. 48: KDM. 49: by L.S. Sutcliffe, courtesy of Ken Grayson, Lexington. 51: KDM. 57: KDM. 58: KDM. 59: Martin F. Schmidt, Louisville. 62: FC. 63: KDM. 67: KDM. 70: (l) FC, (r) KDM. 71: KDM. 72-73: FC. 74: LC. 77: FC. 78: FC. 80: FC. 81: UKKL. 83: FC. 84: by Clark Capps, KDM.

NEW LOUISVILLE JOCKEY CLUB

86-87: KL. 91: L&F. 93: R.G. Potter Coll., ULPA. 94: L&F. 95: (both) L&F. 96: KDM. 98: FC. 99: Kentucky State University, Frankfort. 105: George B. Leach Coll., ULPA. 106: courtesy of Mrs. Jean Tower Rennie, Palm Beach. 107: Charles F. Price papers, KDM. 110-111:

Charles F. Price papers, KDM. 113: (a) L&F, (r) post card, courtesy of Eugene Blasi, Louisville. 114: post card, courtesy of Eugene Blasi, Louisville. 115: (a) L&F, (r) post card, courtesy of Eugene Blasi, Louisville. 119: UKKL. 120: by James Mullen, Lexington, KL. 122: R.G. Potter Coll., ULPA. 123: Long/Bashford Manor scrapbook, KDM. 124-125: Charles F. Price papers, KDM. 129: KDM. 130: R.G. Potter Coll., ULPA. 133: by Royal Photo Co., KDM. 134-135: by Royal Photo Co., courtesy of Dan Regan, Harry M. Stevens Co. 136: KDM. 137: (t) Thomas P. Hayes scrapbook, KDM. 138-139: by Royal Photo Co., KDM. 140-141: FC. 142: post card, KDM. 143: KDM.

COLOR SECTION

144: KDM. 145: KDM. 146: KDM. 147: (both) KDM. 148-149: (all except right) R.G. Potter Coll., ULPA, (r) KDM. 150: (t) by Dan Dry; (above left) by Dan Dry; (above right) by John Nation. 151: (t) by Dan Dry; (above left) KDM; (above right) by John Nation.

KENTUCKY JOCKEY CLUB

152-153: by Royal Photo Co., KDM. 154: KDM. 155: by C&S, KC. 156: FC. 157: (t) Charles F. Price papers, KDM; (b) *Kentucky Derby Lauded*, KDM. 158-159: by C&S, ULPA. 160: *Kentucky Derby Lauded*, KDM. 160-161: section of panorama, 1924 souvenir booklet, KDM. 162-163: by C&S, KC. 163: by C&S, KC. 165: KDM. 166: KDM. 167: by H. C. Ashby, KDM. 168: (t) KDM; (bm) by C&S, ULPA. 169: by C&S, KDM. 170-171: by C&S, KC. 173: by C&S, KC. 175: UKKL.

AMERICAN TURF ASSOCIATION

176-177: by C&S, KC. 178-179: by C&S, KC. 180: (l) by H. C. Ashby, Charles F. Price papers, KDM; (r) FC. 181: by C&S, KC. 182: by C&S, KC. 184: CD. 185: (a) KDM; (b) by Wallace Lowry, *The Courier-Journal*. 186: by Royal Photo Co., ULPA. 187: KDM. 188-189: (all) by C&S, KC. 189: by C&S, KC. 190: R.G. Potter Coll., ULPA. 191: by C&S, KC. 192-193: by C&S, KC. 192: by C&S, KC. 193: (t) by C&S, KC. 194: by C&S, KC. 195: KDM. 196-197: KDM. 197: (inset) by C&S, KC. 198: by H.C. Ashby, Matt J. Winn Coll., KDM. 199: (both) by C&S, KC. 200: C&S, KC. 201: KDM.

CHURCHILL DOWNS, INC.

202-203: by Richard Nugent, *The Courier-Journal*. 204-205: by C&S, KC. 207: (a) by C&S, KC ; (b) KDM. 208-209: by C&S, KC. 210: by C&S, KC. 211: *The Courier-Journal*. 212: (a) by C&S, KC; (b) KDM. 213: *The Courier-Journal*. 214-215: (both) by C&S, KC. 215: courtesy of Kenneth A. Coyte, Louisville. 216: by C&S, KC. 217: courtesy of Warner L. Jones, Jr., Louisville. 218: by Bob Ludwig, KDM. 218-219: by C&S, KC. 219: by Bob Ludwig, KDM. 221: (both) by C&S, KC. 222: KDM. 223: (both) CD. 224: CD. 225: by C&S, KC. 227: CD. 228-229: CD.

Back endpaper: by Royal Photo Co., *Herald-Post* Coll., ULPA.

INDEX

GREYSCALE

BIN TRAVELER FORM

Cut By Mi _____ Qty 2 ____ Date 10/22/24

Scanned By Michael A. Huerta Qty 2 ____ Date 10/22/24

Scanned Batch IDs

938445447   938448445   _____

Notes / Exception

_____

_____

_____

_____

_____